Making a Monster

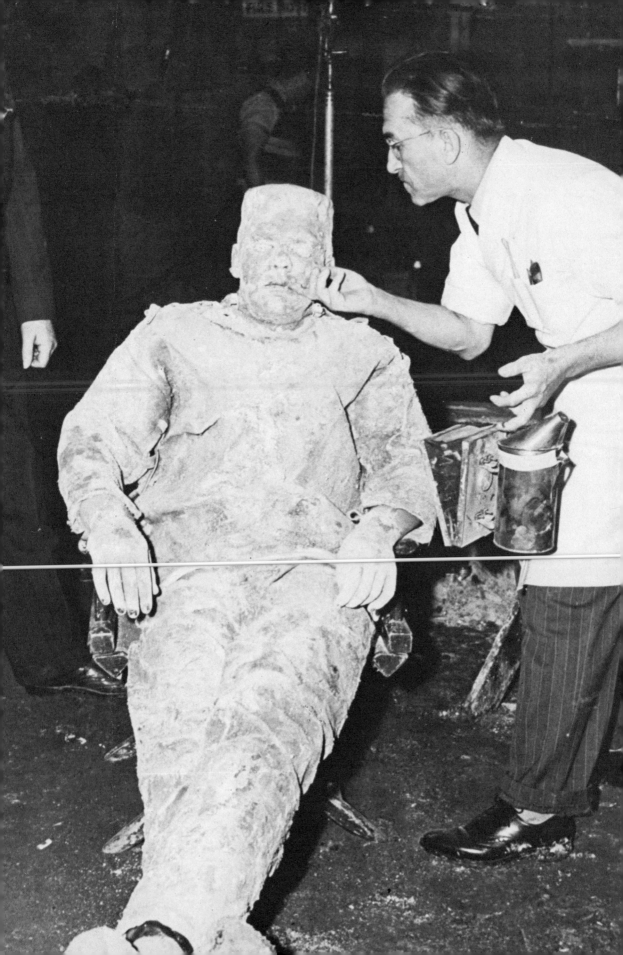

Making a Monster

Al Taylor and Sue Roy

**The Creation of Screen Characters
by the Great Makeup Artists**

Introduction by Christopher Lee

Crown Publishers, Inc. / New York

Printed in the United States of America
Published simultaneously in Canada by General Publishing Company Limited

Designed by Leonard Henderson

Library of Congress Cataloging in Publication Data

Taylor, Al, 1949—
  Making a monster.

  1. Make-up, Theatrical. 2. Horror films—History and criticism. 3. Science fiction films—History and criticism. I. Roy, Sue, joint author.
II. Title.
PN2068.T3   791.43'027   79-16816
ISBN O-517-53456-8

We wish to dedicate this book to the memory
of
CECIL HOLLAND
''the Daddy of Makeup Artists''

Contents

Acknowledgments

Many people have helped in the writing of this book. First of all, the makeup artists who comprise this book are to be given the greatest thanks, for being who they are and for sharing it with us. It has been impossible to include everyone we wanted to include. To those people we've had to leave out, we are painfully sorry but immensely grateful for your time and contributions. We wish to thank all makeup artists, hair stylists, actresses, actors, motion picture studios, television companies, and friends who provided us with photographs, information, and support. We have attempted to list all alphabetically as follows; however, if we have overlooked any, it is with deepest regret.

ABC-TV, Academy of Motion Picture Arts and Sciences, Del Acevedo, Jane Alexander, American International Pictures, Amicus Film Production, Jack Arnold, Roy Ashton, Association of Cinematograph, Television, and Allied Technicians, Association of Theatrical, Television, and Kine Employees, Rick Baker, Roy Ward Baker, Liz Bark, Charles Bates, George Bau, Gordon Bau, Robert Bau, Lee Baygan, Linda Blair, Fred Blau, Les Bowie, Ray Bradbury, Gary Braley, British Film Institute, Georg Stanford Brown, Ricou Browning, Sr., Bryanston Pictures, Tom Burman, Clay Campbell, Nick Carabat, Veronica Carlson, John Carradine, Barbara Carrera, Michael Carreras, Dave Case, CBS-TV, John Chambers, George Chaney, Ken Chase, Christopher Lee International Club, Columbia Pictures, Marty Cooper, Sue and Colin Cowie, Peter Cushing, Dan Curtis Productions, Saul David, Jack Dawn, Robert Dawn, Francio Demura, Dino De Laurentiis Productions, Gary Dorst, Don Feld, Films Incorporated, Terence Fisher, Robert Florey, Fogler Library at the University of Maine at Orono, Stuart Freeborn, Greer Garson, Lawrence Germain, Alan Gibson, John Gillespie, John Gilling, Alan J. Green, Morton K. Greenspoon, O.D., Lee Greenway, Val Guest, Alec Guinness, Hammer Film Productions, Helen Hayes, Her Serene Highness Princess Grace of Monaco, Edward Hermann, Charlton Heston, Anthony Hinds, Cecil Holland, Norma Holland, Hurlock Cine World Incorporated, Liz Kaul, Ruth E. Kennedy, Jack Kevan, Pam Ellen Knox, Elsa Lanchester, Ann Lander, Philip W. N. Leakey, Reginald LeBorg, Christopher Lee, Bill Lenney, Library of Congress, Mort Lickter, Judy Lillie, Stuart Linder, Stephanie Locke, Herbert Lom, Ida Lupino, Roddy McDowall, Maine State Library, Make-up Artists and Hair Stylists Local 706, Jayne Meadows, Ralph Meeker, Metro-Goldwyn-Mayer, Lynne Moody, Dan Morgan, Steve Mountford, Christopher Mueller, Jr., Museum of Modern Art, NBC-TV, Joseph Newman, Gustaf Norin, James Norin, Josef Norin, H. Noune, Ben Nye, Ben Nye, Jr., Dana Nye, Gwen O'Connor, Sir Laurence Olivier, Robert Ozman, George Pal, Syd Pearson, Peter Cushing International Club, Marc Pevers, Jack Pierce, Ingrid Pitt, Walter Plunkett, Vincent Price, Irene Prohaska, Tony Randall, Mark Reedall, Michael Ripper, ROA Films, Margaret Holland Sargent, Saturday Matinee, Robert Schiffer, Peter Sellers, William Shatner, Barbara Shelley, Roy Skeggs, Howard Smit, Dick Smith, Allan "Whitey" Snyder, Dan Striekpeke, Richard Thomas, Thompson Free Library of Dover-Foxcroft, Maine, Christopher Tucker, Josephine Turner, Anita Tuttle, William Tuttle, TV Guide, Twentieth Century-Fox, United Artists, Universal Pictures, Universal 16, Vivienne Walker, Walt Disney Productions, Warner Brothers, John Wayne, Stan Winston, Katherine Wise, Robert Wise, Michael York, and Richard Youman.

And, finally, the authors would like to thank their close relatives, Lawrence, Chris, Missy and Ryan Roy, Anna and the late Aaron Kinney, and Mr. and Mrs. James S. Taylor. Without their enormous faith and understanding, we would never have been able to have completed the challenge of this book.

Introduction

I t is a part of theatrical tradition that in olden times actors and actresses removed their somewhat crude makeup, which consisted mainly of paints and powder, with a form of grease taken from the fat of an animal. This is supposedly the origin of the word *ham*, as it was frequently bacon fat.

We have come a long way since then.

I am not aware of the precise origin of the word *makeup*. To me it would suggest a combination of the word *make-believe* and the process whereby the actor and actresses make themselves "up" into a character.

There is no question but that Lon Chaney, Sr., was an outstanding creator of character in the many versatile roles he played, because he insisted on doing his own makeup. However, there have been many great and brilliant practitioners of the art of makeup in the history of the cinema, whose names within the industry have become household words, who are not actors at all. Of course, there are an equal number of marvelously talented people who have performed miracles in the world of the theatre and the opera—their names are regrettably for the most part unknown, principally because the exploitation and publicity involved in the making of a motion picture can more easily attain worldwide recognition for makeup artists by means of the credits accorded on the screen.

It is customary in the theatre for an actor and actress to do their own makeup. Indeed, many of them prefer to do so. It is generally only in the case of a long and complicated makeup that they call upon the services of an assistant. In motion pictures, due to a variety of valid reasons concerning time available, full employment, and the necessity for specialists, there is always without exception a makeup man involved—and rightly so, for many of them are brilliant creative artists in their own right. Some actors and actresses in films like to apply certain portions of their own makeup, but the overall supervision must be under the control of the specialist. Today the value of an outstanding makeup artist is of such dimensions that he can literally make or break a motion picture through the credibility of his work.

In the early days of the cinema, the Germans generally were considered to be the best, possibly because many German silent films had a quality of surrealism about them which required skilled hands backed by an agile mind. Since the beginning of sound, however, coupled with the increasing technical advances in film stock and photography, makeup has had to become considerably more subtle and credible.

In fact, it would not be an exaggeration to say that many of the finest makeup artists are literally a combination of draftsman, painter, and chemist.

For me, as an actor, makeup can be of value and importance only where it is absolutely necessary to the creation of a believable character. The nearer the audience is to the human face, the more subtle and less obvious the makeup must be, except in essential cases where exaggeration and the use of prosthetic appliances are needed—and today, such is the advance of this art in motion pictures that it is almost impossible to tell how it is done. This is as it should be, because when the audience escapes into another world of enchantment, it should never be affected by a lack of credibility in the appearance of the characters on the screen. In the theatre and opera, it is necessary to exaggerate, as the physical details of the characters concerned must be clearly visible to the entire audience from the front row of the orchestra stalls to the back row of the amphitheatre known in the British theatre as the gods.

The real value of makeup is obviously that it helps the performer "to become" any character required; but no amount of makeup will have any value if there is not a thinking mind behind the mask. A true professional uses makeup; he or she is never smothered by it.

In the course of thirty-one years as an actor and singer in the theatre, the opera, and motion pictures, I have worn a considerable number of makeups, which have ranged from the fantastic to the uncomfortable, but I have never felt weighed down by any of these makeups to the point of embarrassment. All actors and actresses carry within them this sense of, and delight in, make-believe. It is always with a slight tingle of anticipation that we settle into our chairs in front of the mirror in the theatre dressing room, and apply the first touches of Five and Nine, or await the hands of a makeup artist, in the making of a film. The thrill is always there— the excitement never ends. And, I believe, that this is communicated to the audience, and contributes toward their enjoyment of what they see. The enchanter waves his wand, and "before your very eyes, ladies and gentlemen," the magic starts to work.

—CHRISTOPHER LEE

Chapter 1

CECIL HOLLAND

Cecil Holland was born in 1887 in England, the son of a Thames river pilot. Attempting to follow in his father's footsteps, Holland decided to become a deep-sea captain, and at the age of fourteen he shipped out to sea on a sailing vessel. For the first two weeks of that one-hundred-and-eight-day voyage, Holland was seasick. During his lifetime, Holland visited nearly every land in the world, and he never knew what it was to leave port without being seasick. This quite probably was the reason he didn't follow in his father's footsteps.

It is doubtful that a stage and film career even flickered in Holland's young mind. He found work as a laborer on a farm and was content to save his wages for the day when he could go to the city and learn a trade.

In 1904, after lending fifty dollars of his hard-earned cash to a deadbeat, Holland chased him to America and finally found himself in Seattle, Washington. He never recovered the loan, but he did have in his possession a letter of introduction from a fellow farm worker to a relative who was playing juvenile parts in a stock company. Holland stayed around the theatre until they allowed him to be a spear carrier. Holland was soon made the leader of the mob, and they eventually gave him small speaking parts in the plays.

Holland also worked as a property man, shifting scenes as soon as the curtain fell. It was during these years that Holland recognized that he did not have the stature or the looks to become a leading man, so he concentrated on perfecting his makeup so that he could excel in the portrayal of character roles. Holland secured larger parts with the company and went "on the road." For several years he toured the West with these small traveling road shows.

All too often the traveling shows would go broke on the road and Holland would find himself stranded in unfamiliar towns, sleeping in vacant lots or on park benches. This didn't appeal to Holland's British upbringing, and he decided to leave the stage and learn a "more sensible" trade. For two years he studied the art of engraving, followed by etching. He became an expert in both fields.

In 1913 the new world of motion pictures beckoned and Holland began his career in earnest with the Selig Company, which, at that time, was one of the greatest companies in the business. He was soon promoted from a three-dollar-a-day extra to a stock player. One of his earliest famous characterizations was as General Sherman in *The Crisis* (1916), a twelve-reel feature produced by Colin Campbell.

To get into character for his role as General Sherman, Holland was fortunate in being able to discuss the general's mannerisms with older men who had actually known Sherman. Holland recognized that in this relatively new medium of film, as opposed to theatre, he would have to strive for realism in his character. The eye of the camera missed little. He allowed his beard and moustache to grow but shaved a part of his head, cut his hair short on top, and shaved half his eyebrows off.

While working on this film, Holland received a letter from a group of women in London requesting that the actors in the film send them autographed pictures which would be sold at a fair in London and the proceeds donated to a fund for wounded soldiers. Holland secured and sent off at least one hundred pictures.

While on location in the heat of a Missis-

Actors who were exceptionally talented in makeup as well would assemble a montage of their work as an advertisement. Here Cecil Holland displays his talents as a pirate, a sheik, a Russian, an Oriental, an old fisherman, a drunk, and a sea captain. (*Photo courtesy of Mrs. Norma Holland*)

sippi summer in 1916, Holland was asked to describe the art of character makeup.

"I have played hundreds of different parts, and I speak the truth when I say I have never made up two just alike. A movie character man is least known to the public, for each picture you see him in a different character but do not recognize him, and unless his character and name appear on the screen, you would never know him. At times, I have not been recognized even by people in the company. That to me is a great compliment, for then I know I am entirely away from myself."

A very interesting yet most challenging character Holland was required to play was that of death itself for *The Man with the Iron Heart* (1915). Holland used a skull for his model, which enabled him to decide the best means by which to create a skull over his own features. He purchased false teeth and set them onto strips of hard rubber, attaching them to his face with wires and hooking them over his ears. He covered his hair with the top of a ladies' silk stocking, and then used about a pound of nose putty to model the appearance of a skull onto his face. The nose putty also served to cover the wires and further secure the false teeth.

Cecil Holland as a one-eyed hunchback. (*Mrs. Norma Holland*)

Holland's answer to priceless jewels was simply to paint them on. (*Mrs. Norma Holland*)

5

Holland used brown paint to create the illusion of the skull's cavities, and when he moved his mouth, the jaws of the skull moved realistically. He wore black silk stockings and black gloves, on which he painted bones in white. He completed his death characterization by adding a cowl. Holland would drink a combination of milk and egg, sucked through a straw, in order to obtain nourishment while wearing this cumbersome makeup. It took him nearly three hours to put the makeup on the first time, but with practice he was able to do it more quickly.

Holland's experience with dentistry for his death characterization led to his experimenting further with making teeth. Holland would create teeth in his own design, setting them in rubber and then embedding them in dental wax, which he would soften with hot water. He would place this in his mouth, forming it to fit the roof of his mouth. Once cooled, the dental wax with the embedded teeth again became hard and could be placed in his mouth whenever needed for the appropriate characterization. Using this type of false teeth became passé, however, when talkies entered the scene, as they would not permit the wearer to speak effectively.

From the drama of make-believe, Holland faced the drama of reality when he was called to war. Early in 1917 Holland joined the 316th Engineers, Company C, Ninety-first Division. He was soon involved in some of the heaviest fighting of the war and led his men ''over the top'' in the Argonne district of France.

Holland and several of his company formed a theatrical troupe and entertained

Cecil Holland as Death himself in *The Man with the Iron Heart*. (*Mrs. Norma Holland*)

Holland adds a monocle to Pete the Pup of *Our Gang* fame. (*Mrs. Norma Holland*)

their fellow soldiers while still in France. After the war, Holland returned to the motion picture industry. He would often find himself looking back to his war years and drawing on the realism he saw there for his makeup work.

Holland employed an unusual effect in *The Love Light* (1921), which starred Mary Pickford. Raymond Bloomer portrayed the part of a blinded soldier, and Holland used the skin of an eggshell to achieve the blind look. After carefully removing the egg skin, Holland cut it into a circle just large enough to cover the eyeball. With Bloomer's head thrown back but with him looking downward, the eyelid was then lifted and the skin placed under it. Holland used tweezers to hold the edge of the skin. The skin that remained was allowed to rest on the eyeball. With the skin in that position, Bloomer then raised his eye to the ceiling, which drew the skin up under the upper eyelid. The upper eyelid was then lowered over the skin, and at the same time the lower lid was pulled out gently. Bloomer then looked straight ahead and the eyelid was released, covering the pupil and giving the eye a whitish cataract appearance. Although this procedure was not painful or dangerous, it did cause the wearer to experience a rather unnatural feeling.

Holland, of course, tried this procedure on himself first, to assure himself it was safe. It is believed that Lon Chaney used this procedure in his portrayal of Singapore Joe in *The Road to Mandalay* (1926). A blinded eye was but one of the startling makeup effects Chaney employed in this role.

In 1924 Holland wrote in *The Truth about the Movies by the Stars* about the art of screen makeup, explaining that greasepaint was used to cover the skin because the blood beneath the skin's surface would cause the face to photograph dark without the greasepaint. He noted that even though a person might have a dark or ruddy complexion, he should not necessarily use a lighter greasepaint. He did feel, however, that there was no way to accurately judge this result without first testing the makeup photographically.

Shading around the eye was very common in the films of the twenties. Holland explained the reason this was necessary was that once the face was made up with greasepaint, it would photograph almost the same shade as the whites of one's eyes. A line drawn around the edge of the eye acted to separate the skin from the whites of the eyes. Holland also noted that the only time a shadow should be used over the eye was to eliminate puffiness in the eyelid, as the shading would add depth to the eye. Actors who did not understand the reasoning behind such makeup techniques would often add the shadowing, but only because they saw others doing so, not because it was required of their makeup at the time.

Holland considered the art of makeup vital to the actor. The makeup had to be the same each day, or the audience would de-

The ape makeup that Holland created on Bull Montana in *The Lost World* bears very little resemblance to the makeup John Chambers created for *Planet of the Apes*. (*Mrs. Norma Holland*)

tect the difference and lose all confidence in the actor's portrayal.

The ape makeup that Holland created on Bull Montana in *The Lost World* (1925) bears very little resemblance to the makeup John Chambers created for *Planet of the Apes* (1967). Whereas Chambers had sophisticated products and techniques to aid him, Holland relied heavily on cotton wool for many of his creations. Using cotton wool, Holland built up Montana's forehead, giving him projecting brows. He also employed the cotton in other areas as well, including creating bags under the eyes.

By 1927 Holland had totally relinquished his acting career and had created the first official position for a makeup artist in a studio by becoming head of the Makeup Department at Metro-Goldwyn-Mayer. It had been Cecil Holland who had coined the phrase "Man of a Thousand Faces" for his work as an actor with an excellent gift for makeup, but Holland generously gave his idea to Lon Chaney, his counterpart in those early days of makeup, when Holland left the acting world for a world of makeup only.

When Helen Hayes took her character of Madelon Claudet from the New York stage play *The Lullaby* and went to Hollywood to re-create the role for her first talkie feature, it was Cecil Holland who did her makeup for *The Sin of Madelon Claudet* (1931).

Holland's makeup required eighteen hours of testing on Ms. Hayes. He would later describe the procedure as one of using her face much as a painter would use his canvas, trying an effect and then rubbing it out if it didn't achieve what he was striving for.

He built Hayes's nose out slightly on each side to buffer the sharp, clean contours of her youthful appearance. Hayes had to sit with her head tilted back for nearly half an hour while Holland created the appearance of tight neck cords with highlight and shadow. He used a plastic compound to effect sagging skin, cutting the material to give the appearance of wrinkles.

Holland's careful efforts were rewarded in November of 1931 when he received a letter from New York from Helen Hayes, a most gracious lady:

Holland painted over eight hundred separate lines on Nigel de Brulier's face for his role as a ninety-year-old Hindu holy man in *Son of India*. (© *MGM*)

Below: Holland created this scarred tissue, caused by an exploded grenade, for Lewis Stone's role as Dr. Otternschlag in *Grand Hotel*. Director Edmund Goulding watches carefully. (© *MGM*)

DEAR CECIL HOLLAND:

Our nightmare of last summer has turned out to be a triumphant picture here in New York. I have received great praise for my masterful makeup. It makes me feel guilty, so I hereby forward that praise to you, where it belongs. I'm ever so grateful for your patience and artistry.

God bless and good luck,
HELEN HAYES

Holland would employ the plastic compound he used in his Helen Hayes makeup for a middle-aged appearance, but he preferred painting on wrinkles for an extreme old age. For *Son of India* (1931) Holland painted over eight hundred separate lines on Nigel de Brulier's face for his role as a ninety-year-old Hindu holy man. Each appeared perfectly natural. It took an enormously artistic makeup artist to achieve such perfection with a brush.

Nearly every major star at MGM in the thirties appeared in MGM's film *Grand Hotel* (1932), including Lionel Barrymore and Greta Garbo. Holland created a most macabre makeup for Lewis Stone's role in this film.

When Charles Brabin directed all three Barrymores in *Rasputin and the Empress* (1932), Holland had the challenge of destroying Lionel Barrymore's majestic features and making him up as the evil Rasputin. He employed an almost fawn-colored makeup on Barrymore, creating deep penetrating eyes and indentations at the temples with highlight and shadow. He lengthened Barrymore's eyebrows and laid a long beard. He successfully completed the makeup of Barrymore as Rasputin by adding a longish, greasy, unkempt black wig. Barrymore was so pleased with Holland's artistic efforts that he presented Holland with the third of only twenty copies of a self-portrait he did while in the Rasputin makeup.

Holland created Boris Karloff as Fu Manchu in *The Mask of Fu Manchu* (1932). To give Oriental eyes to an American, Holland would employ fish skin. Using two strips about three inches long by five-eighths of an inch wide, he would trim one end of each piece to a round pointed **V**. About an inch and a half back from the outside corners of the eyes, he would paint on spirit gum, also in the shape of a **V**. He would then wait until

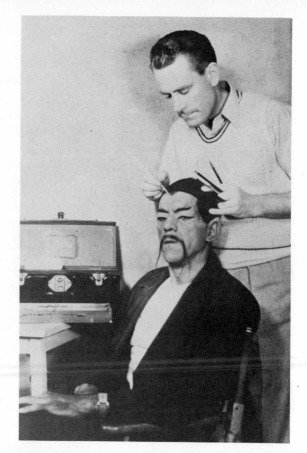

Holland busily turning Boris Karloff into the insidious Fu Manchu in *The Mask of Fu Manchu*. (© *MGM*)

the spirit gum was nearly dry, but not too dry to stick, and place the end of the fish skin on the spirit gum with the point of the **V** toward the eye.

Holland would then cut two strips of three-quarter-inch adhesive tape, each strip long enough to reach around the back of the head from one piece of fish skin to the other. Holland would take one piece, press it to the end of one piece of fish skin, keeping the adhesive side out so that the hair would not stick to it. He would then pull gently on this combination of fish skin and adhesive tape, giving the eye a slanted appearance. He would carry the adhesive around to the other side of the head, pulling back appropriately on the other fish skin until the eye slanted, and then attach the adhesive to that piece of fish skin. Holland would then take the remaining piece of adhesive tape and apply it, with the adhesive side in, over the other piece of tape. This afforded him double protection on the pull of the eye and, at the same time, helped to prevent the hair from sticking to the tape. Once makeup and a wig was added, the fish skin was not noticeable.

Karloff refused to allow this makeup procedure, feeling it would inhibit the movement of his facial muscles, and, instead, small celluloid clips were used, with highlight and shadow employed to aid in the Oriental makeup effect. Shell teeth were fit over his own teeth as well. Long pointed fingernails were also added to the makeup, and to aid in a rather bizarre special effect, copper fingernails were made to fit over them. Ken Strickfaden created a device so Karloff could have lightning playing from his fingernails over the plundered sword of Genghis Khan. Boris Karloff wasn't about to take part in a stunt such as that, so Strickfaden donned Karloff's costume and copper nails and performed the special effect himself. Strickfaden had grounded one of his legs with a piece of wire, but when he moved the ungrounded leg near a metal floor conduit, he went flying.

Because of Holland's expertise in the makeup field he was greatly in demand by all the major studios and left MGM in the midthirties to free-lance. Jack Down succeeded him as head of the Makeup Department. Holland returned to MGM for the filming of *The Good Earth* (1937) and did an excellent job of Oriental makeup for Luise Rainer's role as O-Lan. "Dad was rather stubborn when it came to his profession," Margaret Holland Sargent wrote us. "He won an argument with Miss Rainer, insisting that he apply makeup to her hands when close-ups revealed they were too manicured for a peasant woman."

Makeup wasn't Holland's only forte. He became expert in photography, sculpting, jewelry making, wood carving, engraving, etching, and designing. His hobby of painting became a second profession when he was commissioned to do animal portraits of pets for such celebrities as Betty Grable and Harry James. Neighboring children found him extremely adept at fixing their broken toys.

Despite having left MGM in the midthirties to free-lance, Holland returned to offer his assistance on *The Good Earth*, and he did an excellent job of Oriental makeup for Luise Rainer's role as O-Lan. (© *MGM*)

In 1964 Holland suffered a stroke which left him paralyzed, but with the loving care of his wife he was able to regain the use of the left side of his body, limited use of the right side, and some of his speech. He never lost his sense of humor and, when faced with the inability to express himself verbally, would throw up his hands in the hopelessness of it and became the actor once again, pantomiming his desires. Holland died July 29, 1973, a month after his eighty-sixth birthday, following another stroke and pneumonia.

Cecil Holland's career saw many startling changes in the film industry. It spanned the silent years, the talkies, the musical extravaganzas of the thirties and forties, as well as many of the horror and science fiction films of the fifties. His years as a makeup artist were generous and unassuming ones. His name will come up often throughout the following chapters because, as Howard Smit reflected, "Cecil Holland was a man among men; the Daddy of the makeup profession." He was loved and admired by many.

Chapter 2

JACK PIERCE

It is difficult to believe that the man who created Frankenstein's monster for the movies started his career as a humble theatre projectionist in 1910. After managing theatres for Harry Culver, founder of Culver City, Pierce joined Indian producer Young Deer in 1914 in making films. Pierce then went to Universal Pictures as an assistant cameraman.

One of Pierce's first macabre makeup assignments was for *The Monkey Talks* (1927). Pierce employed chamois and putty, combined with spirit gum and false hair to turn actor Jacques Lerner into a monkey for this Fox production. A wig with leather simian ears sewn into it completed the effect.

Universal Pictures became Pierce's home base for years to come and the studio where his skill as a makeup artist would be repeatedly tested. Over the years, Pierce worked with such well-known stars of the horror genre as Bela Lugosi, Lon Chaney, Jr., and, of course, Boris Karloff.

In 1930 Pierce's assignment was the film *Dracula*, which starred Bela Lugosi. Lugosi's experienced facial muscles, developed for the stage, helped him to create the characterization of a refined gentleman with a touch of seductive evil. The only facial makeup he required—and would allow—for his role as Count Dracula was a light-green greasepaint. Pierce created the makeup for

One of Pierce's first macabre makeup assignments was for *The Monkey Talks*, creating this effective makeup on Jacques Lerner. (© *Fox Film Corporation*)

13

Opposite: Bela Lugosi prepares for his role in *Dracula*. He always applied his own makeup but allowed Pierce to create a special greasepaint of light green for this role. (© *Universal*)

With facial makeup complete, Pierce begins work on the scars on Karloff's wrists for *Frankenstein*. (© *Universal*)

Lugosi, which Max Factor manufactured exclusively. An altered hairline and grayed temples completed the makeup process. Lugosi felt strongly about having his handsome features altered in any way, which was the reason he would turn down the role of Frankenstein's monster the following year.

The 1931 rebirth of the freak penned by Mary Shelley was a definite milestone in the careers of both Pierce and Boris Karloff. The forty-four-year-old Karloff's acting career to date had consisted mainly of undistinguished roles. When James Whale called Karloff to his table during lunch in the studio's commissary, neither man surmised the effect their meeting would have on Karloff's career and Universal's future. Karloff wasn't overly impressed with the role that would totally obliterate his features, but it was work, not to mention the filming of a horror classic.

There were those in years to come who criticized Karloff's becoming stereotyped, but Karloff, the antithesis of his roles, saw his typecasting as an opportunity which offered him the challenge of sinister and evil portrayals.

It was a makeup artist's dream to be faced with the challenge of turning a mortal man into the bits and pieces of Mary Shelley's frightening monster, and Jack P. Pierce rose to the occasion. His first inclination was to read the classic tale for a description of the creature, but his luck was out there. Shelley declined to go into any descriptive narration of her monster's features. Pierce was on his own. Like Dr. Frankenstein, Pierce was faced with creating his own monster.

Using the premise behind Shelley's creature, Pierce is said to have delved into medical and anatomy books, learning the various techniques a surgeon would employ in operating on the human skull. Pierce felt that Dr. Frankenstein would seek the easiest procedure in opening his creature's skull, thus the final version of the flat-topped head with scars and clamps.

Pierce reportedly read that in some early civilizations criminals were bound hand and foot and buried alive. As their bodies decomposed, blood flowed into their extremities, stretching their arms and swelling their hands, feet, and faces to abnormal proportions. Pierce incorporated this bit of knowledge into the makeup design of the Frankenstein monster, which seemed particularly appropriate because the creature was to be composed of the remains of executed criminals.

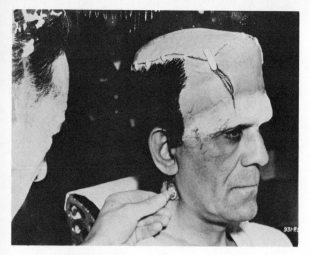

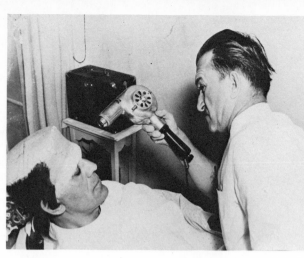

Bolts that were to give the creature his "birth" were embedded so firmly against Karloff's neck with layers of cotton and adhesive that Karloff bore tiny scars from them for years to come. (© *Universal*)

Karloff felt akin to an Egyptian mummy as Pierce built up the square head and enormous forehead with layers and layers of cotton and collodion. (© *Universal*)

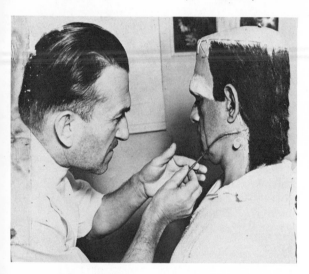

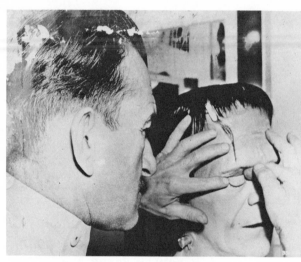

Pierce creates a realistic scar for Karloff. (© *Universal*)

Pierce gave Karloff's monster eyes the weighted dead-look by applying wax caps to his eyelids. (© *Universal*)

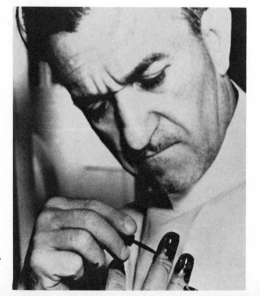

Pierce painted the monster's fingertips black to enhance the appearance of blood having flowed to the extremities. (© *Universal*)

Karloff won lasting fame in his role as the monster, but every time Pierce performed the tedious six-hour makeup application, Karloff paid a dear price. Karloff felt akin to an Egyptian mummy as Pierce built up the square head and enormous forehead with layers and layers of cotton and collodion. Smoking was strictly forbidden because of the flammable quality of the makeup materials, so Karloff wasn't able to seek respite in that area either.

Tiny wires were used to pull the corners of Karloff's mouth out and down. Bolts that were to give the creature his "birth" were embedded so firmly against Karloff's neck with more layers of cotton and adhesive that Karloff bore tiny scars from them for years to come. Pierce's skillfully talented hands created realistic scars on Karloff and gave his eyes the weighted, dead look by applying wax caps to his eyelids.

An appropriate shade of greasepaint was needed to complete the makeup. Pierce needed a color that would give a gray "death mask" appearance to the monster's flesh; however, a gray greaspaint would not film correctly under the Klieg lights. Pierce developed a greasepaint of a greenish hue which photographed correctly and realistically.

Karloff's height was built up to seven and a half feet with the help of heavy boots; and his legs were locked in steel struts, preventing him from bending his knees. It was from this that the famous shuffling walk was developed. Removing the makeup was nearly as challenging as applying it. It required an hour and a half of having oils and acetone applied, a great deal of tugging and pulling, with a certain amount of foul language.

The producer kept the monster's appearance a well-guarded secret, as they wanted to provide a scare Hollywood would long remember. Universal certainly succeeded

there. The picture brought the studio $12 million in theatre rentals alone. When Universal saw the profits from this horror film, they decided to make more. In 1932 Karloff and Pierce were teamed for *The Mummy*.

Pierce discovered that the challenge of wrapping Karloff in the fragile cloth was probably one of the hardest jobs he had encountered in his twenty years in the industry. He had literally cooked the cloth to give it the appearance of having rotted away in some long-forgotten tomb, so there were times when it simply disintegrated in his hands. The proper appearance also required that he wrap Karloff in three directions: horizontally, vertically, and diagonally. This style of wrapping prevented the layers from separating and revealing Karloff's own body.

Once totally wrapped, Karloff's body was then coated with a thin layer of mud. When

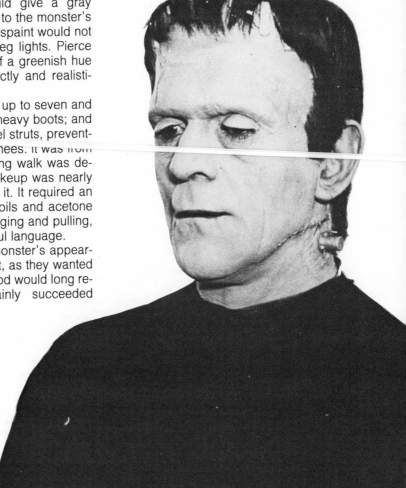

The completed makeup for Frankenstein's Monster.
(© *Universal*)

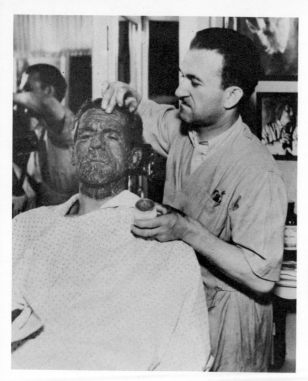

When the producers saw the profits from *Frankenstein*, Pierce and Karloff were teamed again, this time for *The Mummy*. (© *Universal*)

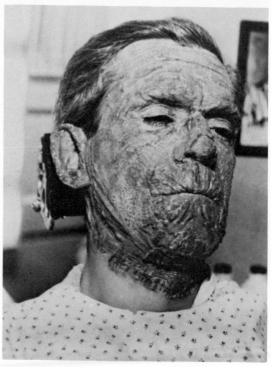

Using cotton and spirit gum, Pierce created a mummified face on Karloff. (© *Universal*)

the mud dried, a coating of glue was painted on. When Karloff opened his eyes and arose from his coffin, the mud and fragile first layer of cotton disintegrated into so much dust, giving an excellent effect.

It remained Karloff's face and hands, however, that had the most startling appearance. Using spirit gum and cotton, Pierce covered Karloff's face, removing the excess cotton with tweezers. With the application of cotton, Pierce was able to create the impression of lines of age. The cotton and spirit gum were dried with an electric heater as Pierce turned his attention to the actor's hands and employed the same technique there.

A layer of greasepaint covered the cotton, and Pierce accentuated the lines of age with a dark-brown pencil. Lighter shades of greasepaint were used to highlight and shadow the foreboding features.

To transform Karloff's own full dark hair into the yellowed decayed hair found on mummies after many centuries in the earth, Pierce used a neutral tone of greasepaint as a base. He then rubbed a mixture of fuller's earth and beauty clay into Karloff's hair, thus achieving the needed effect.

Once on the sound stage, Pierce completely wrapped Karloff's legs together. His eyes were carefully sealed with rice paper. A small slit was made horizontally in the center of the paper. A dark brown pencil accentuated the slit giving a deathlike appearance of slightly opened eyes. Finally, as he lay in the coffin awaiting his cue to be reincarnated, the mummy was complete. Karloff's makeup as the ancient mummy Imhotep took over eight hours to prepare. In the latter part of the film, Karloff played an Egyptian priest—a less grueling makeup.

Until recently it was believed that no makeup artist had received any honor, award, plaque, or Oscar until the late sixties. However, at Universal City Studios a sink was removed from the Makeup Department, and a department head found, attached to the bottom of the sink, an award. It was awarded in 1932 to Jack Pierce by a popular magazine of the day for makeup on *The Mummy*.

Although Karloff had to endure the mummy makeup ordeal only once, Lon Chaney, Jr., who just happened to be Universal's number-one box-office attraction, was not quite so fortunate. Universal

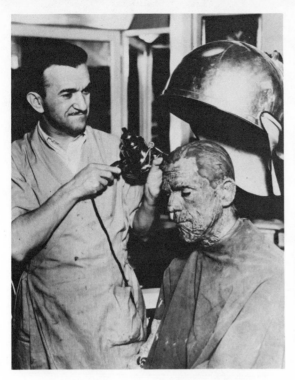

Turning Karloff's own full dark hair into the decayed yellow mass usually expected to be seen on those buried beneath the earth was no easy chore. (© *Universal*)

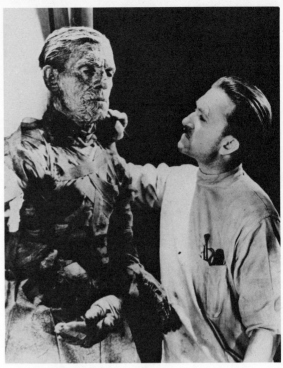

A layer of greasepaint covered the cotton, and Pierce accentuated the lines of age with a dark brown pencil. (© *Universal*)

began a new mummy series in the forties. Pierce followed about the same makeup procedures for Chaney, Jr.'s, portrayals in *The Mummy's Curse* (1944) and *The Mummy's Ghost* (1944). However, in *The Mummy's Tomb* (1942) Pierce created a rubber mask for the mummy role, which was much less effective.

In 1935 Pierce created a bride for the beloved monster in Universal's *Bride of Frankenstein*. Elsa Lanchester was the bride and she told us of the many hours of makeup that were needed to create the marvelous hair style of the bride.

"Jack Pierce was, you might say, very sentimental. When he created a live beauty makeup, he felt about it like a woman feels about her children.

"I was done all in tiny braids—four little braids for the crown of my head. This was my own hair. Then small braids were made on the crown of my head—a false hairpiece about the size of a fruit can was pinned on, then my own hair combed up over that. Then some gray hairpieces were added. It took at least an hour to get all the makeup off me."

Ms. Lanchester was wrapped in cloth and

she remembers that as being "quite bothersome," with the material sometimes coming loose at the knees and other joints.

Because of Karloff's popularity as a result of his heavy character makeup as Frankenstein's monster, Bela Lugosi was willing to don the makeup of Ygor in *Son of Frankenstein* (1939), which nearly obliterated his handsome features. Pierce employed a rubber neck form to simulate the broken neck Ygor received from being hanged—though obviously not "to death." The hoarse, gravel tones Lugosi used for his characterization were immensely convincing and difficult to imagine coming from the same man who played the suave count in 1930.

Pierce fit the rubber neck brace snugly to Lugosi's neck and head, securing it with an elastic strap which ran under Lugosi's right arm. The application of neck appliance and hair took Pierce well over four hours. Once the neck appliance was secured, Pierce began laying layers of yak hair upon Lugosi's face and on the rubber appliance. Once the necessary layers were completed, a wig was added to aid in the transformation process. Pierce then, carefully and diligently, clipped, combed, and curled the hair until

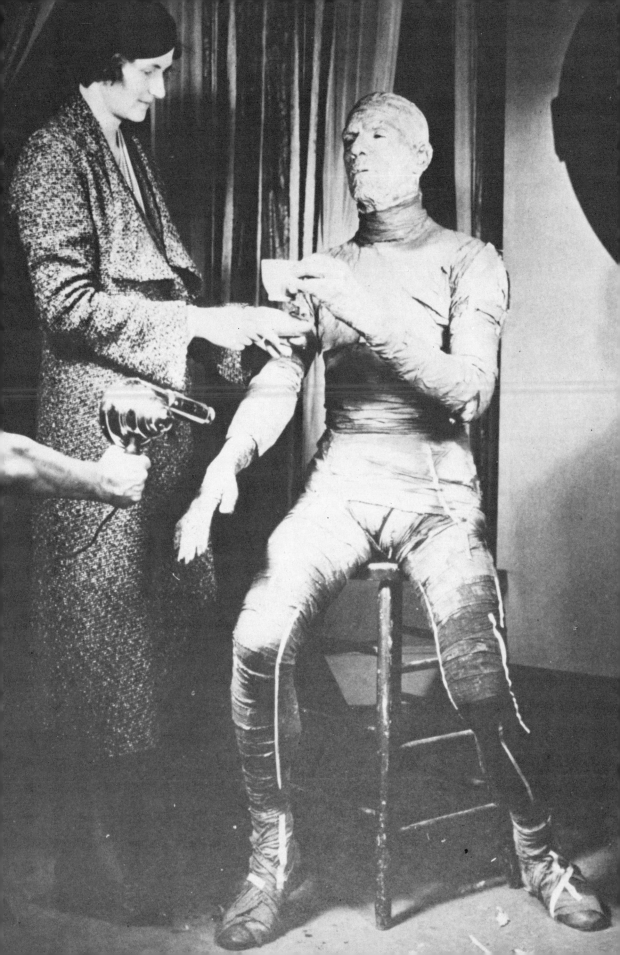

Opposite: Even a mummy has to have a little tea now and then. (© *Universal*)

Lon Chaney, Jr., doesn't appear too pleased with his rags for his role in *The Mummy's Ghost* as Pierce paints his costume. (© *Universal*)

In 1935 Pierce created a bride for the beloved monster in Universal 's *Bride of Frankenstein*. (© *Universal*)

Although Bill Tuttle and John Chambers were the first two makeup artists to win Academy Awards, Pierce was presented with a special Makeup Trophy in 1932 for *The Mummy*. (*John Chambers*)

Pierce adds a wig to Bela Lugosi to aid in his characterization of Ygor in *Son of Frankenstein*. (© *Universal*)

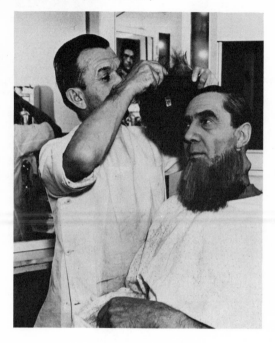

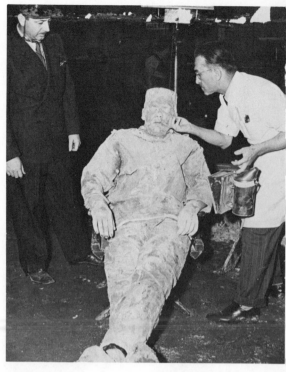

Lon Chaney, Jr., steps into the monster's shoes in *The Ghost of Frankenstein*. Here Pierce checks all aspects of the makeup after Chaney has been effectively dusted. (© *Universal*)

he had created a most realistic beard on Lugosi's face. A moustache was added, and appropriate teeth to give Lugosi the sinister appearance he required for *Son of Frankenstein*.

Lon Chaney, Jr., was cast in the lead of *The Wolf Man* in 1941. *The Wolf Man* was Universal's most important picture that year. Universal had previously made a film covering the subject of lycanthropy in 1935, *The Werewolf of London* starring Henry Hull; however, both films are totally different.

Pierce had worked out a makeup for Henry Hull in *The Werewolf of London* that never materialized because of the long application time, and because Hull did not want his face covered, so a less convincing makeup was utilized. For *The Wolf Man*, though, Pierce was given a free hand. He fashioned a long wolflike snout out of rubber and covered Chaney's face with yak hair

deftly applied a few strands at a time. A thick wig aided the facial transformation, as well as a set of fangs. Hands and feet fit into hairy coverings. Full makeup application took nearly six hours. A shirt and long pants kept Chaney from needing any further makeup on his body.

Transformation scenes were tedious, to say the least. Tiny nails were driven into the skin beside Chaney's hands, holding them immobile. Drapes behind him were starched to remain motionless during the scene. The camera was heavily weighted down to prevent even the tiniest jarring. The needed number of frames were then shot, the film sent immediately for developing, and Chaney's makeup was completely removed. Makeup application would begin again, however, with less makeup applied each time. And Chaney would reposition himself to preserve the film alignment. The

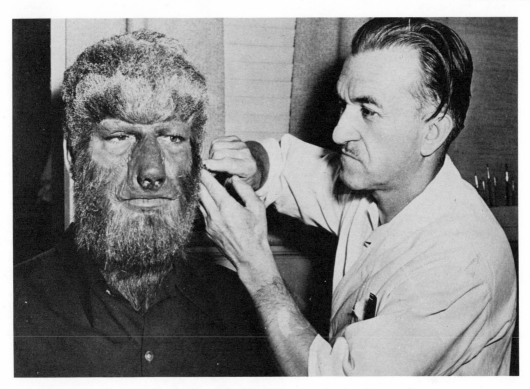

Lon Chaney, Jr., was cast in the lead of *The Wolf Man* in 1941. (© *Universal*)

entire transformation scene, according to Chaney, took twenty-one makeup changes and twenty-two hours to film. Despite the role's tediousness, Chaney was fond of his wolf man and portrayed the character in five films.

In 1942 Lon Chaney, Jr., found himself in the role Karloff had made famous, as he played the monster in *The Ghost of Frankenstein*. Bela Lugosi was at his side, however, continuing his role of Ygor once again.

The Frankenstein monster in *The House of Dracula* (1945) was Pierce's last attempt at a monster makeup. Glenn Strange played the monster and found a great deal of difficulty with the makeup. The skullcap he wore fit so tightly, perspiration was held in. After only a few hours, Strange could simply shake his head and hear the water rattling around inside the cap. The skullcap was only one of his problems. He also had a problem seeing well because the eyelids hung over his own eyes and made seeing difficult as well. And the makeup itself irritated his skin to the point of rawness.

Modern materials such as plastics and foam rubber were replacing the materials Pierce's career had been founded upon, and his use of putty, burlap, collodion, and fuller's earth were outdated. New management came into the Makeup Department in the midforties and time, always a valuable commodity, wouldn't stand still for the slow, methodical makeups Pierce was used to doing. Unwilling to change, Pierce found his services of twenty-two years no longer desired at Universal Studios.

Pierce went on to free-lance in the makeup industry, doing such television productions as ''Fireside Theatre'' and the outstanding historical makeups seen on the popular ''You Are There'' television series of the fifties.

Feisty, stubborn Jack Pierce, one of the pioneer makeup artists of the century, died in 1968 at the age of seventy-nine near the studio where he created our most memorable monster—Frankenstein—who brought terror to many for years to come. His funeral was a pitiful affair with few mourners and only three fellow makeup artists in attendance, and a minister who tried to eulogize a man he'd never met. It would seem that he deserved more recognition than that.

Chapter 3

JACK AND BOB DAWN

When makeup artists speak of films whose makeup work remains outstanding even today, they most invariably mention *The Wizard of Oz* (1939) and the Director of Makeup on that classic, Jack Dawn.

Jack Dawn was born John Wesley Dawn in Covington, Kentucky, in 1889. When he was five, his father was killed and his mother had to take in boarders to make ends meet. Dawn did what he could to help, and by the time he was eight, he was a messenger for Western Union.

Dawn's mother remarried, but the marriage was short-lived. When the parents separated, Dawn remained with his mother. Times were difficult, and eventually the mother had to place him in a boys' school, where Dawn was less than happy. Within a year, Dawn ran away and headed for New York to find his uncle.

Dawn remained with his uncle and found work with a sign painting company. He'd shown a great talent for drawing and painting at a very early age and was an inquisitive youngster, reading every book, magazine, and newspaper he could get his hands on. He read about the blossoming motion picture industry in California, so he saved his money and in 1907, at the age of sixteen, bought a ticket to Hollywood, California.

Jack Dawn at age twenty-eight with several of his own creations. Dawn evidently passed these pictures out as an advertisement for his services; as the back of one reads: "Seven years' experience in picture work. Complete wardrobe. Complete Western outfit with my own horse. Can swim, ride Western or English saddle. Drive any make of car. Very good at character makeup." (*Bob Dawn*)

He had very little money upon his arrival, but he was fortunate in finding work as an extra. Later, he would work as a Keystone Cop with such "unknowns" as Fatty Arbuckle and future director Frank Lloyd. He learned to ride a horse, and this enabled him to become employed as a cowboy actor. It was about this time that Dawn changed his first name from John to Jack. He worked very hard at acting, changing his makeup to suit the roles available. When war broke out in Europe, Dawn went to Canada and enlisted in the Canadian Army; he was sent overseas. He was wounded two years later and returned to Canada.

Dawn remained in Canada until he was separated from the army in 1919. It was during these years that Dawn became even more fascinated by the art of sculpting and created heads of friends. He made a figure of a black man and presented it to the library of the city where he was living.

Although he continued acting, Dawn found more and more work in the makeup field. He became Director of Makeup at Fox Studios and then at a new independent company known as Twentieth Century Pictures. When this company closed, Dawn went to Metro-Goldwyn-Mayer and eventually succeeded Cecil Holland as Director of Makeup.

Throughout Dawn's twenty-five-year career at MGM, he searched for outstanding talent, offering them an opportunity in the makeup field. Some of these men were Bill Tuttle (who would later succeed him as Director of Makeup), Emile LaVigne, Charlie Schram, Jack Young, Eddie Polo, Jack Kevan, Kester Sweeney, and John Truii. Dawn contacted his brother, Lyle, who was an engineer on the Canadian and Pacific Railroad. Lyle Dawn and his family came to Hollywood, and Dawn trained Lyle to sculpt and to do makeup. He employed his half-sister, Edith Mitchell, as a body makeup artist.

A large and demanding film requiring extensive makeup transformations was the 1937 film version of Pearl S. Buck's novel *The Good Earth*. Dawn was called upon by director Irving Thalberg to turn a small army of Americans into Orientals. He succeeded in doing so with the help of the jellylike formula and an enormous amount of work. Cecil Holland did the makeup for Luise Rainer as O-Lan. Charlie Schram, Bill Tuttle, and Emile LaVigne describe their assignments on this film in their chapters; but it was Dawn whose drive and creative expertise put it all together, along with an incredible lab man by the name of Josef Norin and his son, Gustaf.

Dawn did marvelous work in converting Americans to Orientals in *The Good Earth*. (© MGM)

Paul Muni receives a touch-up to his makeup for the character of Wang Lung in *The Good Earth*. (© MGM)

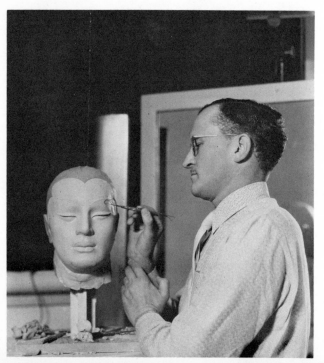

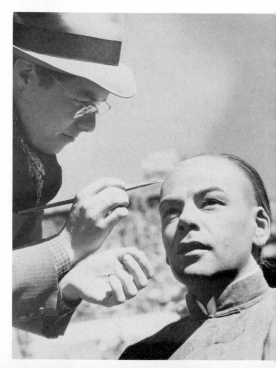

Other films at MGM that year that also took Dawn's specialized skills were *The Firefly* (1937) with Jeanette MacDonald and Warren William, *Conquest* (1937) with Charles Boyer in the role of Napoleon, and *Lost Horizon* (1937). With the help of his lab technicians, Dawn created a remarkable Napoleon out of Charles Boyer and an extremely convincing Talleyrand of Reginald Owen. Dawn employed the death mask of Napoleon as his model and reconstructed Boyer's features, with the aid of appliances and makeup, to match Napoleon identically.

Because of Dawn's marvelous work in converting the Americans to Orientals in *The Good Earth*, and his incredible Napoleon for *Conquest*, he was paid approximately $3,000 for the ten hours of work devoted to Sam Jaffe as the ageless Lama of *Lost Horizon*. However, Jaffe's makeup was actually easier than Boyer's, because Dawn was restricted in constructing the historically familiar face of Napoleon over a well-known star like Boyer. With Jaffe's face, he had a free hand to create an old-age makeup.

Dawn designed the makeup for Reginald Owen's portrayal of Scrooge in the film based on Charles Dickens's novel *A Christmas Carol* (1938). Unlike some authors, Dickens took pains to describe his characters in elaborate detail, and Dawn conceived Owen's makeup from a close study of the pictures and text.

An entirely new coloring was worked out for Jeanette MacDonald in *Sweethearts* (1939). Dawn changed the color of her skin to near white, worked out an entirely new shade of lipstick—after fifteen different color tests for her lips—and changed her eye shadow to a very pale blue/gray. Emile LaVigne worked with Dawn on this. Dawn also created an old-age makeup for Luise Rainer for her role as an eighty-year-old woman in *The Great Waltz* (1938).

A number of onetime vaudevillian headliners were employed in the production of *Babes in Arms* (1939), which starred Judy Garland and Mickey Rooney. Dawn was given the challenge of subtracting twenty years from each of them. After completing such a youthful makeup on Irene Franklin, he asked her if she didn't look just like she did years ago. Ms. Franklin dryly commented, "Almost. One thing that is missing is a certain optimistic expression in the eyes."

Dawn traveled to MGM's English studios on the film *Goodbye, Mr. Chips* (1939), where he created another old-age makeup for Robert Donat's superb characterization of the eighty-three-year-old schoolmaster, Mr. Chipping.

The Wizard of Oz was a new high in makeup artistry. The film was a full nine months in the making, and many makeup artists and lab technicians worked day and night. It was Jack Dawn's intent to use as little makeup as possible to allow the personalities to show through their characterizations. He achieved this effect by designing their characters with the use of appliances, not masks; and he was so successful he had everyone wondering why Bert Lahr hadn't always reminded them of a lion!

Charlie Schram describes the application of Bert Lahr's makeup in his chapter. Lahr's job was probably the hardest, as his costume was created from real lion skins weighing about fifty pounds. After about twenty minutes in costume, he would have to remove it to rest.

The Tin Man's lot wasn't much easier. Jack Haley had to be very careful not to trip and fall because when he did, he couldn't get up without help. It took a welder to get him in and out of his costume. Silver makeup was needed to match the costume, but once applied, it didn't look right through the camera. Dawn discovered that by adding a little washing bluing to the silver, it achieved a tinny look under the cameras, especially when shined up with a soft cloth.

Dawn considered Ray Bolger's makeup the most challenging. As the Scarecrow, Bolger had to appear as though his head were made of burlap, stuffed with straw, and tied up with a rope. The design was molded on a plaster cast of Ray Bolger's face and then cast in foam rubber. Aljean Harmetz explains in her book *The Making of the Wizard of Oz*: "The result was a rubber bag wrinkled to simulate burlap. The bag covered Bolger's entire head except for his eyes, nose, and mouth and then extended down his neck, where it was tied with a piece of rope."

The Wizard was played by Frank Morgan, who had several startling makeup changes; not only as the Wizard but also as the Coachman who drove the Horse of a Different Color in Emerald City, and as Professor Marvel. Judy Garland, who gave a warm

An overwhelming number of skilled makeup
artists and lab technicians were behind the
successful makeup creations in *The Wizard of
Oz:* Jack Dawn, Josef and Gustaf Norin, Bill
Tuttle, Charlie Schram, and Emile LaVigne, to
mention a few. (*Photo courtesy of Gustaf Norin*)

and enchanting performance in her role as Dorothy, wore very little makeup. She was tested in a blond wig, but it was felt that she looked too sexy, so that was eliminated.

In *Joe and Ethel Turp Call on the President* (1939) Dawn had to make up the twenty-two-year-old Marsha Hunt and a forty-year-old Walter Brennan to appear as though their ages were close together. Hunt appeared as herself and then gradually aged. Brennan had to have about fifteen years taken off. Then he had to gradually age to his actual age and beyond.

It was about this time that Jack Dawn formed his own makeup company, "Jack Dawn, Inc.," known as "Third Dimensional Makeup." He received screen credit for the makeup in *Northwest Passage* (1940), which starred Gary Cooper and Preston Foster, and had a startling scene in it in which a decapitated head is pulled from a burlap bag.

Dawn turned his makeup expertise into something more than a means of make-believe when he began to make appliances for maimed soldiers. He built a new nose and cheeks for a young man who had been horribly burned when diving off a burning ship into a sea of flaming oil. The young soldier, who had become deeply embittered, shed tears when he saw his new face for the first time and told Dawn, "Now I can go home and see Mom." Working with Dr. Michael Gurdin and Lieutenant Gordon Bau, Dawn helped begin a prosthetic program for the navy.

Dawn's oldest son, Bob, returned from Europe in 1944. As a fighter pilot, Bob had been shot down several times over Germany and had had some harrowing experiences finding his way to safety through the enemy-filled Black Forest in the dead of night. Bob was studying very hard at UCLA as an aviation engineering student when a makeup apprenticeship opened at MGM.

"I realized that if I worked very hard as an engineer," Bob related, "at the end of ten years I might make as much as I'd make at the end of three years as a makeup man— so I did it for the money!"

Bob joined Terry Miles and Johnny True as apprentices at MGM and found his father a demanding taskmaster. Dawn didn't want to show favor to his son, so he actually treated him harder than the others. Bob didn't appreciate it and would become in-

furiated with his father at times. After all, he was a big hero just home from the war— and yet he had to sweep the floor and not be recognized for what he was.

"It was a good apprenticeship, partially because of Dad. There was a kind of practice session that went on almost every day. We worked on each other, on models; and I probably got to a point where I was as good a makeup man then as I've ever been in my life because of the things we repeatedly did; hair work and various kinds of age makeup. That's when we were very fast, very quick, and very thorough. It's improved technique-wise, but as far as knowing what you're doing, that was probably the best time. My dad took great pride in training the various people that came in there, and some of the better makeup artists came out of MGM."

In 1947 Bob was sent on location to Oregon on the picture *Green Dolphin Street* (1947). He was given the chore of spraying body makeup on the hardy stunt men who played the Indians. There were some extremely cold mornings, and the makeup was rather chilly when he sprayed it on their bodies. Bob took delight in teasing and tormenting these rugged men, calling them babies as they stood there shivering when the cold makeup hit them. When shooting ended, they had their revenge. Stripping Bob naked, they sprayed him completely with makeup about an inch thick, then tossed him into the river.

Jack Dawn retired from a very successful career in 1950, turning the reins of his department over to Bill Tuttle, an extremely gifted makeup artist and an excellent choice for department head.

Dawn took a trip to South America, where he remained for nearly a year, but his health had begun to fail and he entered the Motion Picture Home in San Fernando Valley. He passed away at the age of sixty-seven in 1956. He had lived a full life and given much to the motion picture industry.

After completing his apprenticeship in 1951, Bob remained at MGM until 1954 when he went independent. Dawn was skilled in lab work which he had learned during his apprenticeship, and in 1954 he worked as a lab man on *Creature from the Black Lagoon* with Jack Kevan, an extremely skilled makeup artist.

The "Creature" costume, which was worn by stunt men Ricou Browning, Tom

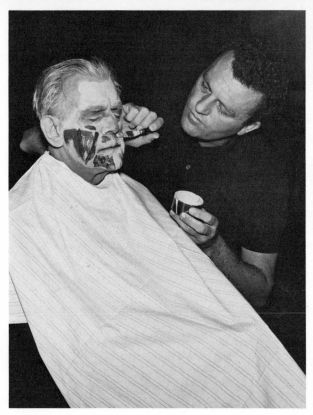

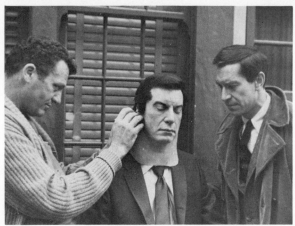

The "Mission: Impossible" show required many pull-off masks, intricate appliances that demand considerable skill to make and apply. Martin Landau watches as Bob Dawn applies a pull-off mask of his face to a double. (*Bob Dawn*)

Boris Karloff must be destroyed by a vat of acid in a "Thriller" television sequence, and Dawn supplied the appropriate makeup, including some Bromo Seltzer and alcohol which bubbled appropriately when sprayed with water. (*Bob Dawn*)

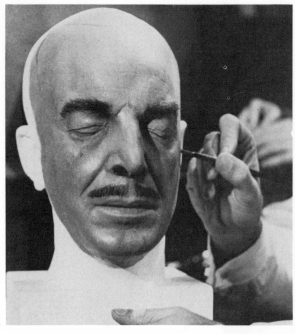

Although on screen Martin Landau could make a pull-off mask of Paul Stevens in a seemingly short time, Dawn's actual construction of the mask took several days for use on "Mission: Impossible." (*Bob Dawn*)

Hennessy, and Ben Chapman, was created of a very soft sponge rubber and could take very little abuse. Bob was always calling Kevan and Tom Case for new pieces and Kevan dubbed him "Push-the-Panic-Button Dawn."

Bob worked on *This Island Earth* (1955) at Universal, *The Ten Commandments* (1956) with Yul Brynner at Paramount, and then again with Brynner on *The King and I* (1956) at Twentieth Century-Fox.

Dawn has spent much of his career in television productions such as "Thriller," "Leave It to Beaver," "Wagon Train," "General Electric Theatre," and the "Alfred Hitchcock Show." In 1960 he worked on *Psycho*. Hitchcock wanted a very quick cut of an actual nude in the shower knifing scene. Janet Leigh, who played the part, would not appear nude, so they found a girl who was similar to Leigh in appearance. It was Bob's assignment to attach a piece of Y-shaped material covering the girl's most intimate parts. This was then blended in with makeup. Bob had to remain close by during the day, as she couldn't visit the rest room without a visit to him first. Bob was the envy of the crew.

Bob Dawn did pilots for "Star Trek" and "Big Valley" and was the makeup artist on seventy-three "Mission: Impossible" programs.

The "Mission: Impossible" show required many pull-off masks, intricate appliances that demand considerable skill to make and apply.

One "Mission: Impossible" show called for an inflatable reproduction of one of the characters. Dawn considers this one of his more challenging and satisfying jobs in the show. He had to construct internal stresses on the inflatable dummy so it would retain the shape of a head and chest. He built ribbons inside the cloth and if the special effects man turned the valve too much, the ribbons went "pop, pop, pop." However, the final performance went perfectly.

In 1974 Dawn worked with Bill Bixby on "The Magician," in 1975 he did *The Missouri Breaks* with Marlon Brando and Jack Nicholson, and in 1976 *Black Sunday* and *The Deep* with Robert Shaw. He continues to be an active participant in the film industry.

One "Mission: Impossible" show called for an inflatable reproduction of the character played by Torin Thatcher. Peter Lupus inflates Dawn's creation. (*Bob Dawn*)

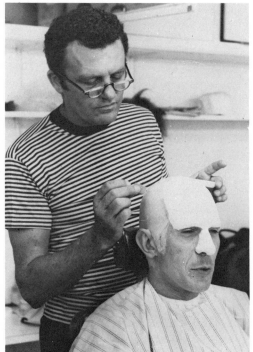

Actor Leonard Nimoy traded his pointed ears from "Star Trek" for numerous disguises on "Mission: Impossible." (*Bob Dawn*)

Chapter 4

THE BAUS

The name *Bau* is nearly synonymous with foam latex appliances in the field of makeup. If George Bau were alive today, he would undoubtedly be a walking encyclopedia of the makeup industry. But mandatory retirement forced Bau out of the industry in 1971 and led to his death in 1974.

George Bau is recognized by most of his fellow makeup artists as having been the appliance genius of the industry, and his generous help to Dick Smith, Rick Baker, and many, many others aided them in the perfection of their craft.

George was born in Minnesota in 1905, and his brother, R. Gordon Bau, was born two years later in 1907. George's son, Robert K. Bau, who also followed his father's footsteps into makeup, was born in California in 1929.

By 1937 George and Gordon were employed by Rubbercraft of Torrance, California. The Baus developed a side business of manufacturing rubber dolls and various other rubber products for the studios, including Oriental eye prosthetics. When George developed a microporous sponge rubber with tissue-thin edges that looked, felt, and wrinkled like skin, it was this new formula that helped revolutionize the makeup industry. Only George Bau knew its formula.

The lab work for the prosthetics for Charles Laughton's portrayal of Quasimodo in *The Hunchback of Notre Dame* (1939), an RKO release, was done at the Warner Brothers lab where Perc Westmore was head of the Makeup Department. George and Gordon were called in as independents to develop these prosthetics.

Perc Westmore set up an elaborate laboratory at Warner Brothers for the development of prosthetics. George specialized in making the foamed latex sponge; and Gordon specialized in latex goods. During their years at Warner Brothers, George invented the foam sponge beater which is still widely used today.

In the film *Juarez* (1939), Paul Muni wore Bau's appliances to achieve the appearance of the Mexican liberator. It was during this film that a problem with Bau's creation became evident. The oils in the makeup would rot the sponge rubber, causing it to deteriorate. The rubber was lacquered first, but this gave Muni a wooden-faced appearance, and too much facial movement caused the appliances to crack.

George created a new makeup formula to use on the rubber pieces. One of the most successful films in which this new formula was employed was MGM's *Arsenic and Old Lace* (1944), which starred Peter Lorre, Cary Grant, Jean Adair, Josephine Hull, and Priscilla Lane. Raymond Massey was disguised in this film as Boris Karloff, as Karloff

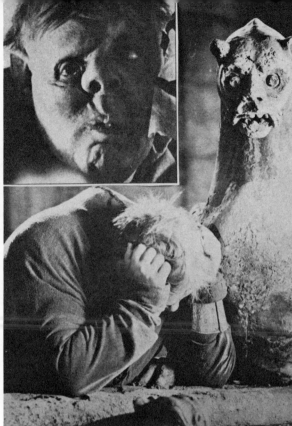

George and an unidentified man in Warner Brothers second makeup lab. Note the hand on the table. It was a cast of George's own hand and was used in the chiller *The Beast with Five Fingers*, which starred Peter Lorre. (© *Warner Bros.*)

George and Gordon Bau's entry into the film industry came when they assisted Perc Westmore at Warner Brothers in the prosthetic appliance work needed for Charles Laughton's portrayal of Quasimodo in RKO's 1939 version of *The Hunchback of Notre Dame*. (© *RKO*)

was unavailable for the film version.

Gordon and George separated when Gordon joined the navy in the early forties. He operated a prosthetic laboratory for the disfigured and amputated. At the end of World War II, Gordon resigned his commission and accepted a position with RKO Studios as Director of Makeup. Gordon remained at RKO for three years. When Perc Westmore was relieved of his position at Warner Brothers, Gordon left RKO and became Director of Makeup at Warner Brothers. After Gordon became head of Makeup at Warner Brothers, a more extensive laboratory was built. Gordon then proceeded to develop the studio's own cosmetic line known as Warner Brothers' Cosmetics.

During George Bau's years at the studios, he continued his many inventions and formulas. In the late forties, he developed the first plastic bald cap. Prior to this, they had all been made from rubber latex. He developed a method to preserve plaster molds so they could be used several times before

they would deteriorate. In the fifties, George used phenolic resins in making masks. This was the basis for the mask he created for Vincent Price in *House of Wax* (1953). He also developed the pressure injection method of inserting foam latex into large-size molds.

George formed Hollywood Latex Products, a side business which catered to individuals outside the studios. It later became known as G. T. Bau Laboratories. This firm sold many items all over the world, specializing in foam latex ingredients, bald plastic caps, and cosmetics for appliances. He also developed a plastic scar material sold in tubes and known as Scarola. He invented the first plastic toupee cement used extensively by the studios. This was known as Invisible and was in great demand by the public and theatre as well.

In 1953 Warner Brothers began to take advantage of the then-popular fad of 3-dimensional movies. They filmed *House of Wax* in 3-D and CinemaScope color, with

Gordon Bau joined the navy in the early forties and operated a prosthetic lab for the disfigured and amputees. Here Gordon (in uniform) shows George the lab. (*Photo courtesy of Bob Bau*)

Top right: Vincent Price in makeup for the role of Henry Jarrod in *House of Wax*. (© *Warner Bros.*)

Center right: Henry Jarrod (Vincent Price) becomes horribly scarred when a devastating fire in the *House of Wax* destroys his handsome features. George Bau created this macabre makeup under the supervision of doctors to ensure its realism as burned flesh. (© *Warner Bros.*)

Bottom right: Makeup application took nearly three hours, as did the removal, and both stages were extremely painful for Price. (© *Warner Bros.*)

MAKING A MONSTER

Carl Switzer, well known for his portrayal of Alfalfa in Hal Roach's *Our Gang* films, was chosen to play the part of a one-hundred-year-old Indian in *Track of the Cat*. (*Bob Bau*)

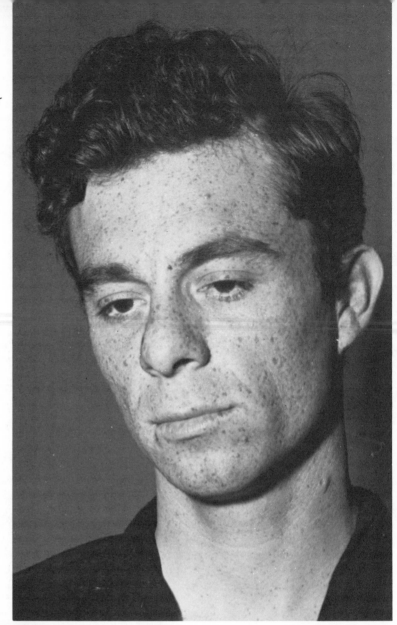

Bottom left: Gauze hides and flattens Switzer's own hair. (*Bob Bau*)

Bottom center: George's foam-latex mask is glued into place. (*Bob Bau*)

Bottom right: George blends in the foam-latex mask with Switzer's own skin. (*Bob Bau*)

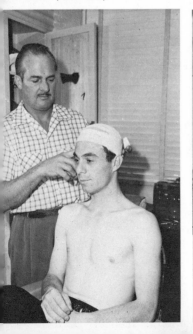
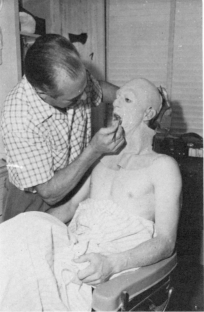
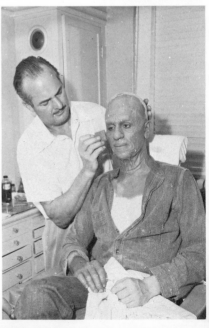

Carl "Alfalfa" Switzer wearing George Bau's old-age Indian makeup for his role in *Track of the Cat*. (*Bob Bau*)

Bottom left: Once the facial makeup is completed, George carefully adds the hand appliances. (*Bob Bau*)

Bottom center: George gently adds the wig. (*Bob Bau*)

Bottom right: Note the completed hand makeup. (*Bob Bau*)

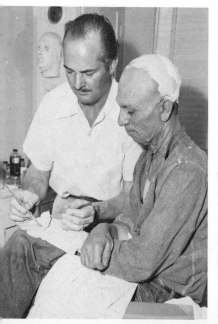

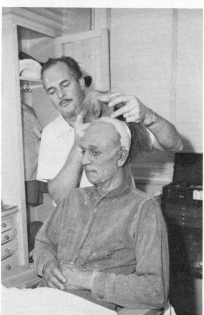

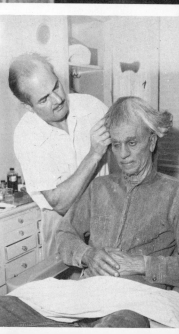

George is obviously pleased with the final results of his wax creations of Bela Lugosi and Lon Chaney, Jr., used for publicity purposes for United Artists release of *The Black Sheep*. (© *United Artists*)

Opposite: George checks off the prestigious cast of wax figures he created for *The Black Sheep* with assistance from son Robert. (© *United Artists*)

Vincent Price starring in a role that seemed tailor-made for him. The story is about Henry Jarrod (Vincent Price), creator and co-owner of a wax museum in New York City in the early 1900s. Price's greedy partner sets the museum on fire in order to collect the insurance money, and Price tries to stop him. Price is knocked unconscious and left for dead as the museum burns.

Price recovers, however, but he has a horribly scarred face. Before setting out to avenge his destroyer, he creates a lifelike mask, identical to his previously unscarred features, in order to hide the grotesque face he must now live with. Having killed both his ex-partner and his ex-partner's girl friend, Carolyn Jones, he must now murder Jones's roommate who discovers her dead roommate's body disguised as the wax figure of Joan of Arc in Price's new museum. As she attempts to fight Price off, she strikes his face and his lifelike mask crumbles, revealing his hideously burned features. The wax life mask and the scarred face were the creation of George Bau. Vincent Price describes his experiences with this makeup and Bau:

"I'm told it was one of the most elaborately real makeups ever done. Two doctors supervised it to be sure the burns were as would be. It took almost three hours to put on and as long to take off . . . and both processes were very painful. Because the picture was scheduled for only thirty days, I sometimes had to wear makeup for ten hours. I couldn't eat because my mouth was partially 'scar tissue,' so I drank many liquids and because of the running around in makeup, I fainted one day from lack of oxygen. Lon Chaney, Sr., only wore his 'creations' for a few hours, but those were the good old days.

"George Bau, who did this makeup, and I became great friends, not only because he was a wonderful man, but we spent six hours a day almost alone together getting to the studio before anyone else and checking them all out at night. George, under the supervision of the two doctors—especially Dr. Gunzberg, an eye specialist who was credited with perfecting the process of 3-D—took great pains, and I don't mean just mine, to study burnt scar tissues. These were then molded in rubber, applied with alcohol, or spirit gum, or collodion, and then tinted with many colors of makeup.

"For the famous scene where the girl strikes my face and it cracks and falls off, showing the burnt face underneath—a wax cast of my own face was made—then another of my burnt face—the "real" one enlarged to fit over the burnt one, and for one hour of horror, I wore two masks while the camera was set up and the director satisfied everything was perfect for hopefully *one* perfect take—it worked and the scene is still remembered as one of the horror highlights of the history of the cinema."

A makeup that Bau always considered his finest was for the film *Track of the Cat* (1954). The studio approached George and explained their dilemma. The film called for an Indian about one hundred years old; however, the role itself was incredibly physical and demanding. Furthermore, the film was to be shot on location at Mount Rainier, Washington, which is 9,000 feet above sea level. It was difficult not only to find a one-hundred-year-old actor to play the part, but one who could survive at 9,000 feet above sea level. They had to find a young, vigorous actor to play the part, and they asked George if he could truly make such an actor look one hundred years old.

His answer was decisive. "Yes, absolutely!" George Bau had that quality of creative insight and showmanship that separates the makeup artist from the makeup man. A makeup artist of any creativity recognizes that it is vital to present your creation in its entirety to the director because even the most experienced director may not truly be able to visualize what the makeup artist can do.

Audiences might be very surprised to learn that the actor chosen to portray this old Indian was the well-known child star Carl "Alfalfa" Switzer, formerly of the *Our Gang* series. He was twenty-six at the time.

George secured the complete wardrobe and a small room at the studio where he completely transformed Switzer into the one-hundred-year-old Indian. He had all the furniture, with the exception of the makeup table, removed from the dressing room and then arranged Switzer, in full makeup, in the corner of the room sitting cross-legged, Indian-style. Then the director walked in and saw this creation. He was impressed and totally satisfied with George's old-age make-

up transformation.

Until Gordon Bau's retirement as Director of Makeup in 1972, many films passed through and out of the Warner Brothers Makeup Department. Gordon's more notable achievements were *The Silver Chalice* (1954), *East of Eden* (1955), *Giant* (1956), *My Fair Lady* (1964), *Who's Afraid of Virginia Woolf?* (1966), and *The Illustrated Man* (1969).

Robert Bau joined his father and uncle in the midfifties and served his apprenticeship from 1954 to 1957. On Robert's first day in the studio, he watched George making up Anne Baxter's lips. He was quivering the line, and in front of Miss Baxter he told Robert that a quivered line looked more natural. After she had left the room, he confessed to Robert that he was suffering from a party hangover and just had the shakes!

Another recollection Robert shared with us was an incident that occurred shortly after he had returned from Korea, where he'd been a front-line combat soldier. He was asleep in George's home one night when George came sneaking into the bedroom wearing a monster mask which was to be used in the next day's shooting.

"He was really hamming it up," Robert went on, "and when I woke up, I was frightened and thought I was back in Korea. I promptly jumped on this monster and beat the hell out of it. Needless to say, the results were one ruined mask and no shooting the next day. I still don't know what excuse he gave the company, but he never tried that again."

After Robert served his apprenticeship, he then became a lab assistant and remained in this position until he served as head of the laboratory from 1970 to 1972, when he left makeup. He does return on occasion to make up such actors as Paul Newman and Jean Simmons or to help out the Local.

George created all the makeup for *The Black Sleep* (1956), and he agreed to create lifelike wax figures from a particularly macabre scene in the film as a publicity stunt. George didn't agree to this at first. He had never been too impressed with the results of wax figures he had seen. But he had the feeling that he could create some very lifelike figures using plastic, and so he agreed to try.

The Black Sleep starred such notables as

Basil Rathbone, John Carradine, Akim Tamiroff, Lon Chaney, Jr., and Tor Johnson. Bela Lugosi accepted the part of the deaf mute servant, despite the lack of dialogue. Lugosi, who had recently fought a long battle against heroin addiction, was trying desperately for a comeback.

Robert worked with George on the creation of the figures. He describes it as a "flat-rate deal" and admits that George lost money on the proposition. But the figures were so absolutely lifelike that it was difficult to distinguish the figures from the real thing.

"He used to poo-poo my hobby of aircraft building," Robert told us, "until I suggested that an epoxy resin I was using might be tried on figures because of its light weight and durability. It was successful on our first try but expensive. It's quite a process. We also used the same process years later in building the mannequin of Rod Steiger for *The Illustrated Man*."

The figures were sent to New York's Loew's Theatre and set up with a beautiful live girl on an operating table with the hideous figures bending over her.

Robert and George also made a mannequin of Donald Crisp for the film *Spencer's Mountain* (1963), from which "The Waltons" television series evolved. This particular mannequin was not used for publicity, though, but for a tree-falling sequence in the film.

Gordon, George, and Robert were extensively involved in the film *Giant* (1956), which starred Elizabeth Taylor, Rock Hudson, James Dean, Mercedes McCambridge, and Chill Wills. The film required twenty-eight makeup artists, with two makeup artists and an assistant assigned for each aging makeup each day. The aging required was not extensive, being only to middle age, but this is often more difficult. George and Robert made all the age appliances, and both did the makeup on Chill Wills.

Dick Smith has been very impressed with George's products and has written the following about him:

"I would say that George Bau was the only person in the makeup industry that helped me to any great extent. Most of the time, I had to teach myself by doing everything the wrong way first. Our relationship was, of course, a commercial one. George alone knew the formulas for his products, and I don't know to this day what the formu-

George and Robert made all the age appliances and did the makeup on fifty-three-year-old Chill Wills for his role in *Giant*. (© *Warner Bros.*)

George proudly displays the mannequin head of Donald Crisp he and Robert created for *Spencer's Mountain*. (*Bob Bau*)

las were. However, he was particularly helpful and generous in teaching the use of foam latex and in the making of molds. He devoted a great deal of time to me in the form of letters. I personally consider George Bau as one of the innovators and contributors in a very substantial way to the art of foam prosthetics, and the pity of it is that I doubt that his name hardly, if ever, got on the screen. It was always someone else who got credit for his really creative work.''

Before work could begin on the film *The Illustrated Man,* it became necessary to find dyes that could be used without danger on Rod Steiger's body. In the film, Steiger played the part of Carl, a former carnival roustabout who has been seduced by Felicia, the skin illustrator. Steiger's wife, Claire Bloom, played the part of the enticing Felicia who lures Carl into her house and tattoos his entire body. Three months of intensive research on rabbits and guinea pigs were conducted at the Applied Biological Sciences Laboratory of Glendale, California.

When the doctors were satisfied that the dyes would have no ill effect on Steiger's body, the studio then went ahead with the film.

George Bau, along with his son Robert, created a life-size mannequin of Steiger, and artist Jim Reynolds painted it with vivid psychedelic tattoos in ten colors as a guide for the makeup men in ''tattooing'' Steiger. Steiger lay on the table in a large sterile room, and the nine makeup artists, with Gordon Blau guiding them, began the intricate and beautiful pattern that became *The Illustrated Man*.

Some of the television series that Gordon Bau supervised, assisted by George and Robert, were ''Casablanca,'' ''Roaring Twenties,'' ''77 Sunset Strip,'' ''Bourbon Street Beat,'' ''Hawaiian Eye,'' ''Alaskans,'' ''Bronco,'' ''Colt 45,'' ''Maverick,'' ''Sugarfoot,'' ''Wendy and Me,'' ''Room for One More,'' ''Hank,'' ''Surfside-Six,'' ''Cheyenne,'' ''Lawman,'' ''Temple Houston,'' and ''F-Troop.''

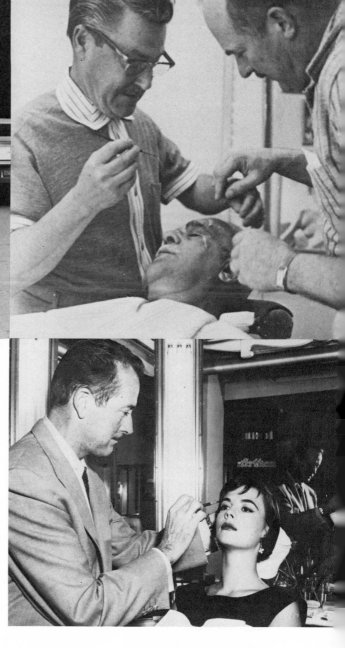

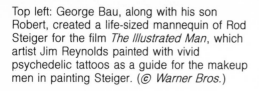

Top left: George Bau, along with his son Robert, created a life-sized mannequin of Rod Steiger for the film *The Illustrated Man*, which artist Jim Reynolds painted with vivid psychedelic tattoos as a guide for the makeup men in painting Steiger. (© *Warner Bros.*)

Top right: George, right, and an unknown makeup artist add scars to Boris Karloff's face for his role in yet another Frankenstein feature: *Frankenstein—1970.* (© *Allied Artists*)

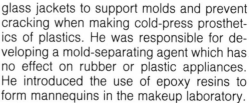

Right: Gordon Bau puts the finishing touches on a beauty makeup for actress Natalie Wood. Probably Gordon's greatest achievements were his cosmetics and the widely used roll-on mascara still in use today. (*Photo courtesy of Bob Bau*)

George was head of makeup on the "Line-up" television series shot in San Francisco and became assistant department head from 1965 to 1970 at Warner Brothers. Gordon retired in 1972, and he died in 1975. Probably Gordon's greatest achievements were his cosmetics and the widely used roll-on mascara still in use today.

Robert refined mold-making techniques by impregnating plaster molds with fiberglass instead of jute fiber, which shrank and cracked molds. He also developed fiber-glass jackets to support molds and prevent cracking when making cold-press prosthetics of plastics. He was responsible for developing a mold-separating agent which has no effect on rubber or plastic appliances. He introduced the use of epoxy resins to form mannequins in the makeup laboratory.

George Bau will always be remembered for his "secret formula" of foam latex, which gave the makeup world the ability to transform the normal into the abnormal, the beautiful into the grotesque, and youth into old age.

Chapter 5

CLAY CAMPBELL

Clay Campbell came to California from Toronto, Canada, in 1922 at the age of twenty-one. He and his widowed mother settled in Whittier, and he commuted daily to the Oates Waxworks in Los Angeles. I was at the Oates Wax Factory, where Campbell learned the skill of wax figure making, a process that was once a guarded secret which was passed from generation to generation, father to son. During his three years of apprenticeship Campbell learned the correct combination of such waxes as ceresin, stearic, carnauba, and beeswax; the temperatures at which each is added to the mix; and the temperature at which the mix is finally poured. It was also during this time, from 1922 to 1932, that Campbell learned how to make casts, molds, and how to paint the wax mannequins.

While at the Oates Wax Factory, Campbell met a wigmaker by the name of George Westmore. Westmore told Campbell that he should go out and join his sons, Perc and Ernest, who were "making it good" in the movie studios, making up the stars. Campbell remembers that George Westmore always gave him a free haircut.

In 1932 the wax studio made the figures for *The Mystery of the Wax Museum* (1933), which starred Fay Wray and Lionel Atwill. At the completion of the job, Campbell was sent to Warner Brothers to "baby-sit" with the figures and repair them when they got broken, which was most of the time. Perc Westmore, head of Warner Brothers' Makeup Department at the time, told him, "If you can paint those wax dummies that good, you can paint the live dummies that act in the pictures." So Campbell chose the profession and became one of Hollywood's most successful makeup artists until his retirement in 1966.

During the filming of *The Mystery of the Wax Museum* Clay was awed by all he saw at Warner Brothers. He took some pictures of the filming and in one picture caught the propman standing with an umbrella over one of the figures that happened to be melting. In 1933 the Technicolor process required many Klieg lights and the sets were extremely hot.

One experience that Campbell had before leaving the wax factory concerned Jack Dawn. Dawn was doing a picture for MGM, where he was the head makeup artist, and this picture required seven different faces for Paul Muni, and one of them had to be a wax mask. Dawn was trying to model the wax himself, but it wasn't coming out so that it could be transposed onto the actor's face. It was decided that a cast would be taken and the mask made at the wax factory, so Campbell and another man from the factory went to the studio to take the cast.

Campbell recalled that they arrived right

in the middle of Dawn's applying the makeup on Muni, and they just walked right in and looked and asked questions, and probably appeared very obnoxious. Little did Campbell realize then that in three or four years he would be the one applying a similar makeup on Muni.

In 1932 Campbell became Perc Westmore's assistant at Warner Brothers. Campbell created an old-age makeup on Aline MacMahon for her role in *As the Earth Turns* (1933). Campbell employed liquid adhesive for this effect. As it was applied to each area of her face, Campbell would stretch and hold her skin while the adhesive was dried with a hand dryer. The skin was then powdered with talc before it was released. Although liquid adhesive was fine for an old-age effect in those early days of makeup, it was a challenge to remove after filming.

Most of Campbell's career was spent making beautiful women more beautiful. He came to be known as one of the best beauty makeup men in the business, so he enjoyed perfecting his technique to a point where it was invisible. When he could create an effect without showing the makeup, he was very happy.

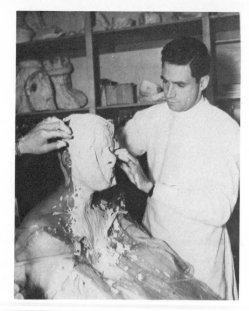

Perc Westmore becomes a willing subject as Campbell applies plaster of Paris to make a face cast. The skin was first lubricated with Vaseline. Campbell never used straws in the nose, as some makeup artists do, but would take special care with that area so the subject would have no trouble breathing. (*Clay Campbell*)

Campbell removes the front half of the head cast, much to Westmore's delight. (*Clay Campbell*)

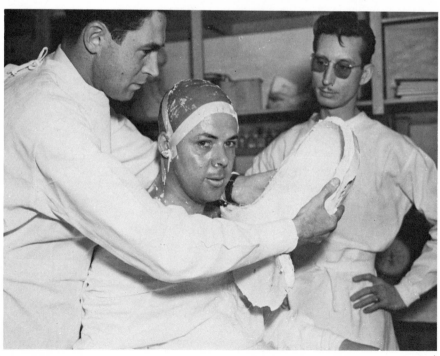

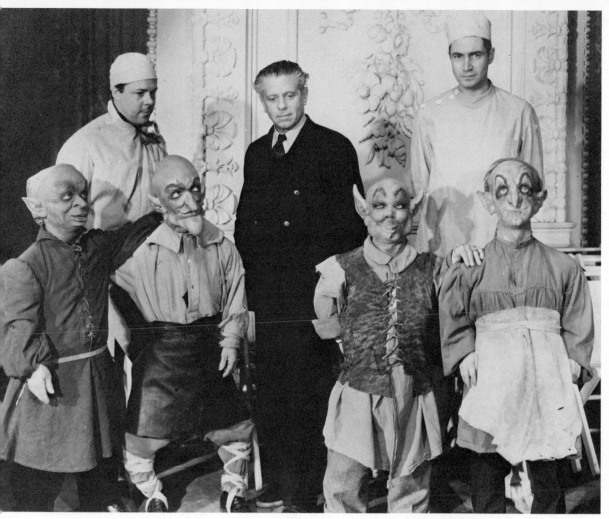

Perc Westmore (*right*), Director Max Reinhardt (*center*), and Clay Campbell (*left*) pose with Westmore's and Campbell's dwarf creations for *A Midsummer Night's Dream*. (© *Warner Bros.*)

A little trick Campbell used to employ created for him a most unusual collection of Hollywood artifacts. Whenever he used to make up a beautiful movie star, he would take a lip impression so that he or anyone else could make her up a second time with very little difficulty. This has resulted in a collection of over two thousand lip imprints of some of the most famous beauties in filmland.

In Max Reinhardt's *A Midsummer Night's Dream* (1935) Perc Westmore and Campbell constructed all the grotesque masks worn by the dwarfs and the donkey head worn by James Cagney. The donkey's head had to be seen forming itself on Cagney's face. This was done with stop-action photography and gave Campbell the idea that he was able to use some twenty years later

in *Son of Dr. Jekyll* (1951).

Campbell and Westmore would make up the cast for *A Midsummer Night's Dream* during the day, and then at night they would work on the construction of the head for Cagney. They would snatch a few hours of sleep during the day between makeups, and then go back to work all night. They didn't see much of their homes for those two weeks.

In *The Story of Louis Pasteur* (1935) Campbell had to go out to Paul Muni's ranch to make him up at six-thirty A.M. and to stay with him until the makeup was removed at night. He also had to take the wig home every night and clean it. On one particular night Muni had removed part of his makeup but didn't wait for Campbell to remove the black wax from his hairline. Muni chose to

45

Campbell adjusts Paul Muni's beard on the set of *The Story of Louis Pasteur*. (© *Warner Bros.*)

Paul Muni in makeup for his role in *The Story of Louis Pasteur*. (© *Warner Bros.*)

shampoo his own hair with acetone. Campbell tried to stop him but to no avail. Three days later, Campbell again arrived to make him up for the start of the picture, and when he looked at him—Muni was yellow! His skin was yellow; his eyeballs were yellow. The acetone had given Muni yellow jaundice. It held up the picture for about a week.

Perc Westmore was a perfectionist. For weeks prior to the actual makeup tests of Muni as Zola in *The Life of Emile Zola* (1937), Muni and Westmore discussed makeup concepts. Campbell was Westmore's assistant and would apply the makeup for the tests under Westmore's supervision. However, when shooting began, Campbell was on his own to apply Westmore's makeup creation with all the care and perfection that Westmore would demand of himself.

Muni was also a perfectionist, and Campbell felt under great strain when working with him. He recalls a day when Muni was very exacting. Everything was wrong, and he wouldn't be pleased, despite the fact that there were several hundred extras on the set. It was a big courtroom scene. The as-

sistants were barking at makeup to hurry, and nothing was going right. One of the tasks Campbell had to accomplish involved an old theatrical trick of raising the forehead with a piece of chamois. Wax was put on the hairline to flatten it down. Then a coating of collodion was applied. Then a piece of chamois about three inches wide and ten inches long was fastened to the back of the head with a small hook and eye. The forehead was covered with collodion and makeup. By the time this was done, Campbell was a wreck. Muni was upset, and taking a last look into the mirror before stepping out onto the set, when he spotted a flaw in his forehead and ripped the whole thing off. When he did this, the hook put a long deep gash into the bridge of his nose. Muni was bleeding on and off for most of the day.

The whole makeup was removed and a new chamois prepared. When the extras and crew came back from lunch, Muni stepped onto the set and did a thirty-minute scene without a cut. With all his eccentricities, Muni was quite an actor.

Claude Rains was just as nervous as Paul

Claude Rains poses in Campbell's makeup for his role as Don Luis in *Anthony Adverse*. (© *Warner Bros.*)

Below right: Campbell made up George Stone to resemble a cat for his role as Sancho in *Anthony Adverse*. (© *Warner Bros.*)

Muni before a scene. Probably more nervous, if that was possible, because in Warner Brothers' *Anthony Adverse* (1936), Rains wore a very simple makeup—a wig and a very small, smart beard—whereas Muni always wore complicated makeup.

In 1938 Campbell went to Twentieth Century-Fox as head of the Makeup Department. Darryl F. Zanuck and Bill Koenig were in charge of Fox at the time. Both Zanuck and Koenig were at Warner Brothers when Campbell was an apprentice, and Campbell felt that he was still being treated like one. Clay was back at Warner Brothers in 1940 after two years with Twentieth Century-Fox. Ulcers!

Perc Westmore stuck by him, though, and helped him to get the position of head of Makeup at Columbia in 1941, and after one year's probation, he was given a five-year contract. He remained with Columbia until he retired in 1966.

While at Twentieth Century-Fox, Campbell had an opportunity to employ his skill in waxworks for the film *Charlie Chan at the Wax Museum* (1939). Life casts were made of three of its stars: Sidney Toler as Chan, Joan Valerie as Lily Latimer, and Mark Lawrence as Steve McBirney. The remaining wax figures used in the film were rented. In order to implant hair into the warm wax, Campbell used an embroidery needle. He would cut the needle off at the middle of the eye. Once cut in half, the needle became a fine prong with which to embed each hair, one at a time. Although a wig was used on

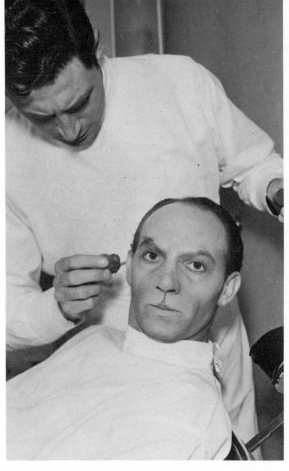

Will the real Sidney Toler please sit down! While at Twentieth Century-Fox, Campbell had an opportunity to employ his skill in waxworks for the film *Charlie Chan at the Wax Museum*. (*Courtesy of Twentieth Century-Fox Film Corporation*)

Joan Valerie's wax double, the eyebrows and eyelashes were real, as were Toler's and Lawrence's.

Campbell made up Henry Fonda as Lincoln in *Young Mr. Lincoln* (1939). Many sketches were made. Campbell employed a special artist for this purpose, and the more sketches they made of Lincoln, the more Lincoln looked like Fonda!

Prior to Campbell's going to Twentieth Century-Fox as head of the Makeup Department, he had taken a trip East and bought a small trunkful of books of all periods anticipating their eventual help in his future characterizations. He was fortunate, indeed, to have found many books that had full pictures of Lincoln. Campbell also sent to Washington for the official casts of Lincoln. Three casts of the nose were made for the physical change in Fonda's face; however, this was the only physical change. The rest was shadow and highlight makeup, which shows us Campbell's skill.

In 1943 Columbia presented Bela Lugosi in *The Return of the Vampire*. Lugosi, playing Dracula, becomes trapped in a London blitz and is unable to return to his coffin be-

fore daylight. Thus, good vampire that he was, he dies and disintegrates before the eyes of a terrified audience. Campbell explains how he created this effect:

"As usually happens when I get working on an idea, the idea expands. New effects suggest themselves and you have to improvise as you go along. This happened on the Lugosi makeup. I had cast two heads, front half only, as thinly as possible, in wax. With a hot iron tool I was thinning it when I realized that when it melted in the scene there would be nothing left. So after getting it as thin as possible, I took wet modeling clay and applied it to the inside of the head to form a mold for a skull. Then, before pouring the plaster into this mold, I had another idea that, if it didn't melt, what would happen? So I rushed down to Special Effects and asked the head man to rig a wire inside the still unpoured plaster skull, so that if necessary, it could be heated enough to help with the melting process.

" 'Not necessary,' he said. So I poured the skull and removed it when it had hardened. There I had a skull and a wax head. Now I had to put the full head of hair, eye-

Joan Valerie (*right*) and her wax double. Although a wig was used on Valerie's wax double, the eyebrows and eyelashes were real. (*Courtesy of Twentieth Century-Fox Film Corporation*)

brows, and eyelashes on the wax head. The hair was stuck into the warm wax, hair by hair. It took a long, long time to do this. When it came time to shoot the disintegration, a dummy figure was dressed in Lugosi's suit. The plaster skull—without the heating unit I might add—was placed and ready for the wax head of Lugosi. I got two glass eyes and put them in the skull's eye sockets, then placed the wax head over the skull.

"They started shooting. Three men turned on portable room heaters. Soon, three more heaters were requisitioned. Two hours later, with the help of even more heaters, the head was finally melting very well. But it required a lot of film and a lot of cutting and editing, whereas a heated skull would have worked, I'm quite sure. But that's the way they do things in the pictures—sometimes."

Campbell created a very effective werewolf makeup for Matt Willis in this same film. As a result Universal Studios started legal proceedings against Columbia alleging that they copied Jack Pierce's makeup for Lon Chaney, Jr., in *The Wolf Man*. It was proved that Columbia's makeup conception was

original, since they used no rubber appliances as Universal did. Campbell feels that his was much better.

There was no time in which to prepare a special wig for Willis, so in order to achieve the effect Campbell wanted, the werewolf makeup was done with loose hair. After the makeup was worked out, Campbell and his assistant began laying the hair. Campbell did one side while his assistant did the other side. Campbell would check both sides, front, and back, adding any necessary touches. The werewolf nose was simply black makeup applied directly to Willis's nose, and the odd shape of the ears was achieved by shaping hair as it was laid on. A set of werewolf teeth were built for Willis by a dentist for $600.

Another actor whom Campbell enjoyed working with was Louis Hayward. In the 1951 film *Son of Dr. Jekyll* Campbell conceived the process by which Hayward's face could change from the good-looking Dr. Jekyll to the horrible Mr. Hyde in one continuous take without remaking his face or using stop-motion photography. He found that by using special filters on cam-

Campbell made up Henry Fonda as Lincoln for *Young Mr. Lincoln*. A nose was the only physical change in Fonda, the rest being achieved with highlight and shadow. (*Clay Campbell*)

eras he could achieve the appearance of continuous change in the actor's face.

Campbell made up Hayward's face, with red rouge and a red lipstick pencil, to look like the creature Hyde. The red pencil was used to draw sharp lines and the rouge was used for delicate shading. When this was viewed with the naked eye, of course, Haywood looked rather funny. But when viewed through a red filter, he looked normal. The illusion of evil was created when viewed through a blue filter, turning the seemingly normal features into the terrifying Mr. Hyde.

Because the whole process was an experiment, Hayward spent many long hours in the makeup chair. The number-one problem was to get a neutral foundation for his face and hands that would have the same look regardless of the filters used. The second problem was to mix a red makeup that would have the same look as the foundation when viewed through the red filter. Then they needed a blue or green filter that would turn the red makeup black without affecting the neutral foundation. In addition, Hayward's clothing had to meet the same requirements. Even the floor had to be of a neutral tone so that it would not change color as the split (blue-green/red) filter went across the lens.

After the foundation was applied and powdered with talc, it was necessary to apply the red Mr. Hyde makeup while looking through a blue-green filter. Quite challenging, to say the least. This ingenious idea worked only with black and white films.

The film *Salome* (1953), starring Rita Hayworth, whom Campbell made up for the entire film, required John the Baptist to be beheaded and was a film that gave Campbell great pleasure. As with all the other character makeups in the film, Campbell came up with sketches of each actor's makeup from reading the script. The studio propman had an old papier-mâché head that he was going to bring in since there were no plans to show the head up close.

Campbell felt a close-up would be a very effective part of the film, and he created a wax head with real hair implanted in the wax that could take a large close-up. At the preview of the film when the severed head was shown on the large silver tray, the audience screamed, and Perc Westmore, sitting about two rows behind Campbell, shouted, "Dig that crazy dessert!"

Campbell had his own idea for creating a monster similar to Frankenstein's. Unlike Frankenstein's monster, who was created from the parts of dead bodies, Campbell's monster would be created from the raw ma-

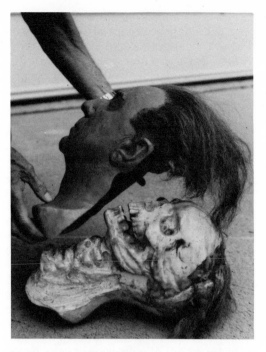

A wax head of Bela Lugosi was created by Campbell to fit over a skull for the disintegration scene in *The Return of the Vampire*. (*Columbia Pictures*)

Campbell created a very effective werewolf makeup on Matt Willis in *The Return of the Vampire* using no rubber appliances. (*Columbia Pictures*)

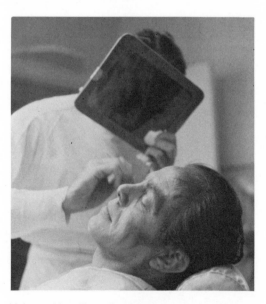

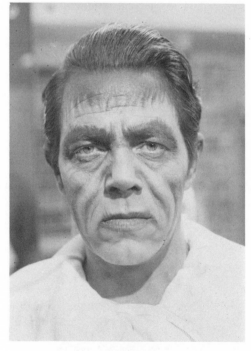

Using a blue filter, Campbell creates the illusion of evil on Louis Hayward for his role in *Son of Dr. Jekyll*. (*Columbia Pictures*)

A red pencil was used to draw sharp lines on Hayward's face, and rouge was used for delicate shading. When viewed through a red filter, Hayward's face appeared normal, but when viewed through a blue filter, he became the hideous Mr. Hyde. (*Columbia Pictures*)

terials in a giant blender.

The camera would shoot straight down into a blender of clear whirling water. As the ingredients are added—a spoonful of this and a cup of that—the clear water becomes muddied. When it is opaque, the camera is stopped and the muddied water is replaced with clear hot water. In the center is placed a wax head without hair and with only half-formed features. The blender is turned on again and turned to the highest heat. The camera runs backward for this part of the effect. When the wax has melted, the waters are muddied up again. When the film is edited, Campbell feels the illusion should be fantastic. He would also have his monster receive many skin grafts to give the monster the scars that all monsters have, of course.

Campbell created a series of aging make-ups on Tyrone Power for his role as Marty Maher in Columbia's *The Long Gray Line* (1955). Campbell made a series of sketches of the forty-one-year-old Power, from youth to old age. He employed rubber jowls, which he considers to have been a major invention in the field of makeup, as well as eye bags, to assist him in the transformation of Power to appear as a man in his seventies. Comparing Campbell's sketches of Power's old-age makeup to the photos of Power in his old-age makeup shows that Campbell is an extremely gifted individual.

A very challenging makeup Campbell accomplished was for *The Five Thousand Fingers of Dr. T.* (1952). This was a story by Dr. Seuss. He illustrates his own books, and the illustrations are nearly impossible to re-create, according to Campbell.

The Dr. Seuss script called for construction of a very strange beard. The beard was to be approximately twenty-five-feet long. It was to be growing from the faces of two men and connected in the middle so that it was considered one very long beard with a man on each end!

The two men who shared the beard were to perform acrobatic feats on roller skates, so this required that the beard be flexible yet remain soft-flowing and natural-appearing. It also had to be strong enough to support the weight of a small child, who would be required to hang on to the middle of the beard. The weight of the child hanging onto the beard would be borne by the two men.

Campbell created a wax head with real hair implanted for John the Baptist in *Salome*. (*Clay Campbell*)

Campbell created a series of aging makeups on forty-one-year-old Tyrone Power for his role in *The Long Gray Line*. He made a series of sketches of Power from youth to old age. (*Clay Campbell*)

Campbell was remarkably successful in transferring his sketch of the makeup to the actual features of Tyrone Power. (*Clay Campbell*)

Campbell designed a ball socket and cable system to be supported by the Peter Pan-type flying harness. This provided the flexibility and strength required of the lengthy beard.

Using several pieces of sponge-rubber seat padding, Campbell cut them into strips to form a long flexible tube. This was tapered from the width of the jaw, which was the widest part of the beard, to the narrowest section, which was the middle area of the complete beard. The jaw areas of the beard were shaped and fitted to each skater's chin and jaw. Each of these sections were about one-and-a-half-feet long from the chin to the first ball socket.

The cable, which was supported by the harness, ran through the flexible tube from ball socket to ball socket. Three different lengths of beard were used, and each section had its own cable and ball socket joint. This enabled the beard to rotate as the skaters did their acrobatic feats yet provided strength and the appearance of a natural free-flowing beard.

Another makeup necessity in *The Five Thousand Fingers of Dr. T.* was the coloring of over thirty dancers green. Campbell employed another technique from his years at the Oates Wax Factory where he learned to use an air gun. Makeup on the dancers began at a chilly five-thirty A.M., and wielding an airbrush, Campbell sprayed them green with makeup.

Campbell has always been interested in the theatre and anything theatrical. He read magazines and bought sticks of Stein's makeup as a child in Toronto. When his family moved to California and settled in Whittier, he joined the Community Players and became star and stage manager for ten years. Campbell suggests that if someone wants to become a makeup artist he should interest himself in everything theatrical, see plays, join community players, and get as close as he can to theatre. He gives us these tips on amateur theatrics:

"My experience has been that amateur theatrics take place on a small stage where the audience is very close to the players.

The Five Thousand Fingers of Dr. T. required Campbell to create a rather unusual beard; a beard with a *man* on each end of it! (*Columbia Pictures*)

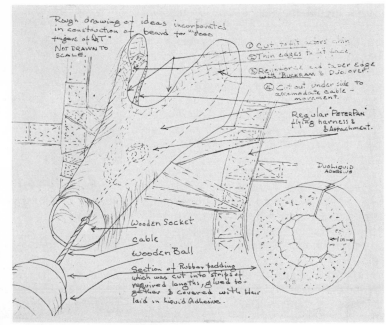

A sketch of the ball socket and cable system Campbell designed to enable the beard in *The Five Thousand Fingers of Dr. T.* to support the weight of a small child. (*Columbia Pictures*)

Campbell wields an air gun, spraying a dancer for *The Five Thousand Fingers of Dr. T.* green. Thirty to forty dancers went through this procedure during shooting each morning at five thirty A.M. (*Columbia Pictures*)

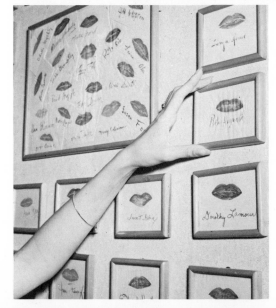

A rather unusual item is Campbell's collection of lip imprints from the many beauties he made up over the years. He has over two thousand lip imprints in his collection. (*Clay Campbell*)

Don't let the makeup show. Professional stage makeup is calculated to carry to the back of the house. It looks terrible in the parish house. The same things go for the amateur motion picture. Stage and motion picture makeup is very different. Stage is very exaggerated; motion picture is very natural. So if you can make your makeup look natural, you will be doing much more than if your makeup sticks out like a sore thumb.''

Campbell may have retired in 1966, but he certainly didn't cease his activity. For eight years he worked as a semiretired expert and commuted from his home in Corona del Mar to Hollywood in charge of the makeup on the ''Donna Reed'' television show.

Campbell began to study at the Laguna Beach School of Art Design in 1968. He has become an accomplished artist. His etchings are highly prized, and he has had many exhibits and won numerous awards. The summer of 1976 found Campbell involved as coordinator of the Print-making Festival at the Orange County Fair.

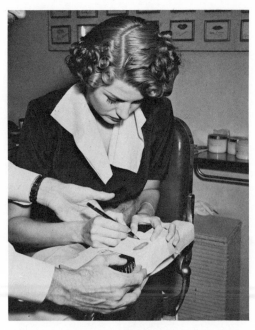

Here, Rita Hayworth adds her lip imprint and signature to Campbell's collection. (*Clay Campbell*)

Chapter 6

LEE GREENWAY

When *The Thing (From Another World)* terrorized audiences in 1951, Director Howard Hawks could thank two men for the film's success—a relatively unknown actor by the name of James Arness, who played the creature, and makeup artist Lee Greenway.

There were no preconceived ideas as to what The Thing should look like. Greenway can't sketch and has never relied on sketches to come up with his ideas, nor does he believe that poring over research books helps. He believes ideas must come from one's own imagination. The fact that *The Thing (From Another World)* has become a classic of science fiction films tends to confirm Lee's philosophy.

Lee worked directly on a live model, building up his creation with mortician's wax. When he had finished a head that he felt might be an acceptable creature, he would pop the actor into the car, leave the studio, and drive out to Howard Hawks's home in the Brentwood section of Beverly Hills. Hawks would take a look and say, "Try something else." Lee would return and try something else.

During one of the many treks to and from Hawks's home, Lee pulled up to a red light. The woman in the next car gazed over, and upon seeing this horrendous creature sitting beside Lee, she promptly fainted.

It took nearly two months before the concept for *The Thing* came into being; however, Hawks had been so impressed with Lee's work on Hawks's *Red River* (1938) that he was very patient. Once the concept had been worked out, it was a different story. Hawks wanted to get busy, and Lee had to really hustle to keep ahead on the appliances. It became necessary to work night and day.

The Thing was created with foam-rubber appliance pieces that had a greenish hue. The hair and head were built up about two inches. Lee made a piece which fit over the actor's nose, cheekbones, around his ear, and down and around his neck. This then went up his forehead and over his head. This was all one piece.

The makeup was actually quite cool and comfortable. Lee constructed an air valve up through the appliance. Colored water ran through the veins in his head, which were connected on each end to a football bladder which contained a small amount of air. A wide belt was constructed to go around Arness's chest—under his clothing—and as Arness breathed, the air would bubble through the veins of colored water. There was also a vein constructed in the back of the head, and as Arness inhaled and exhaled, air would come out around his head, and this helped to keep him cool.

The studio was under strict orders that no

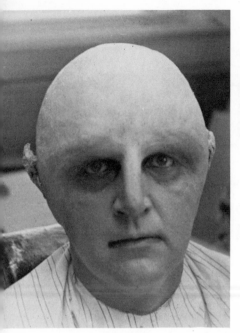

Greenway tried innumerable concepts in his attempt to create a creature for *The Thing*. Here are several concepts that were not used. (*Photos courtesy of Lee Greenway*)

This concept is nearly faceless, almost as though a giant thumb had sprouted a set of eyes and a mouth—more comical than frightening. (*Photo courtesy of Lee Greenway*)

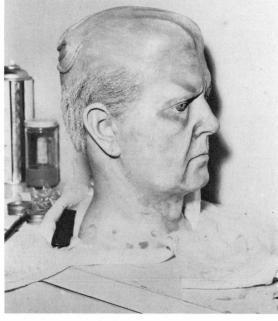

This concept seems to come somewhat closer to Greenway's final creation. (*Photo courtesy of Lee Greenway*)

Arness poses with the midget who would substitute for him during the disintegration scene. (*Photo courtesy of Lee Greenway*)

James Arness, popular television star of the long-running series ''Gunsmoke'' in the horrific vegetable monster design Greenway labored so tediously to achieve. (*Photo courtesy of Lee Greenway*)

one was to see The Thing. Lee took over the entire laboratory and no one was allowed to see the makeup. The set was closed and photographers were taboo. Lunches were sent up from the commissary.

Hands for The Thing were constructed out of a new plastic. Lee contacted the Goodyear Rubber Company to help him with materials as he found that sponge rubber would not hold up.

The hands were constructed like a pair of gloves and went about four or five inches up Arness's arms. Lee would powder Arness's hands with talcum powder, because the gloves would become hot after lengthy use and his hands would sweat. If the actor wasn't extremely careful when removing the gloves, it was easy to pull a finger off.

It took about two hours to do the total makeup. The hands, of course, were just slipped on. The head was sealed down with spirit gum. Lee would then stipple over the edges with a liquid adhesive and use a hand dryer to dry it. He would then make up a rubber grease and cover the stippled liquid adhesive with it. Lee found, though, if the adhesive was touched during the day, it was necessary to retouch it.

In some sequences, Lee had to work with the Special Effects Department in achieving the desired effect.

In one scene the creature catches fire and runs through a window, and it was necessary to come up with a new substance to make the head. Rubber would have burned up. Lee went to Sinclair Paint and came up with a fireproof product he could use. It was capable of withstanding fire for the two or three minutes it would take to film the scene. To Lee's knowledge, it was the first time a man had been completely set on fire in a film.

In another scene The Thing melts out of a huge cake of ice. This was shot in downtown Hollywood in a local icehouse. A dummy was frozen into a large block of ice, the heat turned on, and for a number of days the crew shot film of the large ice block melting.

When the infamous electrocution sequence was filmed, four Things were used. Hefty James Arness himself, a man of average height, a midget, and a twelve-inch miniature were used to effect the disintegration sequence.

When The Thing (From Another World) was ready for its debut, it was felt that a preview might be well advised. The studio chose a little theatre in San Bernardino and billed it as a surprise second feature. They took along a couple of doctors and three or four nurses. It was certainly good that they went prepared, as the audience found the close-up shots of The Thing so grotesque they began passing out right and left, and it became necessary to stop the film.

The film was then cut somewhat, yet on a subsequent showing the audience still found The Thing too gruesome, so in the final version, he is shown very little but enough to become recognized as one of the most horrendous creatures of movie history.

Greenway was employed as a decorator in New York City when his brother, who was already a makeup artist at Warner Brothers, asked him to come to California. Greenway went and became an apprentice painter at Twentieth Century-Fox. At the time, the makeup apprenticeships were filled and the painter apprenticeship was the only one available.

Greenway was something of a prankster at Fox, and Guy Pierce, head of the Makeup Department at the time, once banished him to a tiny room with Cecil Holland for six months.

Because they were under contract, apprentices couldn't be fired and this was all that saved Greenway's job. But Greenway's banishment to Holland's office undoubtedly gave him the knowledge and background for a very successful career.

It was on the film Red River that Howard Hawks first realized Greenway's makeup expertise. Hawks was a demanding director and would call for effects on a very short notice. In one such instance Hawks asked Greenway what he thought would happen to John Wayne's hand were a bullet to hit an object right beside it. Greenway answered that he felt it would quite likely receive burns. Hawks commented that that seemed quite likely to him too, and he would like to see that effected the next day.

Greenway poured raw rubber into Wayne's hand, then splintered up some balsa wood. He slipped this into Wayne's hand while the rubber was drying. They were filming on location in Arizona and the temperature was about 100 degrees, so the rubber dried quite quickly. Greenway added some artificial blood and then darkened Wayne's hand around the edges.

The special effects people drilled a hole in the wagon tongue, which was the object Wayne would be resting his hand on when a .45-caliber bullet would slam into it. They added a small charge and blew off that portion of wagon tongue. They added another small charge and replaced only the surface area they had blown off.

When the scene was filmed, all went smoothly and realistically. As Wayne reached for his gun, he discovered his injured hand. The rubber was by then transparent and all the audience saw was the blood and splinters.

In another scene, Wayne had to shoot at Montgomery Clift, grazing his cheek and shooting his earlobe off. Lee put a scar onto Clift's cheek, which he then covered with a rubber appliance filled with blood on which he had to simulate a three- or four-day growth of beard—no easy task. He folded the earlobe up behind the ear and then added a new one, also filled with blood. He attached all this to a very fine, strong piece of silk which ran down Clift's shirt and sleeve onto his finger, and attached it there. When Wayne fired his gun, Clift snapped the thread, sending the appliances down his shirt collar and leaving a grazed and bloodied cheek and ear.

In *The Black Swan* (1942) with Tyrone Power, Anthony Quinn, Maureen O'Hara, and Thomas Mitchell, Greenway found himself involved in a lot of hairwork. At that time very few people wore their own moustaches, beards, and the like, so in many instances Lee would be doing these. He also had to effect crooked noses, broken noses, and big broken-up thumbs. If they had a rubber nose that would fit, they'd use it. If not, they'd build up the noses with mortician's wax.

Some of the finest makeups in *Bedlam* (1946) were created on the lesser actors in the film. In one instance, the producer told Greenway he wanted a most impressive makeup on one of the prisoners for the next day. It was to be a sunken forehead, and this is one of the most difficult makeups to effect. Greenway worked it out with undertakers; and then making a false forehead, he made a huge indentation to look as though a heavy blow had gone right into the man's brow.

Greenway had a rather unusual assignment in *Annie Get Your Gun* (1950). A sharpshooter in his own right, Lee had

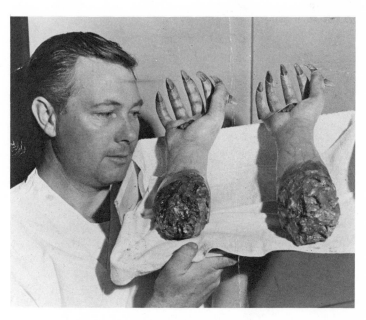

Greenway displays two right hands, hot out of the oven, for the scene when the guard dog tears loose a piece of the vegetable arm. (*Photo courtesy of Lee Greenway*)

Gilbert Roland, whose father and grandfather were bullfighters, is convincing in Greenway's makeup for his role in *The Miracle of Our Lady of Fatima*. (*Lee Greenway*)

taught George Bau and his father to shoot. They called him to MGM to do the sharpshooting for the stars in this film. At one point, there was so much shooting necessary that Lee recruited Jack Harrison and Jules Levant because it was too much for one man to handle.

Targets were thrown right at the camera from about fifteen yards away. Should one of these objects have hit and damaged the camera lens, it would have been an extremely expensive process to repair. However, Lee wasn't about to let that happen and because of his unique marksmanship, it didn't. Lee had to be off-scene, down on the ground, and the camera was located high

on the rocks; so Lee had to be very sure that he busted all the pieces before they reached the camera.

As an assistant department head at RKO, Greenway's duties were to see that all the pictures were done and done well. He supervised not only makeup but hair as well.

At one time, they had a wig made for Arthur Franz for a picture called *The Indian Fighter* (1955), which starred Kirk Douglas. The picture was filmed in Oregon, and Lee had a number of hair stylists and makeup artists with him. Wigs were very expensive, so they had only the one wig made for Franz. In the film, Franz is sitting down having a powwow with the Indians when a

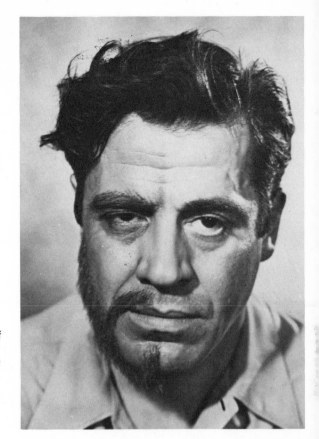

Greenway did only one side of actor Jack LaRue's face in a pirate film whose title he's now forgotten. LaRue required only one side of his face to be made up for a scene where he lay dead on the deck of a pirate vessel. (*Photo courtesy of Lee Greenway*)

This actor received convincing backlashes from the brush of Lee Greenway. (*Photo courtesy of Lee Greenway*)

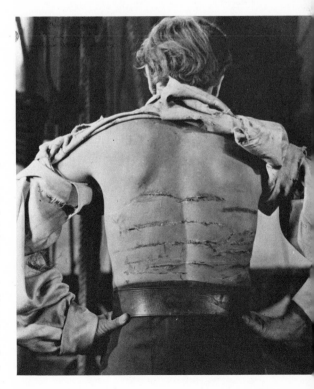

horse and rider jump over him.

Instead of using a stand-in for Franz, they decided to use a trained horse and rider. The hoof glanced off Franz's head, tearing off half the wig and causing him to lose a special contact lens in the process. Fortunately, Franz was not injured. Greenway had to work all night to reconstruct the wig so they could shoot the next day.

After RKO, Greenway became a freelance makeup artist. For a period of about ten years he was often contacted by small production companies to perform "miracles" on small budgets. On one such film, the producer wanted to use a large number of Indians, yet they couldn't afford to buy wigs for them. They were located near a small town in Arizona, so Greenway headed into town, where he bought up all the old-fashioned cotton stockings he could find. Lee and the hairdresser cut up the socks and died them all black. They then cut the socks in strips and braided them halfway down. They would put together two braided stockings to achieve the look of a black braided wig. These were worn by the extras, who were townspeople. Made up in Indian makeup with a red headband and a few feathers, they were quite effective in their cotton-stocking wigs.

Greenway feels that everything about being a makeup artist is exciting. "When you are young, you can go through all those hours and it doesn't bother you." He has enjoyed it all. Some of the actors and actresses Greenway worked with were the finest people he's ever known in his life. Some of them still remain very close friends.

Greenway has left the makeup world, and now he and his wife enjoy traveling. Lee follows the "shooting circuit" now and in the spring of the year leaves for Europe where he competes in the shooting competition.

Chapter 7

WILLIAM TUTTLE

A makeup man has to be not only an accomplished artist in the techniques of his business, but also in public relations and female psychology. Bill Tuttle is an all-around expert in these fields. He has my esteem and admiration.''

This praise of William Tuttle was expressed by Princess Grace of Monaco. The princess stole the hearts of millions during her all-too-brief movie career as Grace Kelly. Bill Tuttle, as head of the Makeup Department at MGM from 1950 through 1969, was responsible for the makeup on Her Serene Highness's films, which included *Mogambo* (1953) with Clark Gable and Ava Gardner; *Green Fire* (1954); *The Swan* (1956); and the musical *High Society* (1956) with Bing Crosby, Frank Sinatra, and Celeste Holm.

Tuttle was born in Jacksonville, Florida, in 1911. Both music and art became Tuttle's interests in early childhood. He began to study the violin at the age of eight. When he was fourteen, his parents separated, and Tuttle assumed the responsibility of providing for his mother and younger brother, Thomas.

Tuttle tried to remain in school and work evenings as a musician, but this became too difficult and he was forced to leave school by the time he was fifteen. He worked with a comedy team playing the violin, did bits onstage, orchestra work in burlesque, and then organized a band and played for dances, radio, and nightclub shows.

Not knowing a solitary soul in California, Tuttle headed for Hollywood when he was only eighteen. He first found a job as a musician, but finally Tuttle went to work for Fox Studios.

Eventually his artistic talent came to the attention of Jack Dawn, who had been head of makeup at Fox but was then head of makeup at a new independent company called Twentieth Century Pictures. Tuttle joined Dawn as his apprentice there for seven months, and when Twentieth Century closed for the summer in 1934, he went to MGM to continue his apprenticeship.

Tuttle created an extremely realistic bullet hole in the right temple of Bela Lugosi's head for *Mark of the Vampire* (1935). When Fox Studios recognized the outstanding work Tuttle had done on this film, they requested his services as a full-fledged makeup artist. Tuttle did three pictures at Fox, then returned to MGM, which remained his ''home'' for over thirty-five years. For eight years he was an assistant to department head Jack Dawn, and for over twenty years he was head of the department after Dawn's retirement.

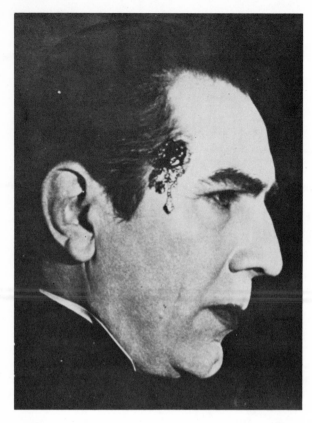

Tuttle created an extremely realistic bullet hole in the right temple of Bela Lugosi's head for *Mark of the Vampire*. (© MGM)

In 1936, when MGM filmed *The Good Earth*, Tuttle's main concern was the makeup on Paul Muni. One problem that occurred frequently was with the cellulose nitrate formula bald caps. When they were exposed to the air for any length of time, they had a tendency to shrink. As the cap shrank, it would creep up, exposing the bare skin that had not been covered by makeup, and eventually the hairline itself would become visible.

Tuttle had to be prepared to cover the bare skin as it became exposed, and to apply a new bald cap when it reached the hairline. Spare bald caps were carried with the artists at all times, sealed in tin cans so the caps wouldn't shrink any before being applied.

One extraordinary actress Tuttle worked with during her many years at MGM was Greer Garson. Ms. Garson has said of Bill Tuttle: "We were lucky at MGM in having a group of really top craftsmen in this field. I was made up by many other members of the department and artists at other studios,

and think of them, each and all of them, with affection and appreciation. But, as William Tuttle was my co-worker on most of my movies, it is a particular pleasure to pay tribute to him here, knowing that all my fellow actors must feel the same way about their associates, the makeup artists.

"The ideal makeup artist has the eye of a caricaturist, the hands of a sculptor, the brush of a portrait painter, and the curiosity of a student. Like the actor, he must study the old masters, the classics of the past, the mechanical marvels of a space-age future, and, most of all, our varied and fascinating world of the present—the faces photographed in the news of today, with all the racial and regional variations of the widespread family of man.

"Bill Tuttle is undoubtedly one of the ideal makeup artists of our day. He can glorify the everyday visage, and if nature has done her part even half well, he can make unremarkable faces look remarkably handsome. He can subtly show, too, the changes due to age, occupation, emotional or physical experiences in a person's countenance. He is recognized as outstanding in the more creative areas of makeup, and where the script allows, he can invent a world of characters varying from the familiar and realistic to the wildly imaginary, the fantastic, the exotic.

"As for my personal experience of working with him, in *Mrs. Parkington* (1944), I played a character who aged from teens to eighties. We studied old family photographs of my Grandmother Greer, producing with the cooperation of wig and costume designers—and aided, I hope, by a little honest acting, too—an illusion so convincing in close-up and striking in long-shot that my kinfolk in Scotland, seeing the movie, gasped at the old lady's first entrance— 'That's Gran!'

"In *Madame Curie* (1943) the time span was shorter, going from a university student to a scientist in her sixties. The portrait, therefore, had to be even more subtle. Bill studied photographs of Madame Curie and compared them to my own features, and helped by Joe Ruttenberg's sensitive camera work, presented not a mask of rubber wrinkles but a believable face, aged more by toil and sorrow than by time.

"I was frequently cast in period pictures which made special demands on the actor's demeanor and appearance. As there were always fashions in faces as in clothes, it is fortunate that Bill knows his pictorial history well. He would never put a contemporary face on a character of some bygone century."

One assignment in particular that Tuttle found rather difficult was for the film *Lili* (1953), which starred Leslie Caron, Mel Ferrer, Jean-Pierre Aumont, and Kurt Kasznar. There were several puppets in the film that were featured as human beings. To transform human features to those of a puppet was very challenging, indeed. Puppets' features are generally quite unlike the proportions of a human face. Noses are usually very short, the upper lip extremely long, and the chins are quite short.

Tuttle achieved a system whereby the actors could move their faces to some extent and yet make the puppets' mouths come out in the right place, then recede back to the mouth of the actor, enabling him to eat, drink, or perhaps smoke a cigarette during the day's work. All of the pieces were in sections and were glued to the face with spirit gum. The one exception was the fox. The top section was immobile and only the lower jaw moved. The eyebrows were manipulated with threads.

Tuttle has found today that many of the newer makeup artists are endeavoring to do prosthetic work long before they learn to do the basics of creating illusions with paint.

An assignment that Tuttle found rather difficult was turning human actors into life-sized puppets for the film *Lili*. (© *MGM*)

"By using highlights and shadow," Tuttle explained, "one can, with some skill, alter the shapes and contours of the face considerably. I feel that they are sort of putting the cart before the horse when they don't make an attempt to perfect these techniques. After all, this was the basis of makeup long ago on the stage, and it's still being used to a great extent in motion pictures today because you frequently have little time to manufacture prosthetics.

"For television, many times you have to create a character on the spot with no suitable prefabricated prosthetics on hand. One must then rely on available materials and techniques. Many makeup artists who have not attempted to develop these skills often find themselves in a real pickle. Correct application of crepe hair is another area that has been sadly neglected. Again, many of the makeup artists of today have been spoiled by prefabricated beards and moustaches, eyebrows, and wigs. Whereas, if they knew the technique of applying crepe hair, they would never be caught short by not having a ready-made beard of the correct color, or the particular type of moustache needed for the characterization. So I say, learn the basics first—and you can spend plenty of time to learn it properly. I would also strongly recommend the amateur study representational life drawing, painting, and sculpture because certainly this is the basic knowledge for any makeup process, be it beautification or characterization."

Tuttle has had occasion to run into the unexpected and recalled an incident early in his career when he was working on both Walter Pidgeon and Henry Hull, who were in different productions on the MGM lot. Walter Pidgeon was required to wear a moustache, which was ready-made; and Henry Hull was wearing a set of ready-made bushy eyebrows.

One morning when Tuttle arrived for work, he discovered to his dismay that Pidgeon's moustache was missing. Not having any time to prepare another, he checked the call sheets to learn that Hull was not working that particular day. Without saying a word about the situation, he scooped up Hull's bushy eyebrows, which fortunately happened to be the same color as the moustache Pidgeon had been wearing, and by turning them upside down and putting them together in the middle, he found he duplicated the moustache very well and no one was the wiser—until he advised them of the switch several days later.

In 1960 both Tuttle and Charlie Schram worked on George Pal's *The Time Machine*, which starred Yvette Mimieux and Rod Taylor. As Schram has mentioned, monkey fur was used for the principal Morlocks. It was a trip to the San Diego Zoo that tipped Tuttle off to using the fur of an East African species of monkey.

It was for his extraordinary makeup on Tony Randall in George Pal's *The Seven Faces of Dr. Lao* (1964) that Tuttle received a special honorary Oscar in April of 1965 from the Academy Awards. Tony Randall took the time to talk about his experiences on this film.

"When we went to work on *The Seven Faces of Dr. Lao*, we were taking a very famous book which had almost a cult following for quite a few years. A number of people had tried to make a movie of it, and twice, if I'm not mistaken, Burgess Meredith had tried to make a play of it. The book is called *The Circus of Dr. Lao* by Charles Finney.

"George Pal, who made the film, had the very theatrical notion that all the creatures in the circus were Dr. Lao himself; thus they could all be played by one man. It was a marvelous idea and, of course, terribly exciting for the actor.

"Bill Tuttle was head of the Makeup Department at MGM, which was a big studio— probably the most powerful and the most well financed. They had a complete makeup building. They had everything you could ever want in the field of makeup: the plant, the equipment, the necessary tools—and they had the trained personnel.

"Tuttle's method was unique. He is an extremely skilled watercolorist; so first he made very beautiful watercolors of each of the seven characters. He just used his imagination. I suppose he conferred a great deal with the director, read the book, of course, and the script.

"Tuttle then made a plaster cast of my head, which he then worked on with mortician's wax. He began to build the faces he had drawn onto the plaster cast of my head. Thus, he was able to work without me.

"When he got the pieces he wanted, that is, the right nose for a certain character, he

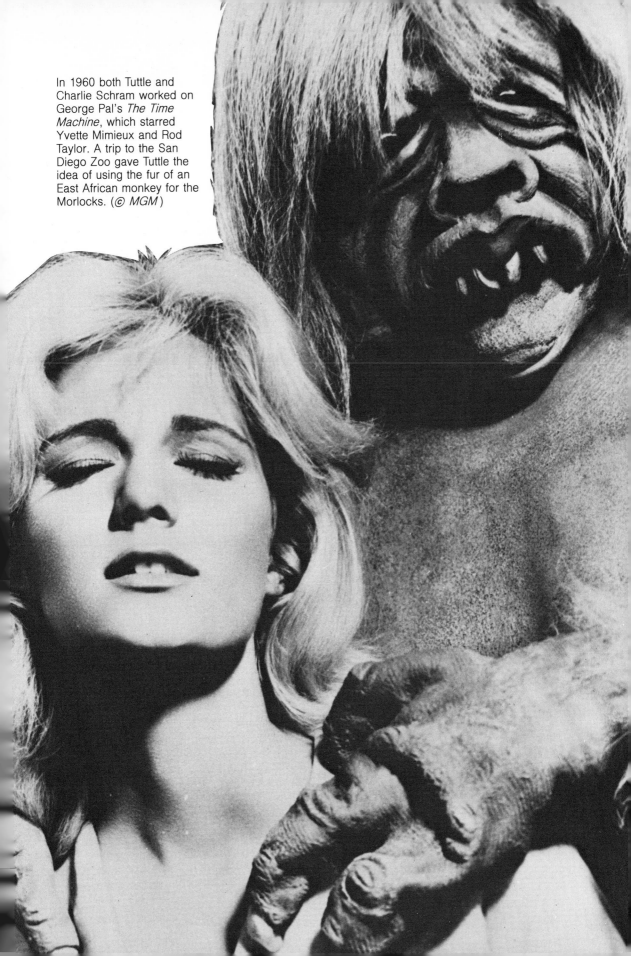

In 1960 both Tuttle and Charlie Schram worked on George Pal's *The Time Machine*, which starred Yvette Mimieux and Rod Taylor. A trip to the San Diego Zoo gave Tuttle the idea of using the fur of an East African monkey for the Morlocks. (© *MGM*)

would take it off and cast it. I suppose it was cast of plaster, as I don't really know. From that, a mold was made, and then from that mold, the pieces were cast again—this time in sponge rubber. These sponge-rubber pieces are the ones you put on your face. They're glued on with spirit gum. Different ones were used every day because they are so fine that they usually tear when they are removed.

"When he had this much done, he then went to work on me. He shaved my head and eyebrows, and put on the various pieces. Now we could begin to see where we had failed. Most of them were damn near perfect the first time, because Bill is extraordinary. He's the best. This was the first time an Academy Award was ever given for makeup.

"I should also mention that I had several pairs of eyes. I had green plastic lenses for the Medusa, blue for the Apollonius of Tyana, and old Merlin had the faded, washed-out light blue. They were extremely uncomfortable to wear because they were so big. They covered not just the pupil as ordinary contact lenses do but the entire iris of the eye.

"The aging for Merlin's face and hands was done by first stretching the skin and then stippling it with liquid adhesive. It's dried by means of an ordinary hair dryer, and then it's powdered. They do several layers this way, and as it dries, it begins to shrivel up to that of an old, old person. Makeup is then applied to that. You have to use a certain kind of makeup over anything with rubber in it because ordinary oil

The Morlocks in their underground world. (© *MGM*)

Sophia Loren from eighteen to eighty in *Lady L* (1966) were two of his fondest achievements. He also had the challenging assignment of turning comedian Dick Martin into a dapper werewolf in Rowan and Martin's *The Maltese Bippy* (1969). Tuttle also supervised all television shows at MGM, with "Twilight Zone" and "One Step Beyond" being the most intricate from the viewpoint of a makeup artist.

Tuttle effected flashing crystals to appear embedded in the palms of the actors in Saul David's *Logan's Run* (1976). False palms were created for each actor. Tuttle reproduced their own palms by casting them in hydrocal. On this impression, he built up the negative side of the mold to a thickness of about one-sixteenth to one-eighth of an inch in the center. This enabled him to reproduce every line in the hand of the actor exactly and the contour conformed very well to their actual palms on the inside. The crystals were embedded in this.

It was necessary to use a flasher for the crystals, and a very fine wire was used because the flasher could not be concealed in the palms. The flashers and crystals were made by the Special Effects Department. The wires had to run up the actors' arms onto their shoulders and into the costume where they could be hidden.

Tuttle's plan went quite well until he discovered that the costumes were designed without sleeves. The wires were so fine they were practically the width of a human hair, but camera angles for each shot had to be carefully determined. They would then place the wire on the "off-camera" side of the arm and commence shooting.

Each time the actors moved, Tuttle and the others held their breath. The wire itself wouldn't show unless a muscle would flex or the actors would use their hands. This movement could cause the wire to buckle, and one could see little ripples along the arm. So each shot took considerable time.

"Then we came to the character of Box (played by Roscoe Lee Browne)," Tuttle went on to explain. "This presented any number of problems. I was much delayed on this process. When I first started on the film, I was told this was to be one of the final shots in the film, and we had lots of time to work out the concept. As always, these

makeup—grease makeup—will rot the rubber. Only a makeup with a castor-oil base will work here. They put the age makeup on top of that. This consists of the liver spots one sees in older skin and the typical ashen color.

"Every makeup would take about two hours to put on, and on some days, I'd be in three different makeups. Charlie Schram, that wiz of a technician who made the pieces and is a marvelous makeup man, was generally the one who applied my makeups. He'd be bent over me for six hours a day. It was really much harder work for the makeup man than for the actor."

The progressive facial changes Tuttle achieved on Paul Newman in the actor's portrayal of Rocky Graziano in *Somebody Up There Likes Me* (1956) and his aging of

Tuttle demonstrates the procedures for making a life-cast. Here Tuttle and Ron Berkeley cool the Negacol for making the mask. (*William Tuttle*)

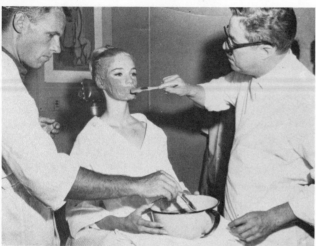

Yvette Mimieux becomes Tuttle's model, and Tuttle and Berkeley paint Negacol over her face. (*William Tuttle*)

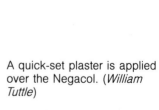

The negative impression is filled with plaster. (*William Tuttle*)

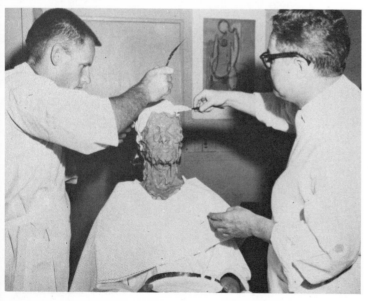

A quick-set plaster is applied over the Negacol. (*William Tuttle*)

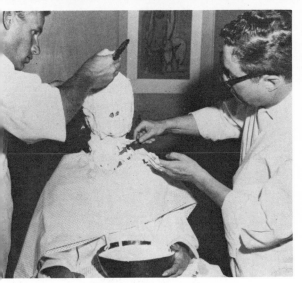

Mimieux is completely covered with the quick-set plaster. (*William Tuttle*)

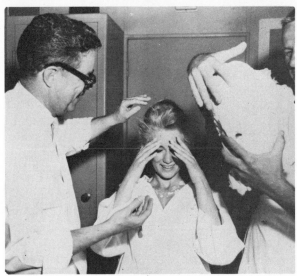

Once the plaster has set, it is carefully removed. Mimieux looks happy to be released from her plaster prison. (*William Tuttle*)

The plaster must fill each indentation, and Tuttle takes great care to make certain of this. (*William Tuttle*)

Yvette Mimieux displays the cast of her features Tuttle has created. (*William Tuttle*)

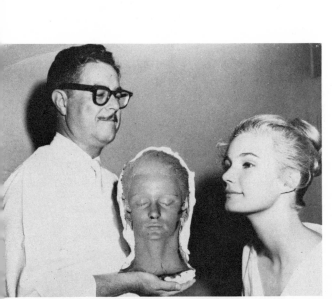

Although this is a negative impression of Mimieux's features, when held in a certain light, it appears to have a positive form. (*William Tuttle*)

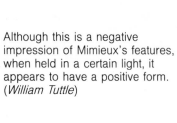

Tony Randall in Tuttle's makeup for *The Seven Faces of Dr. Lao.*

things happen sooner than you expect. Suddenly, 'now' was the time, and unfortunately, I couldn't get a decision on how it should look. Saul David had his ideas; Dale Hennessey, who was production designer, had his; but no one seemed to come to any definite conclusions despite the fact I pursued it to the extent of becoming a pest.

"Everybody got into the act, and the only thing I can take final credit for is the head. In the script, he was described as half-human and half-machine, and unfortunately, I feel, he turned out more like a robot.

"I modeled the complete head much like an African primitive mask, giving it a sculptured effect. Then I covered it with mylar tape, which is flexible in one direction only. So I had to apply it much like a mosaic, enabling it to conform to the contour of the modeling."

Mel Brooks is becoming well known for producing and directing some very funny films, and Tuttle has had the good fortune of being involved on both *Young Frankenstein*

(1975) and *Silent Movie* (1976).

Peter Boyle played the part of the monster. Again, Tuttle had only a very short time in which to prepare the makeup.

"The actor, Peter Boyle, happened to be in New York and was not available at the time for me to make a cast of his face. When he finally arrived, the exact modeling for the characterization had not been determined. Mel Brooks was, of course, very much in on the final decision and had certain preconceived ideas. The production designer had some other ideas but until we saw Boyle in person, it was very difficult to determine the exact look.

"At the same time, we were trying to avoid duplication of the makeup on Boris Karloff. After I made the mask for his face, I made the appliances in such a manner that they could be superimposed to produce several different versions, as there was no time to make major alterations. This worked out quite well. Finally, during the second week of the film, I was able to simplify these

Note the closeness to detail Tuttle was able to maintain in actual transfer. (© MGM)

appliances by combining these variations into one piece, which expedited the application considerably.''

Makeup for *Silent Movie* was basically straight makeup. Tuttle's only comment on this film was ''I must say, working with Mel Brooks is a unique experience in itself.''

In 1976 Tuttle was involved in the film *An Enemy of the People* from the Henrik Ibsen play. The film stars Steve McQueen and is set in the late 1800s. In researching the period, Tuttle discovered it was a very ''bearded'' period when most men wore some type of beard and long hair. With today's styles, very often there is little need for makeup.

However, actors sometimes are involved in finishing another film where they have been clean-shaven, so the use of false beards, eyebrows, etc., will be necessary.

For *An Enemy of the People* Tuttle had at least two full beards to apply and several sets of eyebrows. McQueen had his own beard and long hair, and, as a matter of

fact, his hair was a bit too long and had to be cut somewhat.

Besides remaining active as a free-lancer in the field of makeup, he has also developed a cosmetic line known as Custom Color Cosmetics for both professional and nonprofessional use. Tuttle also teaches at the University of California in the Cinema Department. For the limited amount of time that he has to teach, his class being just two hours a week for sixteen weeks, Tuttle feels it is more a makeup appreciation course than anything else. Many drama students attend his class, and although they do get involved in class, they seem to have little time outside the classroom to practice.

''Only on rare occasions do these young people become makeup artists,'' Tuttle explained. ''For some strange reason, they all have their sights on becoming producers, writers, directors, or something in that area. The ideal training, in my opinion, is through apprenticeship.''

Opposite: Tuttle regards his aging of Sophia Loren from eighteen to eighty in *Lady L* as one of his fondest achievements. (© *MGM*)

Although the character of Box in *Logan's Run* was described in the script as being half-human and half-machine, Tuttle was given little guidance regarding the actual design. It is his feeling that the final character appears more robotlike than humanoid. (© *MGM*)

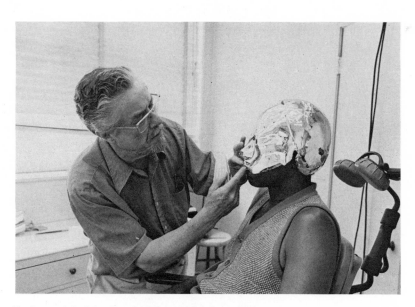

Tuttle modeled the head of Box in the form of an African primitive mask, giving it a sculpted effect. Here he begins the makeup application on actor Roscoe Lee Browne by carefully securing the mask. (© *MGM*)

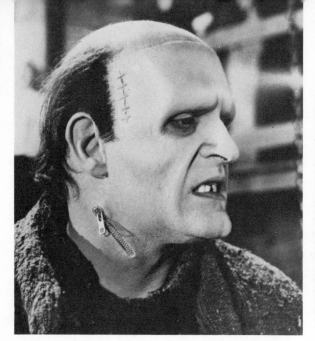

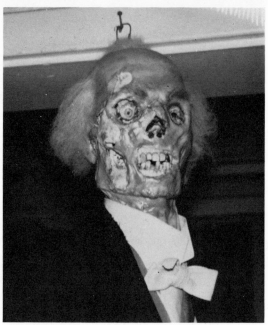

Peter Boyle in Bill Tuttle's makeup for his role in *Young Frankenstein*. Producer-director Mel Brooks wished to avoid any similarity between his Frankenstein and Boris Karloff's.
(© *Twentieth Century-Fox Film Corporation*)

The corpse of old Dr. Frankenstein hangs from its head in *Young Frankenstein*.
(© *Twentieth Century-Fox Film Corporation*)

Marty Feldman, always up to some trick in a Mel Brooks film, models a second head.
(© *Twentieth Century-Fox Film Corporation*)

Chapter 8

EMILE LaVIGNE

Emile LaVigne was working as an assistant propman on a picture entitled *Queen Christina* (1933) when he met Jack Dawn. Dawn was the makeup man on the picture. LaVigne became interested in what Dawn was doing and watched every free moment he had. They became friends and Dawn told him that if and when he took over the Makeup Department at MGM, LaVigne could come and work for him. LaVigne gave this a great deal of thought, as an apprenticeship could go on for a long period of time, and he had been making good progress in the Property Department. However, he met Dawn again after he had taken over the Makeup Department and decided that this was the direction he wanted his career to take, so he became an apprentice, joining the other young people Jack Dawn was gathering around him and training for the future.

While working as an apprentice, he was able to assist Dawn in making up stars like Jeanette MacDonald and Robert Montgomery and after a short time was able to do the makeup himself. LaVigne and Montgomery became friends and Emile did a great many films with him. *Night Must Fall* (1937), *The Earl of Chicago* (1940), and *They Were Expendable* (1945) were just a few.

In 1939 the classic *The Wizard of Oz* with Judy Garland, Jack Haley, Ray Bolger, and Bert Lahr was produced. All of the makeup men involved on it were very young then. Jack Dawn was the guiding light and told LaVigne and his fellow makeup artists "what to do and how to do it," LaVigne explained.

"Joe Norin was the lab technician and sculptor then, and Dawn created the characters in the film. The rest of us did the application. All of the makeup artists worked together on the witches, flying monkeys, and the Munchkins."

LaVigne and the late Lee Stenfield did the makeup for the Tin Man and his double. LaVigne describes this makeup:

"The Tin Man's face and head consisted of three appliances. The funnel formed the top of his head and went down the back of his neck—behind his ears and below his collar. This gave his neck a straight, stiff look and covered his hair, fitting the contour of Jack Haley's head.

"The nose extended slightly into a funnel shape. The third appliance, which was the jaw piece, extended from above his ears, down around his jaw, and moved when he spoke, as if hinged.

"We then put a thick layer of pancake on the exposed skin before applying the silver paint over the appliance and his face. The pancake was used as an undercoat to help protect Haley's skin as constant use of the silver paint directly on his skin proved irritat-

While at MGM, one of LaVigne's assignments was *A Christmas Carol*. Here LaVigne touches up Leo G. Carroll's makeup as Marley's ghost. (© *MGM*)

ing. Talcum powder was used to set the makeup, and a soft powder brush removed the surplus powder.''

As Buddy Ebsen was the first to try the makeup and it proved to be extremely irritating for his skin, great care was taken to prevent the same thing happening to Jack Haley. A double was used whenever possible.

In a way, LaVigne feels that he, Charles Schram, and Bill Tuttle grew up together in the business, all being part of Jack Dawn's group at MGM. They all had the marvelous advantage of working with Cecil Holland.

On *The Good Earth* LaVigne did not spend time on the set as did Bill Tuttle and Charles Schram, although they all helped in the morning to get the actors and actresses out on the set. LaVigne spent most of his time helping Jack Dawn with tests—mainly for the part of the other wife. Tilly Losch finally got the part of Lotus after many actresses tested for it.

For the creation of the Oriental eye, an appliance was modeled that covered the eyelid from the tear duct to the outside of the eyebrow. It was glued on the bottom edge and powder was carefully brushed under the edge. This allowed the lid to move under it and eliminated the eyelid fold of the Western eye, rounding the corner of the inside eye and achieving the Oriental look.

LaVigne tells us that for historical characters he would work from a photograph; in other cases he would talk it over with the director and the actors. Regarding beauty makeup, unless there is some particular look required, Emile sees no reason to look at a book but feels one should be able to pick the good and bad points and start from there.

In 1938 LaVigne ended his apprenticeship when he went with Robert Montgomery to Universal for *Unfinished Business* (1941). It was during this time that he met Jack Pierce and tells us: ''He was a difficult man who had come up the hard way and was, rightfully so, very protective of his work. He did brilliant work during the early period before prosthetics and all the laboratory techniques that are available today.''

Before the picture was completed, Pierce and LaVigne had become good friends, and Pierce became another of LaVigne's teachers. He taught Emile to build a character with cotton and spirit gum and anything that would mold an actor's face into a grotesque nightmare. LaVigne found these lessons invaluable, particularly in some remote location where a director might ask for something that was not in the script and all that was available was imagination and whatever was handy.

In 1948 LaVigne began working on *Abbott and Costello Meet Frankenstein*. The working day would start at about eight o'clock in the morning and end anywhere from eleven to twelve o'clock at night. On those days, LaVigne would do about eight or nine makeups in transforming a man into a wolf. Usually the first two could be done with a little hair and paint but only at the start. Later he would have to remove everything and start with small appliances in the

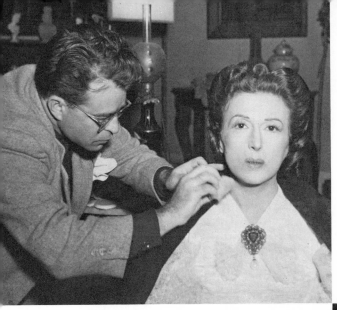

Katina Paxinou portrayed the unfaithful wife and murderer of Raymond Massey in *Mourning Becomes Electra*. (*Emile LaVigne*)

Emile LaVigne (*top right*) and others prepare Ann Blyth for a body cast for her role in *Mr. Peabody and the Mermaid*. (© *Universal*)

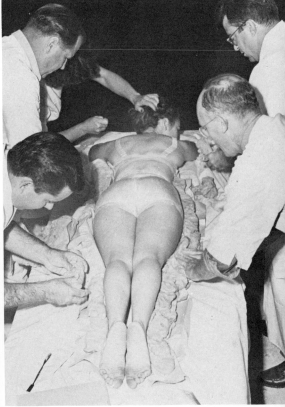

Katharine Hepburn in LaVigne's old-age makeup for a scene in *Song of Love*. (*Emile LaVigne*)

appropriate places, building up the lip and the snout, preparing the forehead so that the hair began to creep down on the face and take the form of a wolf.

The days were long and weary and Lon Chaney, Jr., at times had a little bit too much to drink. LaVigne found that he didn't exactly relish putting glue all over a man Chaney's size when he was a little high.

We asked LaVigne to give us some pointers on different areas. He explained that if he were to do a vampire makeup he would begin with a very light base—bordering on white, a black eyebrow pencil for eyebrows, and a widow's peak coming sharply down on the forehead, and black liner to outline the upper and lower lid of the eye. Mix the black with the base to create a dark gray for use under the eyes. Blend to the light color of the base for the hollowing of cheeks starting under the cheekbone. Use red lip rouge, following the outline of the actor's mouth. Hair should be black and slicked straight back. Crepe hair or a black pencil can be used for a widow's peak.

When putting on a hairlace wig or moustache, LaVigne uses a steel modeling tool and acetone to pick up excess gum. Then he uses a light color and stipple brushed over the lace very lightly.

The careful blending of a bald cap into skin depends on the material the cap is made of, but generally acetone will blend the edge by using a brush or Q-tips.

The first thing an amateur should try with highlights and shadows, LaVigne recommends, would be to paint a skull on someone's face to learn where the bones and hollows are. Age and character makeup are all based on this knowledge.

LaVigne uses whatever the job requires. He feels one can only go so far with paint and powder in aging, perhaps ten to twenty years depending on the subject. Then appliances should be used. He feels that makeup for the screen has changed from a heavy makeup that obscured much of the face to a plain canvas one which the artist pencils and paints the look required for the film. Now a thin, natural look is more the rule, and LaVigne likes to use the minimum amount of makeup, utilizing the actress's or actor's best points to the greatest advantage. He feels that a woman wearing street makeup should use the same rule. It is better to use less than too much.

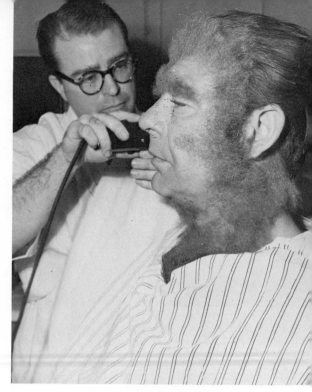

LaVigne was required to do eight or nine different makeups on Chaney in the process of transforming him into a wolf for *Abbott and Costello Meet Frankenstein*. (© *Universal*)

One of the most challenging pictures for LaVigne was *The Land of the Pharaohs* (1955) for Howard Hawks, perhaps because he was less experienced in doing a picture completely on his own, but perhaps also because of its location. The picture was filmed in Egypt and Italy. The crew was away for about nine months. Importing materials and supplies into Egypt was extremely difficult. King Farouk had been recently exiled, and the twenty-day war with Israel had just ended so the Egyptians weren't in any mood to be friendly. LaVigne found that he had to improvise many things.

It was a picture that required a great deal of makeup. When they were shooting the exterior scenes in Egypt, they had dark-skinned people entering the buildings and pyramids, but months later, in Italy, they filmed lighter-skinned Italians walking into the interiors of buildings and pyramids. It was necessary to find a balance. They would lighten the extras used in Egypt and darken the ones in Italy so that the skin tones would be the same and when the two scenes were cut together it flowed smoothly.

LaVigne went on to explain: "Of course, when you go on location to a country where

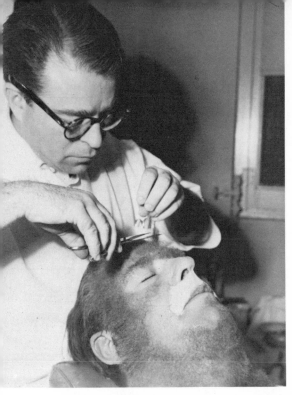

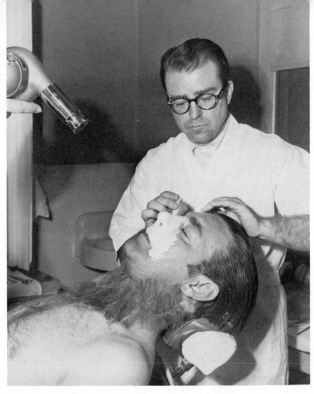

LaVigne carefully trims away any excess hair on Chaney's face. (© *Universal*)

Here the nose appliance has been added to Chaney's features. (© *Universal*)

This side-by-side shot of Jack Kevan and Glenn Strange emphasizes the monster's height. (© *Universal*)

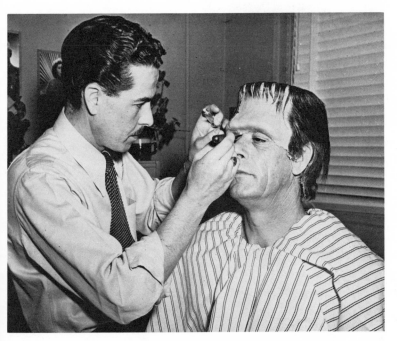

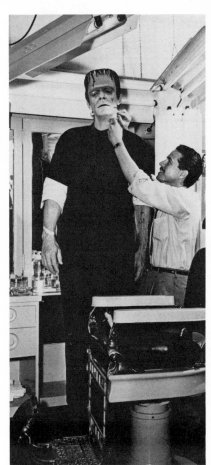

Jack Kevan is another extremely talented makeup artist who was also involved on *Abbott and Costello Meet Frankenstein*. Here Kevan secures the Frankenstein head appliance to Glenn Strange. (© *Universal*)

the picture you are making takes place, some uninformed person announces at the production meeting, 'You won't need much makeup because we're going to use the natives and they are, of course, the right color.' That may be true, but the natives do not go around in loincloths. Their bodies are covered, and the only areas that are dark are their faces, hands, and feet; so when you remove that, you've got two dark hands, a dark face, dark feet—and a white body. It is necessary to tie it all together. The producers rarely count on this so it becomes a struggle to find the equipment needed in the country you are in. We had spraying machines there, and I had about twenty-five guys working on just spraying people and trying to balance the color. It was really a trying job, not being able to get materials for the hundreds and hundreds of people we used and, of course, the color problem. In order to facilitate matters, I bargained to give lessons at the University in Cairo one night a week for about six weeks, so that I could import a few things. I did these things on my own because every department had its own problems. Anyway, to me, that was a challenging picture.''

Following the science-fiction trend in the fifties, Allied Artists released several low-budget features, one of which turned out to be an extraordinary hit due to the care of its

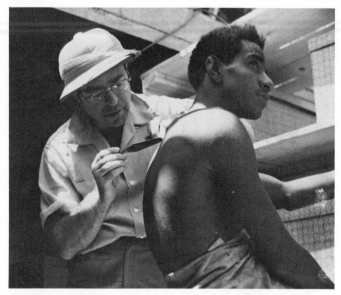

LaVigne found Howard Hawks's *Land of the Pharaohs* a most challenging picture. A great deal of makeup was necessary. The picture was filmed in Egypt and Italy, and importing materials and supplies into Egypt was difficult at the time. (*Emile LaVigne*)

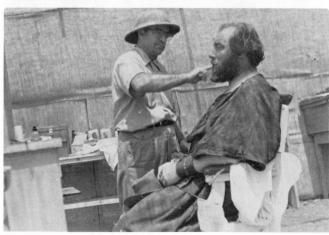

LaVigne completes a makeup on James Robertson Justice for his part in *Land of the Pharaohs*. (*Emile LaVigne*)

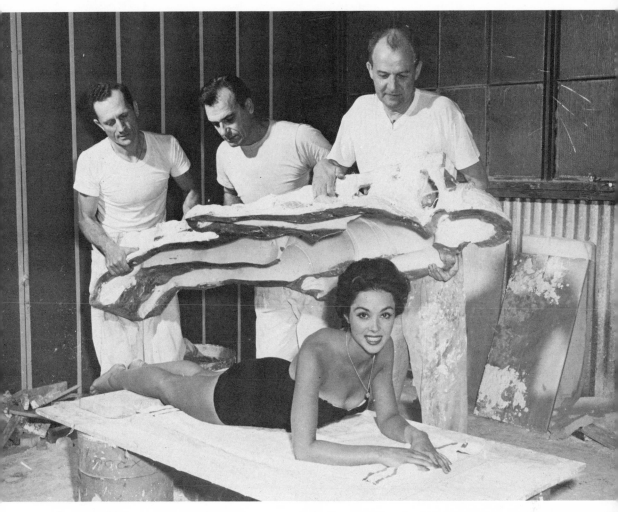

Life-sized casts were made of principals Kevin McCarthy, Dana Wynter, King Donovan, and Carolyn Jones in *Invasion of the Body Snatchers*. Dana Wynter and men from the plaster shop pose with Wynter's completed cast. (© *Allied Artists*)

producer, Walter Wanger. *Invasion of the Body Snatchers* (1956) featured a faceless enemy in the form of spores or life-sized pods which invaded Earth and began to "take over" the bodies and minds of humans.

Life-size casts were made of principals Kevin McCarthy, Dana Wynter, King Donovan, and Carolyn Jones. Body molds were made in two halves—front and back. When the principals were cast for the body molds, the subject was laid on a slant board rather than being laid flat. In this position the breast and muscles fell into their natural position. Keys were put in the first half of the

mold. When the second half was poured over the first half and then separated, they could be brought back together and would fit snugly in the correct position. The head was cast separately in the same manner.

After the molds were dried in an oven, they were treated to accept foam rubber. Because of their size, the body and head molds were poured full of foam rubber and baked at a commercial rubber house.

The heads were attached to their bodies, then hair, glass eyes, and fingernails were added. Skin tones were matched with rubber paint, and every detail was covered, including eyelashes and teeth. The results

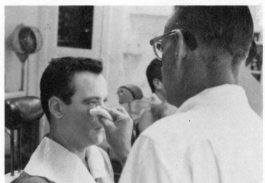

Using a small hairpiece to cover Lemmon's own hair, a moustache, eyebrows, and building his nose out to a little knob on the end, LaVigne disguised Jack Lemmon in *Irma La Douce*. (*Emile LaVigne*)

LaVigne transformed Tony Curtis and Jack Lemmon into females for their roles in *Some Like It Hot*. His biggest problem was to cover their beard growth. A beard cover was mixed and used over what they couldn't shave off. (*Emile LaVigne*)

were lifelike and terrorizing.

By 1958 LaVigne found himself head of the Makeup Department at United Artists. It was at United Artists in 1959 that LaVigne transformed Tony Curtis and Jack Lemmon into females for *Some Like It Hot*.

The biggest problem was their beards. A beard cover was mixed and used over what they couldn't shave off. Many times they would shave two or three times a day in order to keep their faces as clean as possible. A makeup similar to that used by women was needed because they played in the band and did many scenes with Marilyn Monroe and other girls in the cast so they had to blend in with them in coloring and appearance. Tony Curtis looked more feminine than Jack Lemmon, but Jack Lemmon

was supposed to be the clown. It was an enjoyable picture for LaVigne. He feels it turned out very well.

There have been times during LaVigne's career when he would return home from films like *The Magnificent Seven* (1960) or *The Great Escape* (1963) and would be asked why he was taken along on such films. The actors looked so natural. But this is a most flattering remark. His goal on this type of a film is to keep the actor's makeup in balance over a long period of time without it being distracting or obvious.

Much of the cast in *The Great Escape* were English. Their skin coloring was quite pale. On a day off or a weekend, they would head for the mountains and the sun. On Monday, LaVigne had a red face to deal

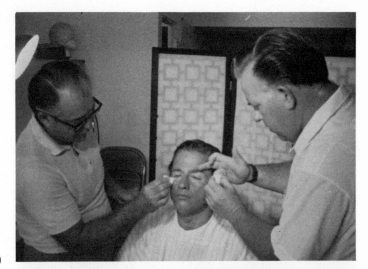

LaVigne and John Chambers make up Lou Antonio for a film test for *Hawaii*. (© *United Artists*)

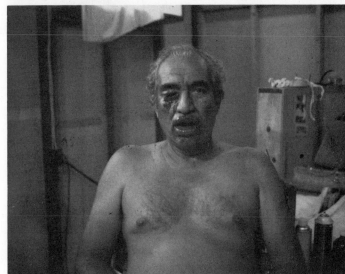

Ted Nobriga becomes a bruised and bloody victim on *Hawaii*. (© *United Artists*)

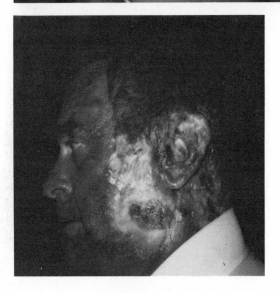

LaVigne created incredibly realistic burned and scarred tissue for the characters in *The Towering Inferno*. (*Emile LaVigne*)

with, on Tuesday and Wednesday the face would either peel or turn darker, and by Thursday it would quite often be pale again. In contrast, the German members of the cast had quite red and ruddy complexions which tended to become more flushed as the day wore on. Americans McQueen, Garner, Bronson, and Coburn had dark tans, so for six months LaVigne found there was a constant changing of color.

Hawaii (1966) was a challenging picture for LaVigne because it spanned so many years. He considered himself fortunate to be able to hire a crew of men that were expert in their field, and they were able to put together a fine picture. John Chambers was LaVigne's lab man and Dan Striekpeke the set man. LaVigne also had a wigmaker there. He had just about everything that would make a picture run smoothly, but toward the end of the production they began to run out of money, and so LaVigne didn't get to use everything that they had planned for. All in all, LaVigne regards it as a beautiful picture, one that required much thought and work.

LaVigne remained with United Artists until 1966, after which he decided to free-lance, doing independent pictures and pictures for Solar Productions and the Steve McQueen Company.

We asked LaVigne to explain the steps he used to achieve the burned and scarred faces for *The Towering Inferno* (1974).

"I used a small piece of glass (8 x 10) and modeled on it with Plastolain the shapes of disfigurement I wanted to use. Plastolain is a material makeup artists use quite often for modeling in place of clay. It separates from the mold and can be re-used. Actually I made many kinds of blisters, open wounds, etc. A half-inch wooden frame was held snugly around the glass. Vaseline was brushed on as a separating agent; then dental stone mixed with water was pounded into the frame and allowed to dry. The two separated early, creating an open mold. Molds should be oven-dryed with a coat of Vaseline brushed on and then allowed to soak into the stone. Plaster cap material can either be brushed in or sprayed—each coat being allowed to dry.

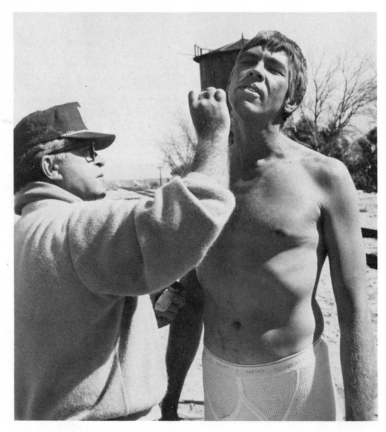

James Coburn and Emile LaVigne on the set of *Waterhole Three*. (*Emile LaVigne*)

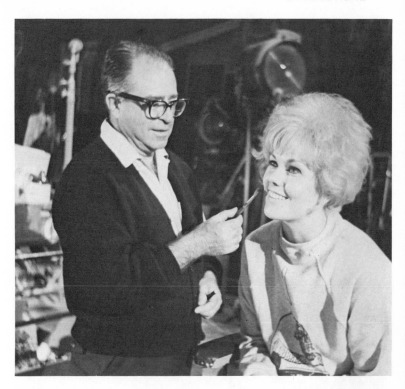

Kim Novak gets a little blusher from LaVigne as she waits for a scene in *Kiss Me Stupid*. (*Emile LaVigne*)

Color may be added to give the effect of a deep burn. Latex can also be used in this type of small mold.

"Spirit gum is used to apply the pieces and acetone to blend the edges, although this type of makeup appliance can be over-lapped and adhered together with acetone. Color is important. Red, yellow, black, etc. Yellow (V.O.) hair cream can be stippled on, giving the oozing look of a deep burn. Hair should be modeled and hair color spray should be applied (brown or yellow) and al-lowed to dry, giving a singed look."

Recently LaVigne has done *Fun with Dick and Jane* (1977) with George Segal and Jane Fonda and *The Great Houdini* for ABC television with Paul Glaser and Sally Struth-ers and *Roller Coaster* (1977) with George Segal, Richard Widmark, and Henry Fonda.

Along with hard work and challenge there is sometimes heartache. Such was the case with *Comes a Horseman* (1978), which starred Jane Fonda, Jason Robards, and James Caan. Segments from this film were featured on NBC's "Stuntman's Special" in October of 1977. Stuntman James Shepard was killed a few days later while doing a stunt for Jason Robards. LaVigne had made

LaVigne and star Jacqueline Bisset as she prepares for her role in *Who Is Killing the Great Chefs of Europe?* (*Emile LaVigne*)

Emile LaVigne is not the only LaVigne on the makeup scene today. Here, daughter Robin Dee LaVigne applies makeup to George Segal under the watchful supervision of her father. (*Photo courtesy of Emile LaVigne*)

him up prior to the stunt. He was a good friend to LaVigne who told us: "Tragedy is also involved in making people up. Many of them, like Jimmy, understand the importance of what we both are trying to do—and we became great friends."

LaVigne found *Who Is Killing the Great Chefs of Europe?* (1978) a very trying film. The film stars George Segal, Robert Morley, and Jacqueline Bisset; it was filmed on location in Venice, Paris, London, and Munich. Shooting was done in the kitchens and the dining rooms of many famous dining places in these cities and had to be filmed either after they were closed for the night or on days they were closed. This made the hours very tedious as well.

Emile LaVigne is not the only LaVigne on the makeup scene today. His daughter, Robin Dee LaVigne, attended the Producers' School for Makeup two evenings a week for eighteen months while working at Universal Studios. These classes are taught by members of the Makeup Union. Robin must share her father's talents because out of seven to eight hundred applicants, only ten were chosen, so one can see it is not an easy school to get into.

Robin is now working at Walt Disney Studios where she employed her craft on Sandy Duncan and Ken Berry in *The Cat from Outer Space* (1978). There are many father and son makeup artist combinations, but Emile and Robin are the first father/daughter team in Hollywood today.

Chapter 9

CHARLES SCHRAM

harles Schram didn't seek a career in the field of makeup; it sought him. Born in Los Angeles in 1911, Schram graduated from U.S.C. In 1935 Jack Dawn, head of makeup at MGM, contacted Schram and several other young men with artistic backgrounds, after seeking recommendations from Schram's dean for sculpturing and painting students that he could train in the art of makeup for the film *The Good Earth*.

For *The Good Earth*, Schram had to experiment with a bald-cap appliance that was to be used extensively to give the illusion of a shaved head. These caps were made from motion picture negative, cellulose nitrate, and were extremely flammable. It was fortunate that there were no accidents.

To make a bald-cap today, a liquid plastic type of material is painted or sprayed over a greased head mold made of either plaster of Paris or metal. The cap becomes a thin, plastic flexible skin very much like a plastic bag, which stretches over the head and is glued all around the edges with the ears sticking out. Makeup is then applied over the cap, and because of the thinness of the edges, it is almost impossible to tell where the edges are on the blended cap.

Oriental eye appliances were also developed for *The Good Earth*. Although the picture was made before sponge latex appliances were developed, the process of making the eye and nose pieces was actually the same as today. Casts were taken of the actors' faces and molds were made from these, but the difference was that instead of pouring foam latex and baking them in the oven, a mixture of melted gelatin and water was poured into cold molds. As the gelatin cooled off, it became a quite flexible jellylike substance.

These appliances were then glued on with spirit gum and the makeup applied over them. The shortcomings of this type of appliance compared to the rubber appliance were that, if the actor perspired a great deal or if it was very hot, the gelatin tended to remelt, and the appliances soon began to run down their faces. Often during a picture in which gelatin appliances were used, they had to be replaced several times during the day.

The next big makeup project at MGM was *The Wizard of Oz*. Makeup artists began months ahead preparing the appliances for the Munchkins, the Wicked Witch, the Flying Monkeys, the Lion, the Tin Man, and the Scarecrow. They made all the appliances with foam rubber, which they found was a great improvement over the gelatin. Casts were taken of all the actors' faces, and then, working from the illustrations in the book, the appliances were modeled with clay on the facial casts.

For *The Wizard of Oz*, Schram worked on Bert Lahr, the cowardly Lion, whose makeup consisted of a bald cap, rubber appliances, an orange tone makeup, false eyebrows, black whiskers, a wig with rubber ears, and a beard. (© *MGM*)

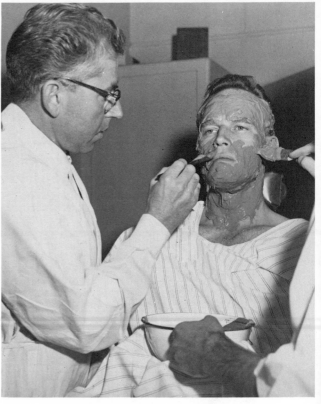

Charles Schram paints a coating of Negacol over Charlton Heston's features as the first step in creating a bust of Heston for the film *Ben-Hur*. (© *MGM*)

Margaret Hamilton's makeup as the Wicked Witch was another that kept Schram extremely busy. (© *MGM*)

These were transferred to the molds into which the rubber was then poured. New appliances were made for each day's shooting. The monkeys wore full-face appliances similar to those used on *Planet of the Apes*.

The actor who kept Schram busy was Bert Lahr, who played the cowardly lion. His daily makeup began with a bald cap over his hair to give him a wide forehead. Next, the rubber appliance went on, which gave him the turned-up nose and the split in the mid-dle of the upper lip. His own eyebrows were then covered over with fine silk, and the whole new face was covered with an orange tone makeup. False eyebrows were stuck on at a slanting angle, and black whiskers were stuck in his upper lip. The wig, with the rubber ears sewn on, was added and the beard then snapped under his chin. His tail wagged by means of a fishline and pole from overhead in the set.

Another makeup that kept Schram ex-

MISS HAMILTON
WITCH
_____   #

10-8-38
RAY BOLGER
SCARECROW

Makeup tests on Bert Lahr,
Ray Bolger, Margaret
Hamilton, and the flying
monkey. (© *MGM*)

tremely busy was that of Margaret Hamilton, who played the Wicked Witch. A life mask was made of her face, and from this, molds were made of her nose and chin. On these the long hooked nose and the long pointed chin with the wart on it were molded in clay and converted into molds for the rubber forms.

The appliances were first glued to her face with spirit gum, and then the whole face was covered with a special grease used whenever rubber appliances are employed. In this instance the grease was a green foundation shade, and the highlights and shadows were painted on her face in dark and light green. Her neck, arms, and hands were also covered with the green makeup.

The makeup was powdered, and the wart on her face, made out of rubber with a hair sticking out of it, was added. Her lips were painted, her teeth darkened, and long green fingernails gave the finishing touch.

The appliances used in *The Wizard of Oz* were very much like the appliances used today. Casts were made of the actors' faces, and appliances molded from these casts were then filled with foam rubber and baked in the same process that is used today. The rubber today, however, is more highly developed than it was in those times. Then making rubber was quite a random experiment. One day it would cure and the next day it would burn up in the oven and be crumbly, and another day it would collapse with big bubbles in it. Today the prosthetics formulas are much more precise, and the foam rubber is quite reliable.

Among the problems Schram had to deal with in his career were those for a picture titled *Three Wise Fools* (1946). In this film a group of midgets worked as leprechauns. They wore cute little rubber noses and long pointed rubber ears. The director wanted their ears to bend forward when they conversed. Schram made small brass pistons and cylinders to go behind each of their ears. These were connected with small rubber tubing to a rubber bulb in their pocket. When they squeezed the bulb, their ears would bend forward and then return.

In *The Time Machine* (1960) George Pal wanted the Morlock's eyes to glow in the dark. The Makeup Department made the rubber appliance faces and painted them green. Small surgical light bulbs, about one-sixteenth in diameter, were put in each eye opening. Fine wires were led down the back of their necks and into a pocket where a battery and push button were located. Flashing these lights on and off in a dimly lighted set gave a very nice effect.

The wigs for the principals were made out of white monkey fur. The background Morlocks wore white synthetic wigs that were bought from a wig manufacturer. The body costumes were made entirely in the Wardrobe Department, since that is their specialty, and they were made from the white fur cloth from which most monsters today are made.

Schram also worked on the television science-fiction series "Twilight Zone." Each week they received a new script with some out-of-this-world creature that had to be ready the following Monday morning. This often meant working late nights and weekends to be ready on time.

In George Pal's *The Seven Faces of Dr. Lao*, Schram found working on all the imaginative characters to be a challenging and exciting project. Bill Tuttle created the makeup concept for Dr. Lao, but Schram did the daily application, applying the eyepieces and so forth. He found Tony Randall a wonderful subject and most cooperative.

Schram also worked on the 1941 version of *Dr. Jekyll and Mr. Hyde*, starring Spencer Tracy. This film was done in black and white and employed the same red/blue filter technique used for the Louis Hayward version.

We asked Schram to talk to us about his experience with the makeup industry.

"In the many years that I have been in motion picture makeup, the cosmetic field has certainly changed. When we started in the thirties, the makeup was a tube of greasepaint makeup made by Max Factor. This was quite thick, heavy, sticky makeup. You squeezed out about half an inch of it in the palm of one hand and rubbed your hands together until they were both covered with makeup. This was then patted on the actor's face and rubbed into his skin, made as smooth as possible. The corrections on their faces were then made with a lighter or darker shade of the same type of makeup applied with brushes perhaps, and blended. Then the whole thing was very heavily powdered and brushed off. This was the makeup that was used in the thirties.

"Then later pancake makeup was

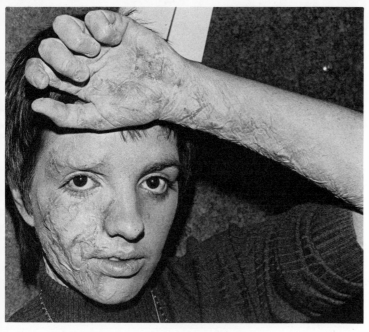

Schram had to simulate acid burns on Liza Minnelli's face and arm for her role in *Tell Me That You Love Me Junie Moon*. (*Charles Schram*)

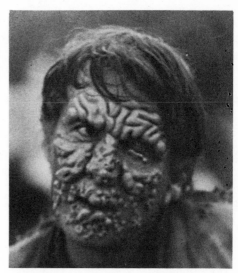

Anthony Zerbe displays an effective leprous makeup that Schram created for his role in *Papillon*. (*Charles Schram*)

brought out by Max Factor, and for quite a few years we all used pancake makeup because it was a quicker process and it was easier for the actor to get off. You only needed soap and water instead of the thick cold cream type of remover needed with the greasepaint makeup.

"Once applied, it dried flat and didn't need much powder. It was quicker and some people liked it better, but it never gave a skin a truly lifelike appearance. It always looked a little flat and dull-looking.

"Eventually cosmetic companies such as Max Factor and the Westmores brought out thinner, lighter makeups that were used for all the actors in the studio during the forties, fifties, and sixties. Different color systems were used because of the different film processes that were being tried.

"As color came in, Technicolor demanded a makeup with absolutely no red in

it. As a matter of fact, the colors that we used in the early Technicolor pictures were very gray. Even pure-gray was used sometimes over skins that were too red, to tone them down so that they would come out lifelike on the screen.

"Then with the advent of Anscocolor we had to add red to the film, and all of our makeups were designed very much on the red side. This was a process that was used until Eastman developed their three-color negative/positive process. Then it seemed for the first time we could use makeups that looked very natural. People now had normal colors on their faces. Now if a person looks good to the eye, he will normally look good on the screen.

"I like to work on the 'cute' makeups, like Bert Lahr, the cowardly lion, or the fairy-tale characters in *Alice in Wonderland*, and so on. I think beauty makeup is a matter of per-

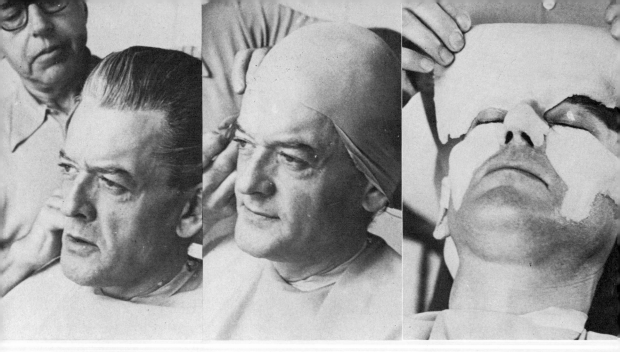

Holbrook prepares to undergo a makeup transformation at the expert hands of Charles Schram for an NBC-TV series on Abraham Lincoln.
(© NBC/Charles Schram)

A bald cap is placed over Holbrook's natural hair to protect it and enable the use of an effective wig.
(© NBC/Charles Schram)

Ear and cheek appliances are already in place as Schram adds the one-piece forehead and nose appliances.
(© NBC/Charles Schram)

sonal taste and cannot be listed as a series of pointers. The application of cosmetics is easily learned, but the evaluation of each face and how best to make it up is a matter of instinct, mainly.

"Recently, in teaching a class of new makeup artists the subjects of old-age makeup, I started by asking each one to name one of the things that happens to a face when it ages. One by one they listed the things which they had noticed in their own observation: the receding hairline, the graying of the hair, the sagging of the muscles, the emergence of the skull through the skin and tissue, the drooping of the eyelids, and the wrinkling of the skin.

"I then proceeded to show them, by painting and blending highlights and shadows onto the face, how makeup can create an illusion of old age on a younger face.

"Next I demonstrated the use of the stretch-skin and liquid adhesive to create the wrinkles on the skin, and thirdly I told them of the appliance technique of old age, where the face is actually resculptured to what nature does in the aging process. It is

very nearly impossible to learn these techniques from a textbook. I feel that the demonstration and practice, with an instructor's criticism, is the only way to actually learn it.

"Life masks are made by applying a flexible covering—either Negacol or Geltrate—over the person's face, leaving openings for him to breathe through. Then, this is covered with a thin coating of plaster of Paris to hold it in shape. When this has set, the whole cast is removed from the face of the actor and is then turned over on a bench and filled with plaster of Paris to create the positive mask.

"When this inside has set, the outside coating is then cracked and removed. The actor's face, reproduced in plaster, emerges at this time. It then has to be pointed up with knives or plaster tools to take off the imperfections caused by the mold making.

"The makeup techniques of the early monster films would look very fake and false on the screen today. Thanks to the use of rubber appliances, actual characters are now created in three dimensions and are

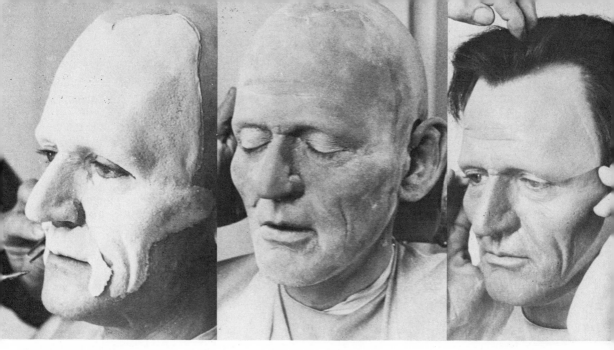

The upper lip appliance is now added. (© NBC/Charles Schram)

Once the basic facial appearance has been completed, makeup and hair will be added. (© NBC/Charles Schram)

A cream makeup, which did not require powder, was used. It left a natural glow instead of a greasy glitter. The wig was then added. (© NBC/Charles Schram)

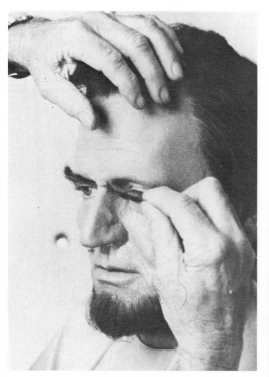

A hairlace beard and thick eyebrows were then added to complete the makeup transformation. (© NBC/Charles Schram)

Hal Holbrook in Charles Schram's complete Lincoln makeup. (© NBC/Charles Schram)

photographed with the film processes of today as an actual creature would be.''

Charles Schram worked at MGM for thirty years under the direction of two department heads, Jack Dawn and William Tuttle. During that time he did the major part of the laboratory work. He made the molds and the rubber appliances, and along with several other makeup artists, he did the many difficult character makeups. He also made up many of the stars under contract on a regular basis.

Since leaving MGM in 1965, he has worked on several independent productions. The first was Otto Preminger's *Tell Me That You Love Me Junie Moon* (1970). For this film, Schram had to simulate acid burns on Liza Minnelli's face and arm. He made thin rubber scars to cover one whole side of Minnelli's face and one arm and hand. These were applied each day, then covered with a makeup to look like burn scars. The scars were copied from an actual burn patient in a hospital.

In 1972 Schram changed Richard Benjamin from a young boy to an adult man in *Portnoy's Complaint*. In *Carnal Knowledge* (1971), he changed Jack Nicholson and Art Garfunkel from schoolboys into middle-aged men, and in *Papillon* (1974) he changed Steve McQueen from a vital young prisoner into the emaciated creature the protagonist became after five years of solitary confinement on Devil's Island.

On September 6, 1975, NBC-TV began its Sandburg's Lincoln series starring Hal Holbrook as Lincoln and Sada Thompson as Mary Todd Lincoln. Schram considers this the film he has most enjoyed working on because of the wonderful cooperation he had from Holbrook, director George Schaeffer, and the cameraman, Howard Schwartz.

Because of the vast structural differences between Lincoln and the actor, Schram made a complete head and neck cast of Hal Holbrook. He had a copy of the life mask of Lincoln, made in 1860, and a photo book with every known photograph of him.

He then proceeded to model a bust of Lincoln right over the bust of Hal Holbrook.

When everyone was satisfied with the structural changes necessary to transform Holbrook into Lincoln, he proceeded to make the individual molds and modeling necessary for the rubber appliances. These were modeled in small detail on their individual casts taken from the bust, and the final set of molds included the forehead and nose on one mold, separate cheekbones and jowls, and separate molds for the upper and lower lips.

The daily three-hour makeup consisted first of a bald cap to cover Hal Holbrook's full head of hair. Next, the forehead and nose appliances were applied; then the cheekbones and nasal folds, with the well-known mole on the right side, were glued on. This was followed by adhering the upper lip and lower lip. By now Holbrook's entire face, with the exception of his eyelids, was covered with rubber appliances. Makeup was applied over the rubber.

The makeup was a cream that required little or no powder, leaving a natural glow instead of a greasy glitter. It was applied very thinly and did not build up in the facial lines or creases. It had the ability to lighten dark skin, subdue sunburn redness, or darken light skin without photographic side effects. Bill Tuttle created this makeup, which is called Custom Color Foundation.

Following this, the wig, beard, and eyebrows were glued on, and the sixteenth President of the United States was reborn. After the second or third day of wearing this extensive makeup, Holbrook became quite used to it, feeling no restrictions on his facial movements. He was even able to carefully eat an apple with his rubber lips!

The bust Schram modeled of Holbrook as Lincoln was bronzed and used in the opening credits of the shows.

In addition to his career as an active makeup artist, Schram owns and operates the Windsor Hills Make-up Laboratory at 5226 Maymont Drive, Los Angeles, California, where he supplies many of the motion picture makeup artists in Hollywood, New York, and London with the latex and curing compounds needed for their appliance work.

Chapter 10

THE NORINS

One of the many skills essential to a good makeup artist is that of laboratory work. Besides being excellent makeup artists, Josef and his son Gustaf Norin were brilliant lab men and knew a good deal about chemistry. Josef Norin was born in 1883 and died in 1954. In his younger years he was head designer and sculptor for A. B. Bolen & Company—a multimillion-dollar jewelry company in Sweden, which had offices all over Europe.

Gustaf Norin was born in 1905. He was raised and educated in Sweden. Josef came to America in 1924 and was both a landscape and portrait painter, as well as a sketch artist. These skills gave him entry into the motion picture industry as a makeup artist. Gustaf worked with his father in industrial staff shops and in motion picture staff shops until they joined the Metro-Goldwyn-Mayer Makeup Department in 1935, where they worked with Jack Dawn.

Josef and Gustaf worked diligently over the years to perfect the appliance materials needed for such makeup as was seen in *The Good Earth*, *Conquest*, *The Great Waltz*, and *The Wizard of Oz*.

"My father and I were eight to nine months preparing *The Wizard of Oz*," Gustaf related. "There were many molds that would burn out, crack, or dry up, that had to be remade. We had to overstock our ovens to cure the rubber, which put the molds a little too close to the fire at times. We had some apprentices in the studio at the time; one of whom was Jack Kevan who later became a very well-known makeup artist.

"My father and I didn't do any characters throughout the picture because we were too tied up in the laboratory with remakes or remodelings for the film. I think my father started to do the Scarecrow, but I don't think he did it throughout the film. I know there were days and nights that we never got home. I remember one instance when I worked two nights and three days straight without going home. I don't think we ever worked so hard on any film as we did on *The Wizard of Oz*. I'm certain that Bill Tuttle and Charlie Schram made up some of the more important characters, as they were some of our finer makeup artists working on that film."

At United Artists the Norins did such films as *The Moon and Sixpence* (1942) and *Blood on the Sun* (1945). John Emery's makeup as Tanaka was sculptured and applied by Josef Norin. They did *Along Came Jones* (1945) for RKO, as well as *The Bachelor's Daughters* (1946) and *The Private Affairs of Bel Ami* (1947).

More time was spent on eyes and lips in those days. Ernie Westmore and Gustaf worked together a great deal then and

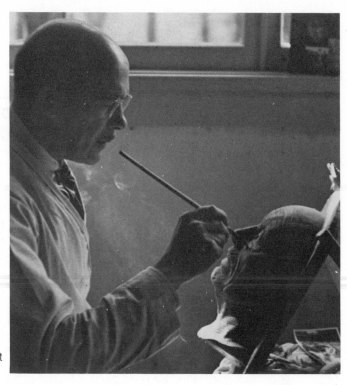

Josef Norin at work on a cast of John Emery. *(Gus Norin)*

Westmore designed a makeup for women's eyes that Gustaf has usually followed throughout his career. Westmore would paint a black line close to the eyelid, using quite a broad stroke, and then blend it gradually upward. He would add brown to that and blend it out into nothingness. When the eyes were opened, they appeared much larger than normal.

In 1948 the Norins were involved in *Arch of Triumph,* which starred Ingrid Bergman, Charles Boyer, Charles Laughton, and Louis Calhern. Calhern's makeup began with sketches from the Art Department, followed by highlights and shadows to bring about the character prescribed. Then hair was laid on the face with spirit gum to make the beard. This was then modeled with a hot curling iron, to shape it, style it, and remodel it.

"I recall a funny incident that happened while shooting *Arch of Triumph,*" Gustaf related. "Director Lewis Milestone was a very good friend of mine and one day I went to his house and spent an hour with him having lunch. We'd been told by many people that we looked very much alike. We were both stocky and had accents, mine Swedish and his Russian. Otherwise, I could never see any resemblance. But as I left the house and opened the front door to step out to my car, I met Norma Shearer. She said, 'Hello, Darling' and kissed me. Well, who am I to refuse a kiss from a beautiful lady! Later that afternoon, I talked to Milestone on the phone and he was *still* laughing. Norma had come upstairs to visit with his wife and was shocked when she saw Milestone upstairs. 'My Lord,' she said, 'who was the man that I kissed downstairs?' "

In 1949 Gustaf's lab skills were used to create progressively worsening facial changes on Kirk Douglas for his portrayal of a struggling young boxer who became a middleweight champion in *Champion*. The first step Gustaf employed was to take a complete impression of Douglas's face, which was then reproduced in plaster. He created several castings from this, from which he reproduced section molds. A face model is generally divided up into seven or more sections. Gustaf then used the original facial cast to model the scars and bruises essential for Douglas's role as Midge Kelly.

A great deal of trial and error went into the making of the nose for José Ferrer in his

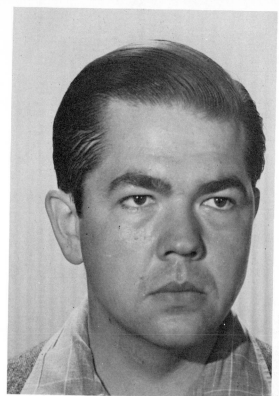

Before-and-after shots of Marvin Miller for his role in *Blood on the Sun*. (*Gus Norin*)

John Emery in costume and makeup by Josef Norin, for his portrayal of Tanaka in *Blood on the Sun*. (*Gus Norin*)

The handsome French actor
Charles Boyer prior to
makeup for his role in
Conquest. *(Gus Norin).*

role in *Cyrano de Bergerac* (1950), which
Josef Norin eventually accomplished.

Other films that the Norins were involved
in during the early fifties were *The Men*
(1950), *He Ran All the Way* (1951), *High
Noon* (1952), and *The Indian Fighter* (1955).

In 1956 Michael Todd shot *Around the
World in Eighty Days* in Todd-AO, a new film
process first used in *Oklahoma!* (1955). It
required only one camera and one projector
in contrast to Cinerama's three of each. On
a picture of this magnitude, problems were
to be expected, and Gustaf Norin had his
share. One was turning a short-haired, blue-
eyed Shirley MacLaine into a dark-eyed,
dark-skinned Indian princess. With the aid
of contact lenses, hair, and makeup, he
achieved the look needed.

"Todd, at times, was a very strange person," Gustaf told us. "Before we left Hollywood to go on location, he called me into
the office and said, 'We're going to need
about a thousand Japanese wigs, even
though the script doesn't call for that many. I
wanted to tell you about that now. We'll be
using them for about a week, possibly two.'

So I immediately set forth to scurry around
town and find some wigs. I couldn't pick up
more than forty or fifty wigs in Hollywood at
Max Factor's, but Max Factor's offered me
a deal. They would bring the wigs into
America from Japan after having them
made over there. The wigs would cost about
thirty to thirty-five dollars a week to rent, but
I'd have to guarantee them three weeks
rental.

"I went back to the studio with the good
news, or the horrible news, depending on
your outlook. Everybody just shook their
heads, and Todd said, 'Look, we don't have
to worry about it right now. We're not going
to shoot this sequence until much later in
the film, and we can make our minds up
then.'

"These wigs were known as 'hard-
shelled wigs'—some of them were geisha
wigs, and some peasant wigs, so there was
no similarity between them and the wigs we
have here in America.

"We went to our Colorado location and
completed that, then came home. The second day I was home, Todd called me into

Boyer as Napoleon in
Conquest. (Gus Norin)

his office and said, 'Incidentally, Gus, next week we are going to shoot that Japanese sequence, and as I told you, we'll need a thousand wigs.' Well, of course, you couldn't bring a thousand wigs from Japan in a week's time. To get them made alone would take at least a month or a month and a half. Shipping them here would take an additional week, and getting them through customs would take quite a bit of time. I explained this to Todd, who said, 'Gus, that's not my worry—that's *your* worry. You just see to it that we have the wigs when we need them!'

"I went back to the department and was discussing the problem with my two assistants when someone overheard me. He was from India and had done some technical work on our film. He said, 'You know, I think I can help you. If your put me on a makeup artist's salary, I can get the wigs together for you in a week's time.' There are Japanese clubs in San Diego, Los Angeles, San Francisco, Sacramento, all along the West Coast—and these club members have their own wigs. He offered to gather them to-gether for me in a week, and I said, 'Fine! You're on salary right now. Take off! When do I see you?' He said, 'Pretty quickly—won't be long.' Before the week was over, he was back with a thousand wigs that he had gathered throughout California.

"I set the hairdressers to work numbering the wigs and recording who they belonged to. We used the wigs for a week and the charge was only ten dollars per wig, plus the man's salary for three weeks. When Todd got wind that the expenditure on the wigs was only a little over ten thousand dollars he came to me and said, 'What in the world did you do? How did you get them?' and I said, 'Mike, you told me it was *my* worry. So it's *my* business. Forget it."

A new generation of Norins have followed their father and grandfather into the field of makeup. Bob Norin was born in 1938, and John was born in 1944. Although Bob grew up around makeup, he never thought he wanted to be involved in it and attended Pierce College in Woodland Hills, California, where he studied business education. At one point he worked in the staff plaster shop

Gustaf Norin's lab skills were used on Kirk Douglas in *Champion*. (*Gus Norin*)

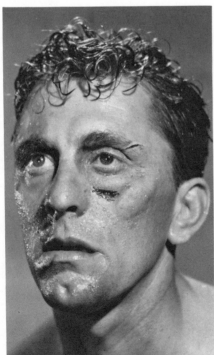

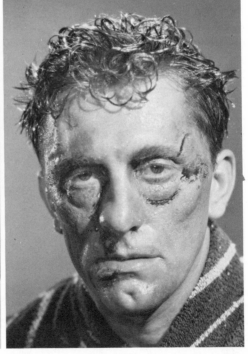

Douglas needed progressively worsening features for his role as middleweight champion Midge Kelly. (*Gus Norin*)

José Ferrer in makeup for his role in *Cyrano de Bergerac*. (*Gus Norin*)

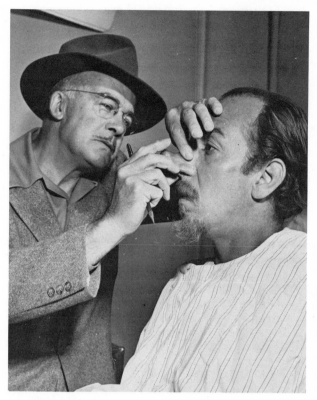

Gustaf Norin applies the famous nose to José Ferrer. (*Gus Norin*)

at Desilu Studios and learned how to make molds and cast items. A year or so later a chance came up to work with his father in making some mermaid tails for a television show that was shot in Florida. Bob would paint the mermaid tails at night, and during the day he would work under the water with the actress's double on the underwater scenes. The tails were made in a period of eight to ten weeks and cost about $20,000. This was in 1965, and Gustaf told Bob that in the 1948–49 period it would have taken about six months to make and cost twice as much.

After this venture, Bob began to seriously consider the makeup profession, and he decided to see if he could do it. He joined Gustaf on a film that he was doing in Kanab, Utah, in 1965, and Gustaf began to teach

his son his profession. When they returned to Hollywood, Bob continued to work at other studios and proceeded to learn from many of the other older, more experienced artists. Bob could feel that he was enjoying what he was doing and the comments he received on his makeup from others indicated that he was on the right track.

Under the guidance of Bill Tuttle, Bob did several feature pictures, and later, in 1966, he did two television pilots for CBS. In 1967 Bob worked on *Planet of the Apes* and in 1968 he spent ten months on *Paint Your Wagon* (1969) as makeup artist and lab technician. Gustaf also worked on this film. Bob made numerous bald caps and other appliances for *The Hawaiians* in 1969.

In 1971 Bob assisted Bill Tuttle again in the prosthetic appliance preproduction work and makeup tests for *The Life and Times of Judge Roy Bean* (1971), which starred Paul Newman. Both Bob and Gustaf also worked on the film *Papillon* (1973). They made all the necessary prosthetic appliances and hairwork. They made a complete working body for the guillotine execution. On location they worked out of a portable lab set up for fabricating appliances as demand necessitated. Bob tells us about one of his favorite makeup creations to date:

"One thing that stands out in my mind is the leper sequence from *Papillon*. We had about ten lepers who were created with appliances, and when they were placed in their spots for the scene, it was a sight that gave me the creeps."

Bob has been an active member of Local 706, the makeup artists' union, for twelve years and has worked on numerous television and movie films, including *The Towering Inferno* (1974), where he worked with Emile LaVigne, "J. E.'s Revenge," "Sybil," "Blue Collar Journal," and *Sorcerer* (1977), in which he assisted Ben Nye, Jr., with makeup effects for a dynamite blast sequence.

Gustaf's younger son, John, studied business administration for three years and then took a year of air-conditioning and refrigeration engineering. He found difficulty finding work in this field, and because he'd always shown artistic abilities throughout high school and college, and also because he knew he had a wonderful instructor in his father, he decided to enter the makeup field.

In 1964, under the direction of Bill Tuttle at MGM, he was given the opportunity to do the makeup on various television pilots such as "Jericho" and "Riot on Sunset Strip." For about one year he worked on the "Hondo" series and on the film *Love-In* (1966), until he was drafted. When he returned from Vietnam, he went back to MGM, where he did "The Courtship of Eddie's Father," a very successful television series, and the film *The Moonshine War* (1970).

Most of John's makeup career to date has been on television, and although he has done some movies, he would like to do more. There is no one favorite creation that he has done, but he enjoys doing old-age character makeups, either with or without prosthetics. Hairwork is a particular favorite, and he is becoming quite skilled in the art of laying on hair.

In 1974 John did the ninety-minute ABC special, "Huckleberry Finn." Royal Dano played "Mark Twain," and John found that Dano's face lent itself to the role perfectly. John devoted his skills to the hairwork, which included coloring and the laying over of the eyebrows and moustache. All hairwork on the actors in "Huckleberry Finn" was raw hand-laid hair, not the lace beards that are commonly used.

In doing research for his character, John discovered that Twain changed his moustache length and hair length many times, so John tried to achieve a characterization of Twain that would fit the majority's mental picture of the famous man.

In 1974 John worked on "Korg 70,000 B.C.," a television series which depicted early man and required considerable prosthetic appliance work for the characters. When a makeup artist is faced with a film that requires extensive prosthetic work the producer will want to know how long a particular makeup will take. John advises that a makeup artist should allot the maximum time needed. This way, after he has done the makeup for three or four days and can get the time down on it, the producer is happier than if the artist has told him it will take only an hour and a half and it ends up taking two and a half.

On the latter part of the film, the producers wanted to cut back on the $150 per appliance per actor per day, and so John and his partner had to come up with some new ideas for concealing the edges so they could use the appliances for two days rather than the one. This could be done for a television film but would never work for a movie, where the image is blown up so large on the screen.

A person must be extremely careful in making a life mask, John cautions, because if the material is not used correctly or in the right sequence, it can be dangerous. Negacol is an old material made in Europe and is still available in various places. It is a plastic which is heated up, melted down, and then painted on the face as a warm material. Sometimes a bald cap is put over the hair to protect it and so the material can be applied further up into the hairline, and there are times when the eyes must be left uncovered or the actor will become claustrophobic. Normally the eyes are closed, though, and they breathe through their nose.

Gustaf and Josef Norin at work in their lab. (*Gus Norin*)

Geltrate is a modern material which is also used. It is the same material used by dentists.

John created interesting old-age makeups for Robert Preston in 1974 for the television feature "My Father's House" and for the 1975 television pilot "Jigsaw John" based on the strangulation murders of old ladies in the Wilshire District of Los Angeles. John re-created the victims, complete with grotesque neck bruises and the smeared lipstick which was the killer's trademark. John also worked on the "Bronk" series and in 1976 did such television series as "Captain Marvel," "Isis," and "Ark II."

John and Bob represent a new generation of makeup artists. The expansive studio makeup departments are gone. John cited the film *Easy Rider* (1969) as a turning point in the industry. Everyone thought they could make a movie for nothing after that and tried to hire makeup artists very cheaply. They

didn't want to spend money for appliances and hair. When the makeup artists were moved out of the studios, they had to do their makeup outside the "honey-wagons"—another name for the portable toilets—on a table. This was far from suitable. Makeup applied on a cold morning would become blotchy under the lights; a room with good lighting is essential to realistic makeup.

John feels that during this period, movies went down. A lot of the experienced producers retired, and the new producers were just that—new—and didn't always know what was going on. Gradually, though, the new producers became good, and the ones that weren't fell by the wayside. The union became stronger and helped their artists cope with these new problems. The manufacturers of the "honey-wagons" understood the makeup artists' problems and are building new "honey-wagons" with rooms in them specifically designed for makeup, with the proper lighting and space. The industry is growing and changing, as it has since its inception.

We asked John to comment on his father, Gustaf, and his grandfather, Josef.

"I think my father and grandfather were the forerunners in the field of makeup. My dad and grandfather invented many things. The formula for one of the best bald caps still used today was designed by my father. Certain types of appliances were created and used by them. They invented more things through the years than I can even remember.

"My grandfather was a true artist in every sense. He could do anything—drawings, sketches, painting, sculpturing, casting—he was phenomenal. He could carve too. I have replicas today of a carving of Greta Garbo he did out of hardwood. I have a bronze statue my grandfather did of Will Rogers, which is thin-wall casting. This is a lost art.

"My father is also a great artist and can cast, sculpt, and design. I think my father could think of things faster than any other makeup artist in his time, and create them faster. When he read the script or was told by the producer what they wanted, he would know exactly what he was going to do and have it going and done while any other makeup artist would still be shaking his head and worrying about how to do it; or how somebody else did it. He was very, very fast, and very good."

It would seem that the makeup profession remains in very professional and competent hands today, and that it is most fortunate to have two such gifted young makeup artists as Robert and John Norin, who have had the opportunity of learning their craft from such a skilled source as their father, Gustaf Norin.

Chapter 11

BEN NYE, SR.

Ben Nye headed for the sunny skies of California in the early twenties and landed a job in the art department of a department store. Although his father had recommended the study of geology at the University of Nebraska, after a year there, his professors recommended art school. Nye had always been the makeup artist for the plays in high school and later at the university, but he didn't have any formal art training when Los Angeles beckoned.

When the crash of '29 hit, like many others, Nye found himself out of work. He was more fortunate than most, because his uncle worked in the Music Department at Fox Studios, and Nye got a job in the photostat section making copies of sheet music for individual orchestra members. It was a boring, repetitious job, but times were tough and Nye held onto the job for three years.

The studio became very busy in the midthirties, and Nye heard about the apprenticeship program being offered by the Makeup Department.

He began his apprenticeship in 1935, and for the first time no longer had to supplement his income with outside jobs. Ernie Westmore was the department head for the first two years of Nye's apprenticeship, but Nye received most of his training from Ernie's brother, Monty. During his apprenticeship, Nye found he really had to hustle around the department to get a good education, and because of that, it helped him in later years to design an excellent apprenticeship program at Twentieth Century-Fox.

Finishing his training in 1937, Nye passed the rigorous union exam and was now a "journeyman" makeup artist. When he began working on films, there were the "A" movies and the "B" movies. The "B" movies, of course, were very low budget films and appeared as second bill. They were also done very quickly, which meant the hours were extremely long. Nye had to do many of these before he was allowed to do an "A" movie. He loved his work, though. Going to the studio everyday was a thrill to him, and he found that a strong feeling of community existed in those days.

Clay Campbell came to Fox in 1938 and became the new department head. He and Nye got along well, and Nye soon discovered that this made a great deal of difference when it came to film assignments.

Fox was soon going into production with a film about the legendary *Jesse James* (1939), and Campbell asked Nye if he wanted to do the film. This was the first film for which Nye was entirely responsible for the makeup, and he soon found himself packing for Noel, Missouri. The entire shooting schedule was only six weeks, but he was used to working hard from all those "B" movies.

Nye regards his first film as a success. He had three makeup artists working for him and putting his limited experience to work; he quickly learned to coordinate his personnel, break down the script, prepare for each day's work, and, most importantly, practice his craft as a makeup artist.

There were many bruises, cuts, and gunshot wounds to prepare. The actors had to look dirty most of the time. Nye had to lay a beard on Tyrone Power that the actor would be wearing when he was shot near the end of the film. Nye used real hair and laid it on thinly. The beard was a success, and through the years, Nye achieved a reputation for natural-appearing hairwork.

It was in 1939 that Monty Westmore, Sr., was asked to direct the makeup for *Gone With the Wind,* which David O. Selznick would produce at Selznick International Pictures. This was Nye's first assignment away from Fox, and he began work on the film in February. It went straight through until August of that same year.

Westmore asked Nye to take care of Leslie Howard, Thomas Mitchell, Hattie McDaniel, and Olivia de Havilland. Westmore did Vivien Leigh's makeup each morning, but Nye was also responsible for her makeup for the rest of the day.

These were some of the most hectic days of Nye's life. He was the first one on the set when the cameras rolled each day, and if he thought he had worked hard then, he really worked hard when they "burned Atlanta." Reaching the department at five-thirty A.M. and making sure that all the principals were getting made up on time, Nye then made up Leslie Howard and other principals working that day. The rest of the day was spent on the set until about one P.M., when he would leave for lunch with his wife and a quick nap.

He would then return to the studio to prepare for the second unit company that would be filming all night. Many evenings there were hundreds of extras working. They required cuts and burns and a general "dirty allover" look. One of the biggest problems they faced on these days was being sure all the people were "in makeup" by the time it got dark enough to begin shooting.

Leslie Howard wore a very thin stubble beard when he was in the thick of the action during the war scenes. Nye hand-laid the

Jesse James was the first film on which Nye was entirely responsible for makeup. Tyrone Power had the title role, and Nye had to lay a beard on him that he would wear when he was shot near the end of the film. (© *Twentieth Century-Fox Film Corporation*)

beard, and he regards it as one of his best. Even Scarlett O'Hara had to get dirty while helping in the hospital in Atlanta, and Nye had to be very careful that Vivien Leigh looked just right for her portrayal of these scenes. Hattie McDaniel, a wonderful woman to work with, became a good friend of Nye's for many years. Nye became acutely aware that there were not any good makeups for the black performers. When he made McDaniel up, he had to carefully blend several colors together so she wouldn't appear red or pasty.

Nye made Ingrid Bergman up for her first role in the United States in the film *Intermezzo* (1939). It also starred Leslie Howard, whom Nye knew from his year with *Gone With the Wind. Rebecca* (1940) turned out to be a wonderful film starring Judith Anderson. This was Nye's first association with the young director Alfred Hitchcock. Nye spent a full year with David Selznick, and the experience he gained during those twelve months proved to be invaluable throughout his career.

Nye became a free-lancer and spent most of his time between the Warner Brothers Studio and Paramount. He was asked to be assistant on Paramount's now-classic *For Whom the Bell Tolls* (1943), which starred Ingrid Bergman and Gary Cooper. They did the locations in Sonora, California, and Nye found the film a real pleasure to do. He purchased a movie camera and started to film the progress of the film. This proved to be a great form of relaxation, and he still enjoys watching his "home movies" of that film.

In the meantime, Twentieth Century-Fox Studios began to go through some reorganization, and the former production manager at the Selznick Studios had moved to Fox. He remembered the excellent job Nye had done on *Gone With the Wind*, *Intermezzo*, and *Rebecca* and approached him about becoming head of the Makeup Department created by the firing of Guy Pierce.

At age thirty-seven, Nye was ready for a challenge and quickly accepted the position. The first year proved difficult, and Nye was faced with many problems. Not only did he have the typical resentment people are often faced with when filling a position held previously by a friend who got the "ax," but the war was just over and production was

When Monty Westmore was head of makeup on *Gone With the Wind* Nye worked under him and took care of makeup on Leslie Howard and Thomas Mitchell, as well as others. (© *MGM*)

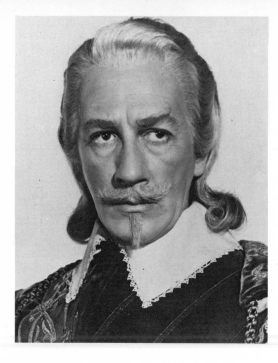

Richard Haydn in costume
and makeup for his role as
the Earl of Radcliffe in
Forever Amber. (*Ben Nye*)

severely curtailed, since they were no longer producing war films. The staff and budget for the department had been large, and suddenly they were drastically reduced. This led to problems in acquiring adequate materials and maintaining a good staff.

Nye proved to those who doubted him that he wasn't quite the young "upstart" they believed him to be. He respected the opinions of his assistants, and he did his homework in getting the department running smoothly. He found that the budgets would remain very tight, and his success in his position partially rested on how well he could stick to them. Fox was still making "A" and "B" films, and now the "A" films were being made almost as quickly as the "B" films. The biggest Westerns were cranked out in two months' time.

After this "shakedown" period was over, Fox made *Forever Amber* (1947). The film took place in England during the period of Charles the Second. It had a large cast and the biggest budget Nye had handled to date. Nearly all of the principals and extras would be wearing wigs and hairpieces, and Nye requested that an entire sound stage be set aside for makeup and hair.

Nye had long curly wigs made which were worn by all the men, with the exception of the commoners, who wore their hair in a short bob. It was the most extravagant film made during this time, and thousands

were spent with Max Factor who made custom-fitted wigs for the principals. Though they had a small stock of wigs in the department, it was necessary to rent most of those required for the extras. The sound stage was divided in half, allowing one side for makeup and the other for hair.

The makeup men were extremely busy with all the beards and moustaches. Lace pieces were made in advance and used and reused an infinite number of times. They could be easily redressed at the end of the day with a curling iron, and they would be ready for use the next day. When a principal would be working close to the camera, they would often overlay the upper edges of the piece with real hair so there would be no chance of a hard edge.

The postwar forties passed quickly, and Nye's next important makeup became *The Mudlark* (1950). When Nye received the script he realized that it posed a real challenge because he would have to create a very close likeness to Queen Victoria. Irene Dunne was cast for the part and unfortunately, bore no resemblance to the queen. The queen had a very full face; one could actually call it a fat round face, and Nye recognized that prosthetics were going to have to be very complete.

Fox had an excellent research library with a full-time librarian. Nye visited her and they found some excellent pictures that could serve as his models. He then arranged for Miss Dunne to spend a few hours in the lab so they could take a full-face impression.

After making a positive cast of her face, Nye began to sculpt what was to become a one-piece prosthetic appliance. The main part of the appliance gave her full cheeks and jowls. After the sculpting was complete, Nye created a new cast, and soon after sponge rubber was pumped into the special mold. The important technical point about the mask was that it was one piece, and there would be no seams between the jowls and cheeks that could come apart during the production. When the makeup was finally applied, Miss Dunne looked every bit the part. The prosthetic piece fit her like a glove. The sponge rubber was light and allowed her natural facial movements. She had no difficulty talking normally, which gave her more confidence.

After applying the piece with spirit gum, Nye then colored it with a normal cream-base type of makeup. Normally, a makeup artist would use castor grease to protect the sponge rubber, but Nye never liked castor color because he couldn't keep it looking "dull" enough. Nye's technique was to seal the appliance with a polyvinyl plastic, spreading it very thinly with a brush. He would then powder the plastic to subdue any shininess and then use a regular cream-type makeup. At the time, they used Max Factor panstick. He found this technique worked very well for him.

Miss Dunne's forehead was blocked out with a partial or three-quarter plastic cap. A wig was made that would correspond to the particular headdress she would be wearing throughout the film. Nye's lab man made the caps and the one-piece appliance in Hollywood and forwarded them to Nye in England as he needed them. The caps were outstanding because they were sprayed so that the edges were very thin. After finishing the cap, the wig and headdress were applied.

Miss Dunne's eyes were not deep-set,

Nearly all the principals and extras in *Forever Amber* would be wearing wigs and hairpieces, and Nye requested an entire sound stage be set up for makeup and hair. (*Ben Nye*)

and they needed a minimum of aging. Nye convinced the producer and director to shoot Miss Dunne's close-ups each day in the morning when the makeup was still fresh. This way they could go after their master or medium shots later on when her makeup would have "aged" some. This produced marvelous results on the screen.

Of course, no matter how well the prosthetic is applied, it will need maintenance and repair during the day. And because these pieces could not be used over again, Nye started fresh each day. After seeing the film in its first cut, Nye knew that his creation was a success.

The years of the fifties were busy ones, and Fox made grand musicals, including *Oklahoma!*, *South Pacific* (1958), and *The King and I* (1956). These films had large budgets and Nye had dozens of makeup artists working for him.

In 1957 Nye got a call to read the script for *The Fly* (1958). Fox hadn't made anything closely resembling science fiction or horror films, and Nye was told they were going into production in two months. It didn't give him long to figure out what to do.

The story was about a scientist who had figured out a way to send any matter, even a human being, from one place to another by somehow breaking down their bodies into molecules for an instant. He constructed a chamber to test his research, and the test was to be on himself. Unbeknownst to him, there was a fly in the chamber with him. When his molecules were reconstructed in the adjacent chamber, he ended up with the head of a fly, and the fly with the scientist's head. The film starred David Hedison as the scientist and Vincent Price as the scientist's concerned brother.

Nye and his assistant got Hedison into the lab and made the necessary cast of his face. They agreed that they would have to create a skin to fit tightly over the actor's head. On this skin, they would eventually glue the various components that would create the fly head. They sculptured the head and began making latex sponge pieces. After settling on a definite design, they secured the pieces and cut the mask in back. The Wardrobe Department sewed in a zipper. This would later be hidden by a wig, and the rear seam would remain unseen. There were now only six weeks left prior to production, and they still had to design the eyes, the proboscis (the tubular sucking organ of the fly), tie the entire mask together, and make a camera test.

Nye could only imagine what the eyes would look like. Knowing there were multiple eye cells in fly eyes, he decided upon a beaded look. The Prop Department constructed some metal frames, covered with a fine wire mesh, in a convex curve.

Nye had left a definite shape in the mask into which the eyes would be secured. They bought 14-mm pearl-type beads. Nye and his staff began applying the beads to the wire mesh frames. They colored the eyes with an airbrush, using iridescent colors in beige, yellow, and green. It had taken two very hectic weeks, but the eyes seemed to be done and Hedison could see through them, which was a help in moving around since it was a very confining mask. The eyes also helped bring in air, aiding him in breathing normally.

The proboscis was sculpted from clay. It had a V-shape look from the front, with a sucker tip on the end. It was supported internally by a wooden core which would be held in Hedison's mouth. This was the only point of articulation in the mask. The exterior was cast in sponge rubber.

Feelers were attached to each side of the headpiece. Turkey feathers were cut in such a way that portions of the feathers had an airy look. Nye painted the feathers a metallic green, blue, and black to get a variegated effect. Finally, at the top of the proboscis, he added little hairs which were constructed out of tiny plastic rods. These were applied with rubber cement into the sponge rubber. Hedison could hold the proboscis in his mouth comfortably during each shot. However, when the scientist discovered he had a fly head, he placed a white cloth over his head, and much of the detail was never seen.

When it was time to ready the mask a week before the test, Nye painted the rubber head with metallic green, blue, and black paints. He decided there would be a better definition of the face if he defined what might be considered a "jawline," and he accomplished this by using more black beneath the mouth from ear to ear. Over this, he added what looked like whiskers, which were also made from tiny plastic rods. These whiskers really gave the mask an eerie effect. With the eyes in place, the fly began to take on a very mysterious quality.

With the eyes in place, the proboscis ready, and the mask entirely colored, Nye was now ready for the wig. He had a special one made by Max Factor, and it was probably the strangest order they had ever received. A plaster head of Hedison was sent over so that they could fit him perfectly. What was so unusual about this wig was the different pattern into which the hair was laid. Nye wanted a sparse effect and ordered the individual hairs knotted in the netting about three-eighths to one-half inch apart. They could see through it when it arrived, and this gave it a surreal look.

After all this preparation, there was only one day to test the mask. The test is very important and extremely revealing. The cameraman took some very close shots, and when they saw the "rushes," they felt that the mask looked great, but the eyes looked exactly like what they were—beads applied in a pattern and painted iridescent colors. Back to the drawing boards.

After several days, Nye decided that he would create convex eyes out of plastic shells. Doing some experimentation, he discovered that if he used two very thin plastic shells, made especially for him by the Prop Department, he could set one within the other and paint them to look semilucid. The effect was perfect. After getting the final version made, being careful that they conformed to the eye spaces left in the mask, Nye began using luminous paint. He used a light orchid on the inner shell and a light green on the outer shell. He also applied a yellow and a green paint around the edges of the shell eyes to give them an even more mystical effect.

It was tested again, and it was accepted. Everyone was pleased except Hedison. They still had not figured out how he was going to see easily enough to walk naturally in each scene. The plastic shells were semiopaque, and Nye couldn't lighten the coloring since the camera might then be able to see inside to his real eyes. While testing, Hedison got hot and they opened the lower part of the shells slightly, giving him a bit more ventilation. When they started testing again, Hedison asked if they could be left open a bit more, and this proved to be exactly what he needed, giving him just enough space to look down and walk around naturally throughout the filming.

The scientist also had one hand which was changed into a fly's leg during the molecular transformation, and Nye decided the concept should be a clawlike appendage. The Special Effects Department made the claw with a movable thumb. This gave Hedison the freedom to hold onto an object if necessary. Nye made a rubber sleeve to fit over the rear of the claw, and he painted it to match, using iridescent black, blue, and green again. After hair was applied to the rubber sleeve, the claw looked very menacing.

In 1961 Fox released a film called *The Comancheros*, which starred Lee Marvin. In the story, Marvin portrays a renegade gun runner who lived with and sold guns to the Indians. He somehow got into an Indian fight and was supposed to have been partially scalped. The script called for a scar to appear conspicuously at a place near the front of the hairline. Marvin sat down with Nye, and they talked about the possibilities. The actor said he would be open to cutting his hair higher to create the illusion of a higher hairline. Nye then chose chamois as the base for this horrible-looking scar. Stretching chamois over a plastic head, Nye wet it and pinned it down with fine nails, allowing it to dry and conform to the shape of the skull. He marked out the area on the chamois which fit very well to the rubber head. He had a thick polyvinyl plastic that he used for scars, and taking an artist's knife, he applied this thick formula in a swirled fashion. When it dried, it gave the appearance of a keloid, or raised scar. He used tints of light purple and maroon to color the plastic. Nye finished the appliance by laying hair in such a fashion that it looked like it had healed into the scar. The entire piece was irregular in shape, and the hair was long enough to comb into Marvin's hair.

The scene in which the scar finally appears was visually quite dramatic. When Nye saw it in the rushes he was totally satisfied. Marvin enters his hotel room with a bottle of whiskey. He had been wearing a hat during every sequence so far. He flops down on the bed, removing his hat and thus revealing the scar for the first time. Nye recalls that everyone in the screening room reacted the same way—with a general sigh of disgust at this horrible-looking scar.

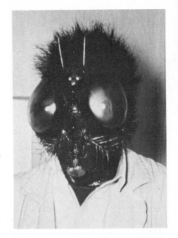

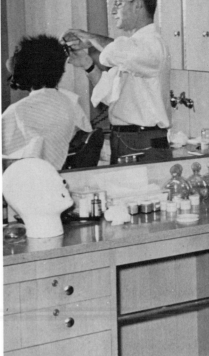

David Hedison as *The Fly*, a scientist whose own molecules become intertwined with that of a fly during an experiment. (*Photo by Ben Nye*)

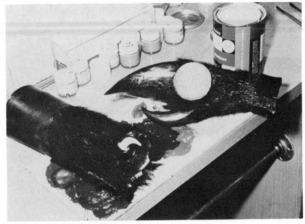

The scientist's arm also becomes that of a fly. These are the appliances employed for the arm and the hand. (*Photo by Ben Nye*)

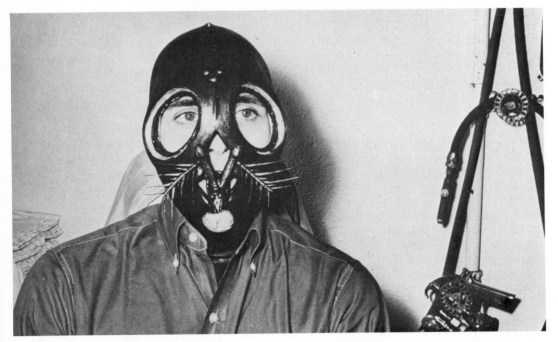

The basic head appliance of *The Fly*. A zipper was sewn in the back so that the actor could remove the appliance. (*Photo by Ben Nye*)

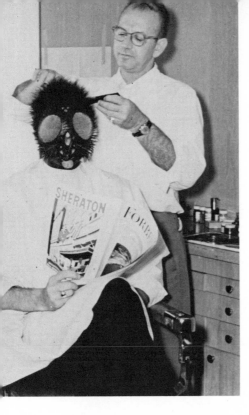

Nye lays hair on the head appliance. (*Photo by Ben Nye*)

In *The Flight of the Phoenix* (1966), a band of people are stranded in the Sahara Desert after their plane crashes. The most dramatic visual aspect of the film was their struggle against the hot sun and the lack of water. Nye made up their faces to look parched, burned, and peeled.

In one scene, Peter Finch goes berserk from the many days in the sun and attempts to walk out of the desert. A rescue party leaves to find him, only to discover that his throat had been slit by some traveling bedouins. Nye designed a rubber piece with an uneven slit which he laid thinly over Finch's neck. He then colored it with a maroon, purple, and dried blood coloring. He added a Texas Dirt formula over the neck and face, giving it real authenticity.

Nye also worked with George C. Scott on *The Flim Flam Man* (1967). Although Scott was thirty-seven at the time, he had to be made to appear in his late sixties or early seventies. Fortunately, he had the right bone structure, and Nye knew he could transform him. Michael Sarrazin played his young apprentice, and the chemistry between the two was very good.

Nye was told that Scott would refuse to wear any special rubber makeup or appliances. He told Nye he had had an unpleas-

ant experience when another makeup artist had tried to make him look old and failed. Nye considered Scott a discriminating actor who knew when things were right or wrong for him. Nye mentioned his Old Age Plastic as one possibility, and Scott seemed to become more confident in Nye's approach.

Nye settled on a simple approach and designed some very small rubber pieces which would fit easily beneath his eyes to create the illusion of puffy wrinkled eye sockets. Though Nye usually had a sketch artist make character renderings for all the important films, they didn't have the time or the budget on this film. However, Nye could visualize his character conception.

In preparation for the screen test he experimented with several people in his department. He applied the Old Age Plastic around the eyes while stretching it. It dried quickly, and the aging, wrinkling effect turned out to be very good. On the day of the test, Nye had Del Acevedo help him prepare Scott. They used the plastic from the hairline down. By applying it section by section on the face, always stretching it before it dried, they made the wrinkles quite impressive and natural. They were to find out that the longer Scott wore the plastic, the greater were the wrinkles. The plastic actu-

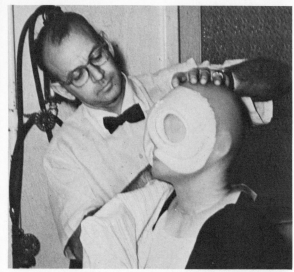

Nye and his assistant agreed that they would have to create a skin to fit tightly over the actor's head, and then glue onto it the various components that would create the fly. (*Photo by Ben Nye*)

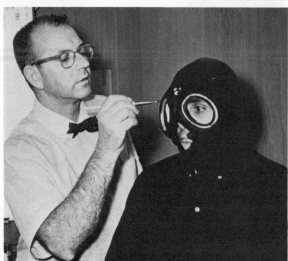

Ben Nye adds paint to the appliance as actor David Hedison serenely accepts a role of heavy makeup. (*Photo by Ben Nye*)

Sculpting begins for the design of *The Fly*, one of the first science-fiction films Twentieth Century-Fox had ever undertaken. (*Photo by Ben Nye*)

In the final scene, the fly with the head of a man becomes caught in a spider's web. Taking two 2 x 4s about 8 inches long, Nye put a coating of white glue between the two. After rubbing them together, he pulled them apart, and the glue formed thin strands that resembled the web of a spider. (*Photo by Ben Nye*)

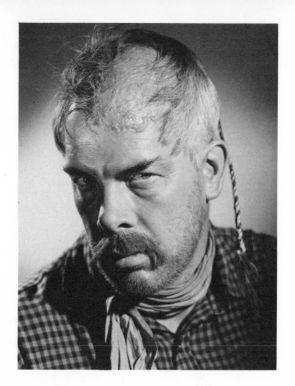

Lee Marvin displays the grotesquely realistic scar Ben Nye created for him for his role as a partially scalped renegade in *The Comancheros*. (*Ben Nye*)

ally aged as it became firmer.

The film was done almost entirely on location in Lexington, Kentucky. The makeup team were to discover the disastrous effect of hot, humid weather on Scott's special makeup. The producer had scheduled another test to make sure his idea of Scott's character still matched Nye's. The day of the test was very hot, and Scott's makeup began to fall apart. He was a ball of sweat, as was everyone else. The test turned out horrible. Word went back to the makeup room asking "what went wrong."

Nye's people talked about ways to keep Scott's makeup together. They realized that each day could prove different. Some days would be hotter than others, others terribly humid, or they might have a sudden rainstorm.

Finally the Old Age Plastic was used to make lower eye bags. The foam latex eye bags were discarded because they wouldn't adhere well under the weather conditions, and Scott was uncomfortable wearing them. Making eyepieces from a plastic mold, Nye slightly recarved them so they would accommodate the Old Age Plastic. He used an eyedropper to place the plastic in the molds. The material had an acetone base, and though it dried quickly, Nye allowed the molds to cure overnight. Many sets were needed because they could not be reused.

The total makeup took about two hours each morning. Touch-ups required another two hours or less during the day.

The plastic eyepieces worked very well, since they were made out of the same material that was brushed onto his face. Since the two materials were exactly the same, they bonded well. The old-age effects on this young man looked just about as good as Nye could get.

Hair coloring was very important for the total look. Nye grayed Scott's hair with a special formula, his Silver Hair Gray, that he had been making for several years. The problem with hair coloring, especially gray, is that it often has a blue tint which looks very unnatural. Nye's formula had an ochre tint that cut the blue, and he applied the hair coloring with a coarse bristle toothbrush. Nye likes to remove every other row or reduce the thickness of each row so that he has more control when he applies the hair coloring. Scott's hair was naturally dark, and Nye allowed a certain amount of this to show. The coloring was very natural, and again, due to the extreme heat, it was necessary to reapply some coloring during the day.

Just one year after completing *The Flim Flam Man*, Nye prepared to leave Twentieth Century-Fox to start another career, the introduction of his own line of motion picture

119

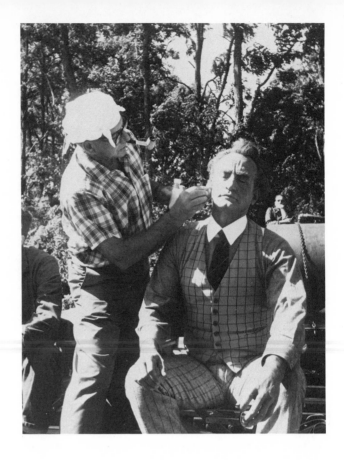

The Flim Flam Man was filmed almost entirely on location in Lexington, Kentucky, and the hot, humid weather took its toll on the makeup. (*Ben Nye*)

makeup. However, he lingered on at Fox until he became involved in *Planet of the Apes.*

When production actually began on *Planet of the Apes*, Nye's department was a beehive of activity. Early that year he hired the talented John Chambers to take charge of the lab as they prepared for this production. Chambers received an Oscar for his makeup in this film. Nye regarded Chambers as perfect for this job, and Chambers, in turn, proved to be a brilliant leader in the lab.

In April of 1967 Nye named his successor, Dan Striekpeke. Striekpeke and Nye worked closely together as *Planet of the Apes* went into production.

One of Nye's final responsibilities was designing colors for each type of ape appliance. He made literally gallons of castor grease colors that would be used to blend the edges of the appliances into the skin.

During Nye's career with Twentieth Century-Fox, he had been personally responsible for training thirty-two makeup artists, and he's proud to say that a Fox apprentice left his three years of training with a very sound background with which to enter the industry as a journeyman makeup artist.

Nye had three apprentices at a time in various stages of training, and each apprentice learned how to keep the entire department running. They often practiced on each other. Nye also invited them in at most times to watch and assist him as he worked. They soon realized that they could even assist him when he was doing a more complicated old-age or prosthetic makeup.

The next step in Nye's program was to introduce the apprentices to the preparation and application of both wool and human hair. In the later years, the price of human or yak hair became very expensive, so there were many instances when a beard, sideburns, or moustache were created out of crepe wool. This wool came from England, and the quality had to be very good. Nye always told his "boys" that if they could learn

George C. Scott in Ben Nye's makeup for his role in *The Flim Flam Man*. (*Ben Nye*)

to lay a good crepe beard, they had mastered the art of laying hair.

Some of Nye's apprentices who have established themselves in today's craft include Harry Maret, Lynn Reynolds, Roy Stork, Dick Blair, Bruce Hutchinson, and Tom Burman. He knew that when these people left his department they could go just about anywhere and do a first-class job. Most of them have remained close friends and many remained as part of Nye's staff over the years.

Nye was always his worst critic, and he was most demanding about the results of his efforts. One of those areas where he began to judge very carefully was the quality of the makeups that he was using in his department. They were bought almost exclusively from Max Factor. Although Max Factor made some colors for Nye that were quite valuable to him, Nye wanted to develop his own color series. He was lucky to have the cooperation of the leading pigment

manufacturer in the country, and he began to use his eye for color to formulate a series of foundation colors that would appear to be natural on the screen. He actually began this project about ten years prior to leaving Fox in 1967, and when he began his makeup business, his colors had been thoroughly tested.

Throughout that period, Nye carefully watched the results of each color, and when they needed a reformulation, he would spend the necessary time to bring the colors into proper balance. He now has two sons who have assisted him in the blending and formulation of Ben Nye Makeup. His oldest son, Ben Nye, Jr., is currently building his reputation as a Hollywood makeup artist. Though he has been busy doing a variety of assignments, his latest work has been for *Marathon Man* (1976) and *Sorcerer*. He serves as an adviser to his father now. Nye's youngest son, Dana, joined him in 1970. Also a makeup artist, Dana has now become the president of Nye's makeup company, as this allows Nye the necessary freedom to design and watch the quality control.

Nye's collection has colors designed for every skin tone, and he asserts that he has the most complete color set for the black performer. Recalling his frustrations on *Gone With the Wind* when making up Hattie McDaniel, he developed the "Twenty Series" which ranges in colors from light olive to rich dark brown. These colors may also be used for Asian and Mexican performers.

Nye has mentioned using his Old Age Plastic and Sealer many times. This is a polyvinyl product that can create very subtle wrinkles on the face by stretching the skin. When Topol portrayed Tevye in *Fiddler on the Roof* (1971), he was in his late thirties, and makeup artist Del Armstrong did a beautiful job turning him into a charming old man. He used Nye's Old Age Plastic exclusively for the entire film. The Plastic material has been used extensively in Los Angeles and New York. Dick Smith used it for some old-age work on Marlon Brando in *The Godfather* (1971).

As the man responsible for the makeup for over five hundred feature films, Nye has made every attempt to share the secrets of his craft. He hopes those people now working in this field are better from the knowledge that he has shared. Though he has retired from active work in the studios, he is still active as an adviser to makeup artists in Los Angeles and is busy creating new products for the industry as he realizes its needs.

Chapter 12

HOWARD SMIT

Howard J. Smit is today the business representative for Make-up Artists and Hair Stylists Local 706. This is an elected two-year term, and he is the only paid officer of the local.

Born in Chicago, Illinois, in 1911, Smit was a small child growing up in Chicago in the twenties when Cecil Holland, Jack Dawn, George Westmore, Perc Westmore, Jack Pierce, Harry Pringle, and Festus B. Phillips, among others, joined ranks and formed the first organization for makeup artists. It was known as the "Hollywood Motion Picture Make-up Artists Association." This group encompassed not only the makeup artists but the hair stylists. They worked very diligently over the years trying to build their profession and to get into organized labor.

Getting into organized labor was a big problem, however. In those early days, organized labor was strictly for laboring people. Not that the makeup artists didn't labor. The makeup artist started out for a flat salary, and although it was a good one compared to the average pay scale of the day, the makeup artist had to work unlimited days and hours for that flat salary. Many times they were worked seven days a week, and so many hours a day that they were bleary-eyed the next morning and could barely see whom they were making up. Organized labor didn't know where to put this

group of talented people. So, for some time they functioned simply as the H.M.P.M.A.A.

Then, in the early thirties, there was a breakthrough. They were offered their first charter as a makeup artists and hair stylists' union; and it was offered to them by the painters. This was the only way in which they could get into organized labor. The painters rationalized that the makeup artists used brushes, too!

Howard Smit moved to Los Angeles with his parents and decided to pursue a career in law. Finding innumerable odd jobs to help finance his education, it was through an attorney friend that Smit was able to find a part-time job with RKO Studios as a makeup man. He helped out on the extras, doing the body makeups for the mob scenes. He soon began to spend endless hours in the practice of makeup. Smit and the other apprentices would do makeups on each other and photograph them, then criticize their work, thereby learning and growing with their craft. By Smit's senior year of law school he was completely in love with the makeup profession and discovered that the challenges and excitement in his life came not from the law but from the makeup room.

On request of the Max Factor Corporation, Smit was sent out to do the makeup for an opera at the Pasadena Community Playhouse. The opera required difficult squared-off Egyptian beard work, and Smit had his

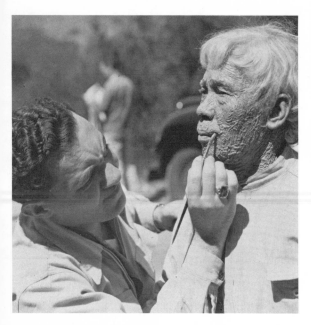

Smit took this unidentified actor from his forties to the age of one hundred and seven years. (*Howard Smit*)

makeup cases spread throughout the room, putting on makeup and beards as fast as possible. The last actors were finally completed about forty-five minutes before the finish of the opera, and Smit was busily cleaning up his supplies when the hostess appeared and made a request.

"Mr. Smit, would you do us the honor of being our guest at a banquet at the Pasadena Athletic Club after the performance?"

He was thrilled, but the night wasn't quite over. As he waited in the lobby following the performance, five or six Pasadena debutants approached him and asked him to autograph their programs.

"Me? Why do you want my autograph?"

"Aren't you Howard Smit?" they questioned.

"Yes," he answered.

"Didn't you do the makeup for this performance?"

"Yes, I did."

"Then won't you please autograph our programs?" they persisted.

"Sure!" Smit replied with a radiant grin.

It was that night that Smit recognized one of the many rewards of his profession. Despite driving a battered-up old car with a mere fifteen cents in his pocket, his artistic endeavors were rewarded with autograph seekers and a dinner invitation.

In the early days of Smit's career, he free-lanced, working at such studios as RKO, Metro-Goldwyn-Mayer, and Republic, while garnering the knowledge he would need to take the rigid union exams. One of the early films he recalls with pleasure was *Rainbow on the River* (1936) with Bobby Breen, produced by Sol Lesser. In 1937 he assisted on the film *Ali Baba Goes to Town*, which demanded considerable beard work. Eddie Cantor starred in this film, but Smit was too new in the profession to work on the star.

In 1937 the painters' union went out on strike, and the makeup artists went with them. They weren't making much headway in the strike when the International Alliance of Theatrical Stage Employees offered them a charter. Most of the groups in the motion picture industry were under this union, and after much deliberation by their representatives and officers, the charter was signed on October 21, 1937, and they came under the I.A.T.S.E. as the Motion Picture Make-up Artists and Hair Stylists Local 706. Bert Hadley was the first president of this union.

Smit worked on the film *In Old Chicago* (1938), which starred Alice Faye and Tyrone Power. It was filmed at Twentieth Century-Fox, and Smit recalls working day and night on it. Another early film was *Gunga Din* (1939-RKO) with Douglas Fairbanks, Jr., and Sam Jaffe.

RKO remained Smit's "home base," and he did many films there. One film he fondly recalls was a huge Western with Lucille Ball called *Valley of the Sun* (1942). Smit subsequently wound up at Republic Studios, which became the Western serial sanctuary of the industry. Whenever one thought of Westerns, one thought of Republic Studios, and Smit tells us he did Westerns until they were coming out of his ears. He worked with Sunset Carson, Monty Hale, Don Barry, Gene Autry, Dale Evans, and, of course, the King of the Cowboys—Roy Rogers!

In the meantime, war had been declared, and Smit enlisted in the Air Corps in 1942. He was assigned to the first army motion picture unit of World War II, which took over the Hal Roach Studios. They did all the training and orientation films for the Air Corps, and they were told not to spare a thing in the way of wounds, broken bones, and the like in order to impress the point of the film on the soldier. Though they did many interest-ing things to train the troops, one Smit will never forget was a film on the uses of oxygen at high altitudes.

When one reaches altitudes above ten thousand feet, the air becomes extremely rarefied, and with a lack of sufficient oxygen one develops what is called sinosis. The sinus area, lips, earlobes, and fingernails turn from a light blue to a deep purple. While this is happening, one feels euphoric until completely passing out.

This was a difficult condition to photograph, so Smit had to make an actor up to look as though he had this condition, and then photograph it. In order to know what the actor needed to look like, Smit went into a decompression chamber with one of the army medics. They went up to thirty thousand feet. Smit had oxygen, but the medic was without it in order for Smit to observe the various colors and stages of sinosis.

After Smit was discharged from military service in 1943, he returned to Republic Studios where he continued on the many serials of the day. One such serial was the jungle girl series. Forty or fifty days were involved in shooting the big serials, and on one particular jungle-girl serial Smit recalls the scriptwriter named all the various African tribes and priests. Smit has always been very conscientious when it came to researching his makeup, and this film was no exception. He endeavored to locate the tribes in research books but to no avail. He finally spoke to the producer, telling him of his problem. The producer had a big belly laugh from that one and told Smit the tribes were all a figment of the writer's imagination. That taught Smit one lesson about serials.

Smit worked with John Wayne, whom he knew as "Duke" Morrison, on many of Wayne's early films at Republic. Wayne, Max Trachune, and Ray Corrigan were together on many of those films and were known as the Three Musketeers. The last film Smit did with Wayne was *Wake of the Red Witch* (1948).

Smit also worked with Cecil Holland during Holland's later years at Republic Studios. Smit considers Holland one of the fathers of the makeup profession. Holland would devote every bit of time he could to help the apprentices.

When television came along, Smit's curious nature wouldn't let him stay away. He

Howard Smit and other members of the production crew on *Moonrise*, a Republic feature.
(© *Republic Pictures*)

offered his services to a television station in Los Angeles. Reception was so poor that Smit likened it to looking through a chain-link fence. It was strictly black and white, and colors had a tendency to completely wash out. If he used a red lipstick on an actress, it would disappear completely on the television screen, so they resorted to dark browns and blacks. Hershey's chocolate syrup made a great "blood." Finding the correct makeup for this new medium became quite a challenge, and Smit found it extremely interesting.

When Republic Studios began to fade, Review Productions bought space on the lot and Smit spent many years there involved in television productions. Music Corporation of America owned Review Productions and became so successful that they bought Universal Studios, which is today known as Universal/MCA, one of the giants in the industry.

At this point in his career, Smit felt the Westerns were finally behind him, and he could relax and do indoor makeups instead of being off in the wilderness on location. But Westerns remained everybody's favorite, and television viewers were no exception, so Smit found himself doing such features as "Wagon Train" and "The Restless Gun" with John Payne. Smit created an old-age makeup for John Payne in one series, and has since seen Payne grow to look very much like Smit's makeup creation.

Westerns weren't the only shows Smit did, though. When Rod Steiger played the part of Steinmetz for the television drama "The Electrical Wizard," Smit had to age him from a young man in his early twenties arriving in America from Germany, through his career with General Electric. He employed various hair pieces for the different life stages, using a goatee, then a full beard, then on to steel-gray hair, then to white hair and a beard in his later years. Smit used a tight white clipped head of hair and white beard upon Steinmetz's death.

Smit worked with Jack Webb when he began his "Dragnet" television series and had the pleasure of doing the first thirteen "Dragnet" features with him. Sometimes Smit's makeup wasn't just for the make-believe of television. When the Wilshire area was having a time of it with some youngsters hitting old ladies over the head and taking their purses, Smit, along with some other makeup artists, made up eleven or twelve of the smallest members of the Los Angeles Police Department as little old ladies. When they caught the entire gang on the first night out, Smit was extremely pleased to have played a part in the operation.

The union was always an important part of Smit's career. During his forty years as a makeup artist, he has served for nearly twenty-five years—off and on—on the executive board of Local 706. In 1953 Smit was elected president and in 1955 was re-elected to a second two-year term. Smit found the position extremely time-consuming, and because he put in many long hours as a makeup artist too, he refused to run a third time.

As an aid to the movie industry as a whole, and as a public relations feature of Local 706, Smit conceived and organized the "Deb-Star Ball," which was a highly successful event for fifteen years. Bob Hope was one of their early sponsors, and in the ball's first two years they entertained one thousand two hundred and fifty guests at the Embassy Room of the Ambassador Hotel with dinner, dancing, and a show. It became so popular that two years later they had outgrown the Embassy Room, and for the remaining thirteen years, it was held at the Hollywood Paladium.

One of the features of the "Deb-Star Ball" were the "Debs" chosen by the Make-up Artists and Hair Stylists, who, in their opinion, were most likely to achieve stardom. Twelve to fourteen "Debs" were usually chosen each year, and some of those chosen were Kim Novak, Anita Ekberg, Dolores Hart, Carol Lynley, Jill St. John, Tuesday Weld, Yvette Mimieux, Shirley Knight, and Paula Prentiss, just to name a few.

Smit did many television features with Alfred Hitchcock, but by far his most unusual assignment was *The Birds* (1963). It wasn't that the makeup assignment itself was so uncommon, but the discussions with Hitchcock, the preparations prior to filming, and the many days of shooting were unusual. The entire cast and crew were even sworn to secrecy as to the film's plot. Smit believes he learned a great deal from Hitchcock and that Smit himself contributed much to the film.

Smit created a nasty bruise on Lee Marvin for an early "Dragnet" television segment. (*Howard Smit*)

"I found that in doing *The Birds* it was again something that had to be 'right.' It had to be real, it had to be believable," Smit emphasized. "If it wasn't, it would have blown the whole film. So I set out to do what I felt should be done. In the beginning when we were doing tests, I worked closely with Mr. Hitchcock to see what he had in mind because, after all, he was the creator of the screenplay. It had been only a thirty- or forty-page short story which Hitchcock built into this fantastic piece of entertainment.

"It was so much fun to do this film, because once you had read the script and knew what was required, you had to figure out how it should look. I've had so many people say to me, 'That is so well executed from a makeup standpoint that it is just absolutely frightening.' That's what it was meant to be! That's what it was designed for, and if people felt that way about it, believe me, it made me feel good.

"I made my bird pecks in all different shapes and sizes. Tippi Hedren starred in this film, which was her first, and she was a lovely person. I had Tippi in my makeup chair preparing her for the scene where the birds come through the attic and attack her in the upstairs of the house. They swarm all over her, covering her with pecks, cuts, and bruises. As she sat in my makeup chair I covered her with bird pecks, blood, scratches, and bruises. She happened to look in the mirror for a moment, and suddenly she pushed my arm aside and graciously said, 'Pardon me for a moment, Howard.' She ran outside and threw up! Well, as far as I was concerned, I knew if the makeup had that effect on her, I had achieved what was required for that scene. Even though I felt badly that she got sick, I was pretty happy I had been able to make it so realistic and convincing."

When Ben Nye, Sr., Dan Striekpeke, and John Chambers were working feverishly on *Planet of the Apes* in 1967, Smit joined them for about a month before the shooting in making the original tests. Smit enjoyed this enormously because in his entire career he had never had the opportunity to go into the prosthetic work that all three of these men had done so beautifully. Smit had been asked to remain on and do the film when he was contacted by the Thomas/Spelling organization.

This was Danny Thomas and Aaron Spelling. Smit joined them for the next ten years. They began with the "Danny Thomas

Smit gives Jackie Coogan a black eye. (*Howard Smit*)

Show," which had a one-hour format. Smit believes they did thirteen. The show wasn't picked up for another season, and Smit was asked to remain with them to do a test. If the test "went," they wanted Smit to remain on and do the series. The series turned out to be the very popular "Mod Squad," which ran for five years on television.

Before one Mod Squad episode, one of the stars, Mike Cole, returned from a personal appearance tour and was injured in an automobile accident. Aaron Spelling called Smit to go to the hospital and see if he could make Cole's face up enough to disguise the injuries the actor had suffered in order to proceed with the filming. Cole had gone through the windshield of his car and suffered a nasty gash that extended from his forehead, through his eyebrow, and eyelid. Cole was extremely fortunate that he didn't lose his eye.

After looking at the injuries, Smit knew he'd have problems, but he was certain it could be accomplished in a few weeks when they would be ready to shoot, and he reported this to Spelling. After filling in, highlighting, and shadowing all of the various depressions and cuts, Smit pulled Cole's eyelid up by about a quarter to a half inch

until such time as Cole could have plastic surgery. He has been told that no one viewing Michael Cole on the television screen ever realized he had been in the accident.

After finishing the five years of "Mod Squad," Smit remained with Aaron Spelling until he was elected business representative of the Make-up Artists and Hair Stylists Local 706.

Smit has found the position of business representative for the union an extremely interesting and busy one. Smit has combined his years of experience as a makeup artist in the motion picture and television industry with his education in the law to his fullest advantage in representing his union in contract negotiations, grievances against producers, and arbitrations.

Smit has worked to see that the fine art of makeup is not lost as a result of the great studios becoming "no more" and their apprenticeship programs being lost to the industry. He has negotiated a deal with the Producers Association whereby the top makeup artists in the industry train ten people at a time, and when Smit says train, he does mean *train.*

When this program opened up, there were five hundred applicants to choose the

Smit found *The Birds* to be a most unusual assignment. Here director Alfred Hitchcock swears the crew to secrecy. (© *Universal*)

ten from. Smit hopes to see the same sort of program designed for the hair stylists. Even though they are very well trained when they complete their state board of exams, there is much to learn regarding period hair styles, lace wigs, iron curling, and innumerable skills that are required in the motion picture and television industry.

"Within Local 706," Smit explained, "we have a third group which you seldom hear about. They are the body makeup women. These are the women who take care of the female bodies and enhance the beauty of the average actress's body whenever need

be. Many times they are called upon to do something unusual. For instance, when Esther Williams worked under water, the makeup that was applied to her body had to be of a special type that would enhance her body under water and, although wet, would remain on. It takes a special skill to apply such makeup. Her hair was treated in such a manner that it would look real and flowing when she was under water, also.

"Usually the male makeup artist will do any unusual makeup on the men." Smit says, "I recall a makeup we designed for Red McCarthy, an ice skater for the Ice

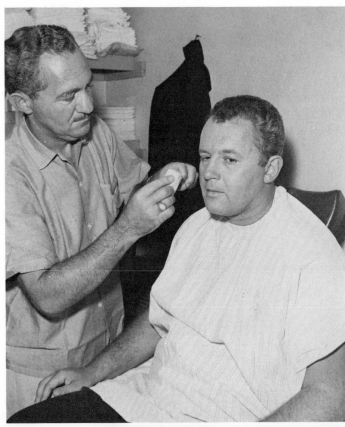

Smit prepares Rod Steiger for his role as Charles Steinmetz in the television drama "The Electrical Wizard." (*Howard Smit*)

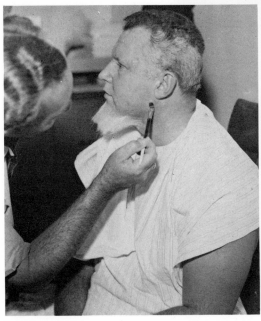

Spirit gum is applied for Steiger's beard. (*Howard Smit*)

Rod Steiger in complete makeup. (*Howard Smit*)

Hollywood's attention to detail can sometimes border on the ridiculous, as Smit here grooms a calf before filming. (*Howard Smit*)

Capades. We covered his body completely with an albolite-type material and then sprinkled it with particles of glass. When you saw him with the lights on, he was one mass of reflective glass. He would dive through a hoop of fire, and it was a beautiful thing to behold. No one realized that the effect was caused by the type of makeup that covered his body. And because it can be fatal to cover the pores of a person's body for too long, he could wear the makeup only for thirty minutes at a time. He would come back to us, we would remove it completely, then reapply it when he was ready for another take."

Smit has a business organization now that he says he rather "backed into." It's called Stage Ten Cosmetics. Over the years, Smit was faced with a problem that many makeup artists have come in contact with, and that is that the faces of those he made up were often either very dry in spots or very moist. There were times, after the makeup was applied, when Smit would see it literally disappear into the skin. He reached the conclusion that if he could develop something that he could cover the skin with first—a kind of base coat—that he would solve his problem.

He wanted something for his "base coat" that would be good for the actor's skin because it was put on under makeup and would very often remain there for twelve to sixteen hours a day. He did considerable re-search over a number of years and finally developed a product with vitamins D and A, combined with a special cream. He went to a pharmaceutical chemist and had the ingredients put together. Every time he used his new base under a makeup, the wearers had a great deal of favorable comments to make about it and immediately wanted to purchase it for their own use, which is how Stage Ten Cosmetics developed.

The moisturizer that Smit developed is called Lemon E Moisturizer and is, in Smit's opinion, one of the greatest products that any man or woman could use on his or her skin, as an under makeup or a night cream. It's sold throughout the country in beauty supply houses and is used by many makeup artists. Eventually, Smit believes it will be available in drug and department stores.

Smit is a Shriner and belongs to one of the smallest working units, which is known as the Masquers. The Masquers do all the makeup and costumes for the ceremonials based on biblical characters. There are only about fourteen members of this unit. Smit was elected president of the Show Business Shrine Club in January of 1978. This presidency, combined with Smit's election in December of 1977 to his third two-year term as business representative of the Make-up Artists and Hair Stylists Local 706, helps keep Smit an extremely busy man.

Chapter 13

PHILIP W.N. LEAKEY

Philip W. N. Leakey was a long way from his eventual career as one of Britain's top makeup artists when he began as a junior member of the staff with a firm of marine brokers in London. Leakey used to travel there daily from his family's home in Golders Green dressed as a proper city gentleman was expected to dress in those days—a black coat, pin-striped trousers, a bowler hat, and an umbrella. He was forever losing his hat or his umbrella. Leakey must have made a striking impression thus attired as he went about the city taking policies from one insurance broker to another. He enjoyed walking about the city with all its little alleys, courtyards, and Wren churches, but after a year it seemed he would be a very small cog for a very long time.

Leakey didn't choose a film career—it chose him! Before his family moved to Golders Green they resided in nearby Cricklewood where one of the earliest film studios—the Stole Studio—was located. It was managed by Joe Grossman, one of the real old characters of the film industry. In due course, the studio was taken over to make World War I airplanes, and Mr. Grossman became studio manager for British International Pictures.

Grossman and Leakey's father were friends, and one day Leakey was invited to see an interstudio boxing match. Leakey

was keen on boxing in those days, and because his father could not attend, he suggested that Philip go in his place.

Leakey arrived at the studio, wangled his way past the doorman, and got to Grossman's office, but not past his secretary! Eventually she announced that Leakey was there, and after what seemed an extremely long time, the door suddenly swung open and Grossman popped his head out and said, "Hello. Too busy to talk now. Start on Monday. Eight o'clock sharp."

With that, he slammed the door, and Leakey was off the premises in a matter of minutes. He said to himself, "What the hell. So I'll start on Monday." He went home and wrote a letter announcing his resignation to the marine broker's office.

Leakey was accepted into the Sound Department with sighs of resignation from its head. Not knowing a thing about sound—sound being very much in its infancy anyway—Leakey started at the very bottom. Everything went along quite smoothly until the studio caught fire and the central recording room went up in flames. All the equipment was lost, creating a long delay, and the entire junior staff was sacked, including Leakey.

Before leaving Leakey felt he should say good-bye to Grossman. However, before he could utter a word, Grossman announced, "Ah, Philip. Start Monday. Eight o'clock.

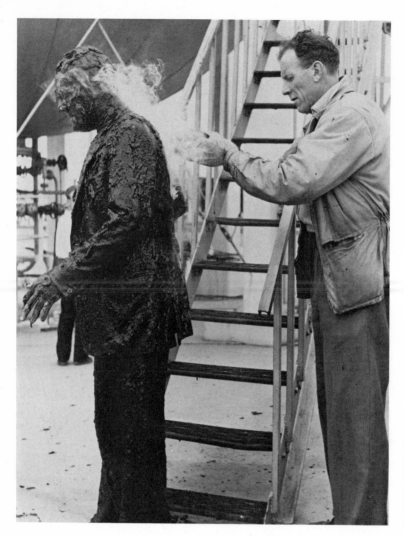

Phil Leakey adds a vapor effect to the makeup on Tom Chatto in *Quatermass II.* (© *Hammer Films*)

Makeup Department.''

When Monday arrived, Leakey was again at the studio ready to begin yet another career. The enthusiasm in the Makeup Department at his arrival was on a par with the enthusiasm he had experienced in the Sound Department. He was told to sit in the corner and watch.

Although there was a good training school for makeup artists at Gaumont Studios, there was no training scheme at British International Pictures. Leakey became very bored and was about to give it all up when help arrived in the form of an American makeup artist who came over with several other Hollywood artists for two or three different films. He wanted someone to assist him. The resident makeup artist wanted nothing to do with him, and so presented him with Leakey.

Leakey describes the experience: ''He made me work for hours, criticizing, encouraging, teaching, scratching it all and making me start again. After a while, the time and the days started to pass quickly. He taught me to use loose hair, make scars, and generally have a good idea about what makes things tick.

''At the end of six months, he felt I was fairly good and could go on and learn if I wanted to. He had a vested interest in my being passably good because he was not very fit from lunchtime onward, and he wanted to be sure I could cope with the unexpected. I cannot for the life of me remember his name. All I can say is that he was

Christopher Lee in makeup as Frankenstein's monster in *The Curse of Frankenstein*. Complete sets of prosthetics were never fully completed, so it was necessary to do most of the work directly on Lee's face as shooting required. (© *Hammer Films*)

very good at his job and I owe him a great deal.''

The next studio Leakey worked at was Shepperton Studios, then known as Sound City. He made a great many films there. It was the age of ''quota'' films, which were brought about by the British government's decision that a certain ''quota'' of films shown in British cinemas be made in Britain in order to keep the film industry alive following World War II. He worked on many films prior to the war as chief makeup artist for George King.

After serving in the armed forces, Leakey worked around the various studios—Denham, Pinewood, Shepperton—getting the feel of things again before he began his ten-year stint with Hammer Films.

In 1955 Hammer Films presented *The Quatermass Experiment,* which had been very successful on television. Brian Donlevy was their Quatermass. It was this film and the later *Quatermass II* in 1957 that launched the ''horror'' films at Hammer.

''It all started with a hand that had supposedly been affected by something from

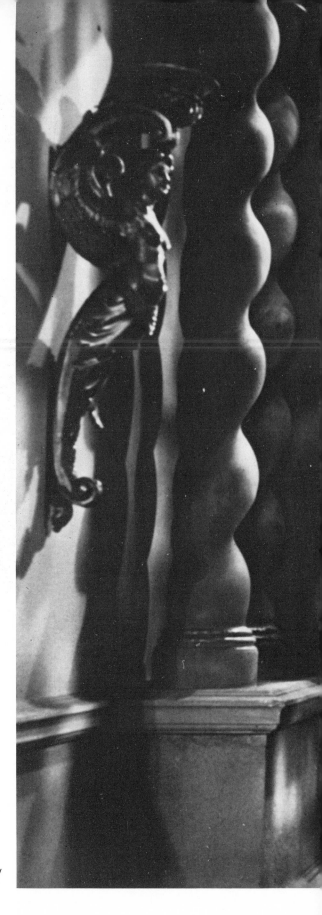

Peter Cushing in *Dracula*. The magnificent
Gothic sets were an important part of the early
Hammer films. (© *Hammer Films*)

outer space. Tony Hinds, the producer at Hammer, wanted me to try and make it look 'nasty,' as he said. I made an arm and hand of sponge rubber, made slits in it and inserted perforated plastic tubes and bits of bone. I hooked it up to a pump and pumped in red-colored carbon tetrachloride. Carbon tet makes foam rubber swell and split, so the general effect was quite good and everybody was happy. From then on the 'horrors' never looked back, and people took delight in thinking up nasty happenings— one after the other. I enjoyed this period, although it got pretty hectic at times. There were days when my home was just as full of arms, legs, heads, and eyes as the makeup room, because in those days we didn't have a very good makeup room, and it wasn't at all well equipped. In fact, just the opposite. I remember the auspicious occasion when I persuaded Tony Hinds to buy a cake mixer for me to make the foam rubber at the studio instead of using my wife's kitchen.

"There were three people in those days who were worth their weight in gold to me. One was Jack Curtis, the head electrician, who was very enthusiastic and liked to make mechanical bits and pieces that worked. The other two were the Banks' brothers, the plasterers.

The Curse of Frankenstein (1957) starred Peter Cushing as Baron Frankenstein and Christopher Lee as the creature. Because of its excellent forerunner and the fact that Hammer had been advised that the Karloff monster was copyrighted, creating this creature presented untold difficulties. Leakey found that anything that remotely resembled Jack Pierce's creation in the 1931 Universal version brought immediate disapproval from the production company.

Leakey took molds and several casts of Christopher Lee's face, trying out several different ideas. The art director made a few sketches and Leakey made many more. There was an atmosphere of anxiety about because the production company was afraid they were going to be held up for violation of copyright. Finally, late on the last evening before shooting began, Leakey worked directly on Lee's face with wax, rubber, cotton wool, and other materials. He was not too pleased with the effect, but the company liked it because it in no way resembled Boris Karloff's makeup. Unfortunately, because they began shooting early

next morning there was no time to make pieces. For the first few days it was extremely uncomfortable for Christopher Lee. He told Leakey he felt certain he would never look the same again, that Leakey was deliberately trying to hurt him and that he most certainly would kill Leakey before the end of the picture.

"We did several tests," Christopher Lee explained to us. "Each one was worse than the previous one. Some of the tests were animallike, rather like *The Island of Dr. Moreau* (1977). Finally, somebody said, 'Look, obviously this character must be as human in appearance as possible because he's put together from human beings.'

"In view of the fact that the monster was supposedly created from bits and pieces of different organs, it had to appear as though it was created in a somewhat crude and hurried manner; hence, the scar tissue, stitches, and contact lens for the blind eye. Considering that somebody once referred to it as looking like a road accident, I think Philip succeeded."

Leakey told us that they never did get complete sets of prosthetics for that particular Frankenstein, and so each day it was necessary to do most of the work directly on Christopher Lee's face.

"Poor Chris suffered quite a bit on that film. He hated having the makeup removed almost as much as having it put on. On the average, the makeup took two and a half to three hours.

Working with a somewhat different theme, Hammer Films wanted *The Abominable Snowman* (1957) to appear awesome but not cruel. Leakey made sketches and came up with the idea of making the creature look just a wee bit like Peter Cushing, who played the part of botanist John Rollason on an expedition in the Himalayas in search of the mysterious beast. With a small resemblance about the eyes and the nose, it was hoped to create a suggestion of affinity between the two. Leakey felt they accomplished this.

It took Leakey about a week before he came up with a sketch that both the director and producer liked, and yet another week to make all the "bits" with the help of the Wardrobe Department.

Real animal skins were used and applied to the outside of what could be described as a sort of boiler suit padded in the right places. The Snowman's claws were made from cotton wool mixed with plastic, hardened and fitted to gloves.

The mountain peak itself, where Cushing and the Snowman confront each other, took Leakey the longest to create. They worked with a mixture of salt and plastic to create the snow scenes. This they discovered to be most uncomfortable because it filtered into their hair and clothes, and they ended up wearing a great deal of it home with them.

When Leakey worked with Cushing his makeup was usually pretty straightforward. Cushing would grow his hair to suit the part or period. Leakey found his features not only ideal for period roles, but that he seemed to be able to add or subtract age even before Leakey started the makeup. He even seemed able to appear pale when the occasion called for it.

Peter Cushing, Christopher Lee, and Leakey were teamed together again in Hammer's *Dracula* (U.S. Title—*Horror of Dracula*) (1958). Christopher Lee, who played the part of the bloodthirsty Count, recalls an amusing behind-the-scenes anecdote:

"I had to pick up a girl from the ground and throw her into a grave. On the very first take, I lost my balance and fell in after her. She was a stunt girl and not exactly a lightweight! This is recorded on film somewhere and it gave a few laughs to the crew."

Since the script called for Van Helsing to pull out his crucifix and force Dracula into the sunlight, Cushing, who played Van Helsing, suggested that they jump off a balcony onto the curtains, pulling them down. It was impossible to construct a balcony, so they came up with the next best thing, a refectory table. Cushing ran along the top of the table, leaped as far as he could, and pulled the curtains down to allow the rays of sunlight to disintegrate Count Dracula. This had a far better effect than simply running to the curtains and pulling them down.

During this period Hammer Films was headquartered at Bray. The work was made easier because the general atmosphere was good, Leakey told us.

"Everybody mucked in to help everybody else. All departments wanted to help—and did. This differs from working with today's large studios where the lines of demarcation are strictly observed."

Special effects man Syd Pearson and Leakey worked closely on the disintegration scene. In discussion with director Terence Fisher, it was decided that the disintegration scene would be aided with a series of cuts. Dracula would be shot in his dying throes, then the camera would cut to Van Helsing, filming his reaction to Dracula's disintegration.

The first rays of the sun strike Dracula's leg. Christopher Lee begins the disintegration by quivering and shaking his leg. The pants leg and shoe were reproduced with a skeleton bone inside. Fuller's earth was employed in the shoe as well. Pearson laid on the floor, out of camera range, and placed his hands inside the pants leg manipulating leg, shoe, and bone.

A cut back to Lee's face in horror, and we view Lee dragging his hands down across his face. Lee's face was made up with dyed mortician's wax, covered with a plastic skin, which allowed Lee to tear "flesh" from his face. The camera then cut to Van Helsing for his reaction as he held the two candlesticks to form a cross, then back to Dracula.

This time Dracula was actually special effects man Syd Pearson whose face was made up with dyed fuller's earth and damp sugar, covered with a mask made from Dracula's features, which allowed the face to continue its disintegration. Pearson held his hands in front of his face in the same manner that Lee had in the master shot. Pearson's hands were made up to deteriorate in this shot, also.

Using a mixture of fuller's earth and acetone, Pearson made a mudpack to cover his hands. The acetone in this mudpack evaporated very quickly, but before it evaporated, Pearson then dipped his hands into warm paraffin wax which coated and sealed in the mudpack. Artificial fingernails were applied and the hands were made up.

When Pearson continued with the gestures Lee had begun in the master shot, the wax "flesh" cracked and disintegrated, allowing the fuller's earth to fall away like dust. Again a cut to Cushing and back to the hands was employed. This time a pair of articulated skeletal hands which had been made up with the same fuller's earth mudpack were used. Operated by remote control levers, this time the bones were seen in the disintegration of the hands.

It was decided that Lee finish up on a prearranged spot. Under this spot they had a small hole through which a probe entered

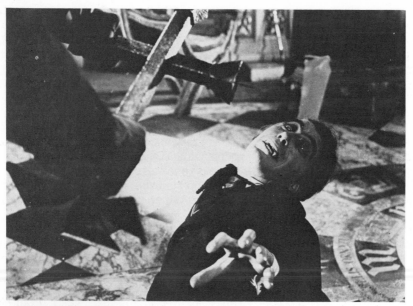

Peter Cushing, as Van Helsing, forces Christopher Lee, as Count Dracula, into a shaft of sunlight to disintegrate before the audience's eyes in *Dracula*. (© *Hammer Films*)

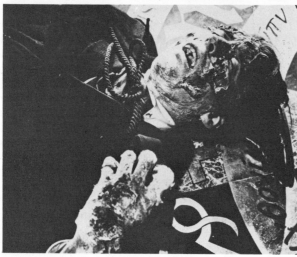

Christopher Lee, as Count Dracula, disintegrates. (© *Hammer Films*)

the head. The probe revolved, breaking down the shape. A few frames were shot, then some skin was removed, showing sugar teeth mixed with sand breaking down; little by little, reducing it to a pile of sand, a skull, and two eyes. Tiny surgical lights were in each of the eye sockets. As the disintegration reached its end, the lights were gradually turned out.

The collapse of the chest was effected by the use of balloons manipulated by someone lying on the floor out of the camera's view. In the end, only Dracula's clothing, ring, and a pile of dust remained. Off screen a wind machine gently blew the dust across the set as the film closed.

In *X—The Unknown* (1956) a character was supposed to be affected by a ray and had to melt before one's eyes. This was done by taking a mold of the actor's face and head, then making the head in two halves with paraffin wax. A complete plaster skull was made, and inserted in the skull in many different places were heating elements such as one would use in flatirons. The skull and eyes were fitted into the paraffin wax face. Skin and hair were added. All the heat was turned on, including a great deal of exterior heat so that the face started to melt. The skin conducted the melted wax down the throat and out of sight. The chin dropped as the wax melted and the skin sagged a bit, gradually revealing the skeleton. Dried granules of red dye had been

Phil Leakey creates a flesh-eating radiation burn on this actor's back for *X—The Unknown*. (© *Hammer Films*)

Leakey adds false hair to Edward G. Robinson's beard in *Sammy Going South* (rereleased as *Boy Ten Feet Tall* in 1965) which was filmed in Kenya. (*Phil Leakey*)

spread all over the wax, turning the wax red as it melted. In order to save film, they frame cut, which is the process of cutting out enough processed film to speed up the action of the melting face. A very powerful fan was used to suck away the smoke that developed.

Leakey left Hammer Films in 1958 and continued to free-lance in his profession. In 1962 he journeyed to Kenya where *Sammy Going South* (1963) was filmed. Edward G. Robinson, who starred in the film, was unavailable for the first three weeks of shooting, so a standby painter, who happened to be about the same size as Robinson, was commandeered to double for him until his arrival. An artist's impressions of the beard Robinson was in the process of growing were forwarded for Leakey's use.

When Robinson finally arrived, Leakey "nearly had a fit." The artist's impressions of Robinson's beard were far from accurate,

and there were noticeable differences. For the remaining week to ten days, Leakey had to make up Edward G. Robinson to look like his double! This was accomplished by adding fake hair to his beard until it caught up in growth to the false beard on the double.

"I don't like horror pictures as such," Leakey says, "and I've only seen a few scenes of one or two, just to have a look at the makeup. To my way of thinking, horror exists only in the mind. One has to have the imagination stirred and the horror must be in the situation and in the dread of seeing something. It's a dead duck if you do see it, because nothing physical can match the imagination.

"In my own career, the part of makeup that I've enjoyed most has been in making up historical characters. Trying to make actors and actresses, if they have been halfway well cast, look like well-known paintings of these same characters. I also enjoy trying to age people gracefully, trying to make them look as I imagine they may look in years to come. I like making prosthetics and a few other things.

In 1971 Leakey and fellow makeup artist Eric Alwright shared makeup credit on the film *Henry VIII*, which was inspired by the BBC's successful television series of the same name. The makeup on Keith Michell as Henry VIII remained the same as it had been in the television series, which was not Leakey's work; however, Leakey and Alwright had enormous pleasure creating the many characters that appeared in the film, including the king's many wives, to look as much as possible like well-known paintings of the historical figures they portrayed.

Leakey's career has taken both he and his wife, Gladys, to many far-off corners of the world. Mrs. Leakey was, in fact, the official hairdresser on many films, as she has considerable knowledge of period hair styles. She worked with Leakey on *Henry VIII*; she retired from films shortly thereafter, but then taught hairdressing to newcomers in the television field. Philip W. N. Leakey has now retired from makeup, and in recent years he and Mrs. Leakey have moved to a small, charming English village and a home known as Lilliput.

Chapter 14

ROY ASHTON

Howard Roy Ashton was born in Perth, West Australia, where he studied art and music. He then studied architecture and worked as an illustrator of architectural subjects and as a commercial artist. Later he came to England and continued his education at the Central School of Arts and Crafts and the Royal Academy of Music. A chance of learning the profession of makeup artist came when he was at the Central School of Arts. He completed his professional training with the Gaumont British Film Corporation and Gainsborough Pictures. Mr. Ashton's film credits span over one hundred pictures.

On Ashton's first picture, which was called *Tudor Rose* (1936), directed by Robert Stevenson, he was responsible for the design and execution of the wigs. It was while working on this project at Gainsborough Pictures that Ashton had the pleasure of meeting and working with the late Boris Karloff.

Ashton's career has been intimately tied to the growth of Hammer Film Productions and the new generation of horror films Hammer started producing in the late fifties and sixties.

Philip Leakey, another great British makeup artist, introduced Ashton to Hammer Films. Leakey called Ashton and told him to come over to Bray Studios one very foggy day. When Ashton arrived at work with Leakey on a Hammer horror project, he couldn't find a place anywhere to park his car. He finally found what he thought was a deserted graveyard and parked it there. "My God," Leakey exclaimed to Ashton, "you can't leave your car there—that's the set we're using!"

Ashton admits that his most challenging job was the horrific makeup for Anton Diffring in Hammer's *The Man Who Could Cheat Death* (1959). It was Ashton's first experience with such a complex makeup, and the experience gleaned on this production led him to create some of filmdom's greatest classic horror characters in the tradition of the grand master of the thirties and forties, Jack Pierce of the United States.

After making arrangements with Universal Pictures, Hammer Films revived the film classic *The Mummy* (1959), to be remade in color with Christopher Lee playing the crumbling Mummy, alive again to destroy.

For *The Mummy*, Ashton first took a cast of Christopher Lee's head. He then modeled a change of outward structure to suggest a shriveled look. On this he started a buildup by utilizing strips of old rags joined by latex, gradually winding them to suggest old and rotten bandaging.

The eyelids were a big problem. The original Mummy had fixed lids, but Ashton made the lids flexible—a kind of flap just resting on the normal lids, allowing the actor to move his lids naturally. The main parts of the trunk and arms were a matter of patient winding and sewing.

Anton Diffring's makeup for *The Man Who Could Cheat Death* was Ashton's first experience with such a complex makeup. He employed sketches to help him achieve the effect he was searching for. Here are two such sketches. (*Hammer Films*)

A preliminary makeup test for *The Man Who Could Cheat Death*. (*Hammer Films*)

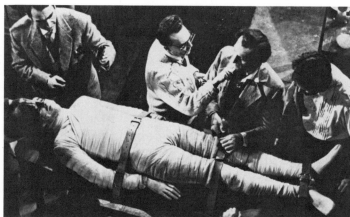

Christopher Lee and Peter Cushing in their respective roles on the set of *The Mummy*. (*Hammer Films*)

Ashton looked back into ancient Egyptian sources for authenticity. Terence Fisher, the director, tells a rather amusing story about an incident that occurred during filming: "The studio hired a noted Egyptologist to help on technical data. He was a very upright scientist and very helpful. But when the scroll was being read to restore the Mummy to life, the scientist turned to me and said, 'You don't know what you're fooling with,' got up, left the set, and never came back. It gave me rather a turn. But everything was okay!"

Christopher Lee also has a favorite behind-the-scenes anecdote from *The Mummy*: "In *The Mummy* someone thoughtfully

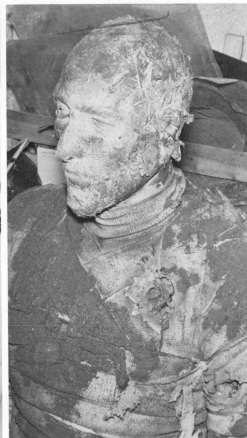

Director Terence Fisher discusses a scene from *The Mummy* with Christopher Lee. (*Hammer Films*)

Top right: The Mummy's eyelids were a big problem. The original Mummy had fixed lids, but Ashton made a flap which rested on Lee's own eyelids. Here Lee takes a brief respite between takes. (*Hammer Films*)

Right: After casting Christopher Lee's head, he modeled sufficient changes to suggest a shriveled look. He then employed strips of old rags joined by latex, winding them to appear like old, rotting bandages. (*Hammer Films*)

locked and bolted the door I had to come through when I strangled Raymond Huntley ... and so I smashed right through it and dislocated my shoulder! Some of the window was made of real glass. Later I was carrying Yvonne Furneaux down the road some eighty-three yards at night, and I pulled every muscle in my neck and shoulders.''

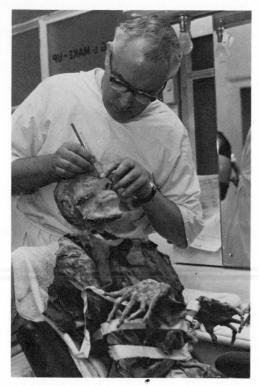

Ashton diligently perfecting a skeletal creation for *Paranoiac*. (*Hammer Films*)

Ashton created dozens of preliminary sketches trying to arrive at a concept for *The Curse of the Werewolf*. Here is a sketch of the final concept. (*Hammer Films*)

The principal structure that changed Oliver Reed's appearance was a plastic dome that fitted from the eye sockets to the back of the skull. Yak hair was used on the head, and the main trunk of Reed's body was fitted with a leotard covered with yak hair. (*Hammer Films*)

Ashton's makeup for Hammer's *The Curse of the Werewolf* (1960) was a crowning achievement in film history. Ashton created dozens and dozens of preliminary sketches. The most difficult problem was to find out what the producers wanted. To create a wolflike appearance on Oliver Reed meant research in the Natural History Museum, drawing and photographing a wolf and setting up a full-size model, then adapting this appearance to a human head. Ashton reproduced Reed's head and modeled the wolf mask onto this cast.

The principal structure that changed Reed was a plastic dome that fitted from the eye sockets to the back of the skull. This was covered with stiffened yak hair. After a few attempts, the ears were attached. The nostrils were dilated with wax inserts, and teeth with extended canines were fitted. A succession of hairfalls, like the overlapping sheaves of a house, were fitted to the back of the neck and toward the shoulders. The main trunk was fitted with a leotard and covered with yak hair to simulate the coat of a wolf. Hands were covered with coarse hair, and fingernails were extended to suggest claws. Contact lenses were inserted for extreme close-up shots.

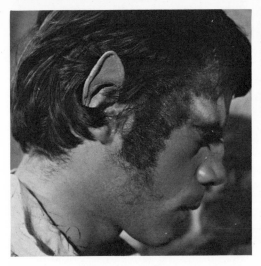

Reed wears the appliance ears that will help effect the beginning of his transformation in *The Curse of the Werewolf.* (*Hammer Films*)

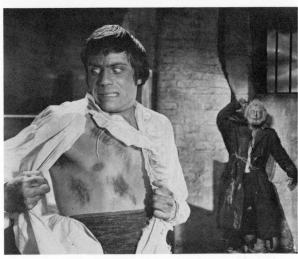

Leon (Oliver Reed) is appalled to see his werewolf transformation beginning. (*Hammer Films*)

Transformation completed, the maddened beast haunts the darkened streets, aided by Roy Ashton's makeup, of course. (*Hammer Films*)

Progressive growths of hair were done by stop-motion photography, locking off the parts to be photographed and putting on more and more hair. A false chest was created. Yak hair was used for the complete makeup job. The only changes were from the small lad—the werewolf of the early scenes—to the awesome appearance of the mature creature.

Undoubtedly this is one of the best films of its type, perhaps only rivaled by the original *Wolf Man* with Lon Chaney, Jr., as the creature. This film has been considered a classic of its genre. Its treatment was based on Guy Endore's famous novel *The Werewolf of Paris*. However, Hammer Films decided to change the scene to Spain instead of Paris.

Ashton made Christopher Lee up as Dracula, the vampire count, and David Peel as the popular Baron Meinster in *Brides of Dracula* (1960). Peel's makeup included a lace wig. Peel was about forty when he played this role, but he looks as if he's in his midtwenties. Ashton did a tremendous makeup job on him—a basic character makeup of highlights and shadows, fangs, bloodshot contact lenses, and the special laced wig. *Brides of Dracula* has been considered by most film fans as the greatest vehicle of its kind and the best in all areas that has been made by Hammer Film Productions to date. Ashton's makeup on Peel, and on Peter Cushing as Dr. Van Helsing, was the frosting on the cake.

To do a vampire makeup, Ashton recommends a pallid face, black hair, and eyebrows joined together. Contact lenses that register eyes engorged with blood should also be used. The face should have a light coloring with highlights on the cheeks. He recommends that you have plenty of pros-

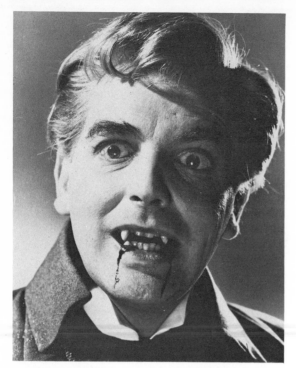

Ashton employed a lace wig to set off David Peel's makeup as the vampire count Baron Meinster in *Brides of Dracula*. With careful inspection, the lace wig can be seen in close-up photography. Peel was about forty when he played this role, but he appears to be a man in his midtwenties with the aid of Ashton's stunning, yet fearsome, makeup. (*Hammer Films*)

thetic vampire "bites" to apply to the victims' necks, and all should be well.

When Hammer Films remade the film version of the immortal Victor Hugo classic *The Phantom of the Opera* in 1962 they employed a professional mask-maker to design the acid-burned appearance of the Phantom. Although the mask-maker came up with several different designs, none were acceptable to the producers. After three weeks of shooting around the scenes that called for the presence of the Phantom, a decision still had not been arrived at. Finally time was up and the scenes needed to be filmed. Ashton was called into service and in approximately five minutes' time while the shooting unit waited, he pulled together what was handy and went to work. The burned tissue effect on this particular Phantom was simply an old bit of cloth, some camera tape, a small piece of gauze, and some rubber, all held together with a bit of string.

The *Phantom* was shot by Hammer Films for release by Universal Pictures, and it was Universal's fiftieth anniversary special film release. Although the makeup was acceptable, it seems that no one has ever rivaled Lon Chaney, Sr.'s, silent version, or the 1943 remake with Claude Rains, which won an Academy Award.

Because Dickie Owen played the role of the mummy in *The Curse of the Mummy's Tomb*, the role originally created by Christopher Lee, Ashton needed to model much more massive temples and cheeks on Owen. Ashton did, however, follow much the same procedure as in the original Christopher Lee version of *The Mummy*. (*Hammer Films*)

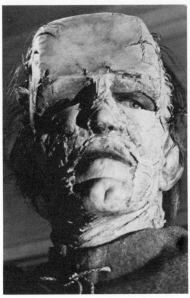

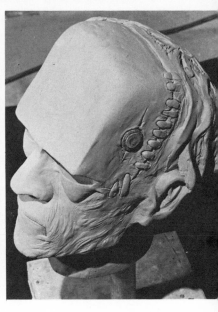

One of only many preliminary sketches of the creature in *The Evil of Frankenstein*, which was portrayed by actor Kiwi Kingston. (*Hammer Films*)

A full-sized reproduction of the actor's head was cast in plaster, and upon this were modeled the alterations to produce the monster's appearance. (*Hammer Films*)

A natural-sized head was decided upon and then modeled in clay. (*Hammer Films*)

The horror cycle went around again, and Hammer Films made another mummy film in 1964 entitled *The Curse of the Mummy's Tomb,* and again Ashton was busy with rotten bandages.

Ashton did have to remodel the mummy makeup after the first screen test. Christopher Lee did not take the title role; in his place was Dickie Owen, who was rather thin. It was decided he needed some strengthening of his facial appearance. Ashton remodeled much more massive temples and cheeks on Owen, but he followed much the same procedure as in the original Christopher Lee version of *The Mummy*.

Ashton recalls during production when the Mummy was floundering in the crumbling sewers with everything falling about him, he lost his footing and fell into the water, getting pretty wet and breathless in the process. Ashton half suspected some mishap was imminent and stood by with a pair of scissors in case of trouble. He leaped into the water and cut Owen free of his facial bandages.

In *The Evil of Frankenstein* (1964), preliminary work was started one month before shooting. Ashton had made and discarded over one hundred and fifty different numbered sketches. He took many shortcuts, cutting down the actual makeup time to about one hour, which included making up the hands.

Peter Cushing played the Baron Frankenstein and shared with us his insights into the character he portrayed.

"I always liken Baron Frankenstein unto the famous, or—as many regarded him during his lifetime—infamous anatomist Doctor Robert Knox, who closed his one good eye to the way in which Burke and Hare supplied him with cadavers, which he needed in order to find out the secrets of the human body, for the eventual good of mankind.

"As in fiction, so it was in real life, both characters being hounded and mobbed by the populace as well as those in authority, forcing them to carry on their work as best they could in secret and, perforce, resorting to ruthless methods in order to pursue their dedicated practice.

"How different today. During the eighteen years which have elapsed since *The Curse of Frankenstein* was produced, medicine has made tremendous advances. In 1967 Christiaan Barnard performed the world's first human heart transplant operation, and, without any doubt at all, the time will come when other organs will undergo similar successful treatment.

"It is rather nice to feel that I 'got there first,' so to speak—thanks to Mary Shelley and the perspicacity of Hammer Film Productions!"

For Hammer's *The Gorgon* (1964), the design for this creature of Greek mythology was taken out of Ashton's hands and given to the Special Effects Department at Bray Studios. Ashton's idea was to base the snakelike looks of the Gorgon on the celebrated sculpture of Cellini. In this marvelous work, the snakes are fairly small. Ashton considered that a writhing effect could be achieved by making vipers from colored wood attached to strips of leather. These are sometimes available as children's toys. However, the special effects people made fairly large snakes which were remotely activated by cables attached to cams. The Gorgon's facial makeup was startling, complete with red contact lenses.

Also in 1964, Ashton experienced some amusing incidents creating the vampires in *Kiss of the Vampire*. He employed a British dentist, who took impressions of the teeth of Noel Willman and the eleven other would-be vampires, made caps to fit over the regular eyeteeth, and formed the plastic fangs on the caps. "You might say I really get my teeth into the part," observed Willman while he wore the appliances.

The fangs were so well designed and so comfortable that the actors often forgot to remove them when they left the set. Isobel Black, who played one of the leading vampires, received a mild reprimand from the studio waitress when she ordered a steak for lunch. "Miss Black," the waitress exclaimed, "you really don't need those things in here. Our steaks are not that tough!"

Ashton faced a very complex makeup problem for the film *She* (1965). Ursula Andress portrayed Ayesha, the queen whose beauty belies her age of two thousand years. John Richardson played Leo Vincey who is believed by Ayesha to be the reincarnated lover she murdered in a jealous rage. In the city of Kuma, Ayesha lures Vincey into the flame of eternal life. When she follows him, her beauty disintegrates, slowly turning her into a two-thousand-year-old skeleton. Ashton explains the aging process he developed for this challenge:

A duplicate head was made of *The Gorgon*, which was to be "severed" by Christopher Lee. Lee actually knocked this head off a dummy and allowed it to roll down the castle stairs.(*Hammer Films*)

Special effects master Syd Pearson works diligently on his design for *The Gorgon*. (*Hammer Films*)

"Since the fundamental idea is shrinkage and emaciation, or shriveling, the original actor can be used only for the first stages of change; that is, to indicate granulation of tissue, burn effects, or preliminary age changes. To apply prosthetics to the face and body beyond this would build it up instead of reducing it.

"I suggest therefore the use of other women of similar bone structure, of increasing age, but diminishing stature, wearing removable dentures, and of a physical condition approximating that which progressively occurs to the body of *She*.

"The progressive facial changes can be taken from original to substitute actor, but general body shrinkage and emaciation can only be indicated by actual bodies—since (according to the script) the body of She is completely exposed.

"The final appearance when dead, however, could be made exactly according to the producer's wishes by modeling, and over this fashioning a skin on a skeleton of appropriate dimensions.

"Suggestions for seven stages of facial change are given—and a possible appearance of the dead and shriveled body. Brief details of the changes are indicated on each sketch."

Another landmark horror creation was achieved by Ashton in Hammer Films' *Plague of the Zombies* (1966). Ashton achieved most of the zombie effects by using latex and single thicknesses of tissues. By crumpling up thin tissue paper, coloring it with fuller's earth or any grayish dust, and then covering it with liquid latex, one can create a very effective illusion of "living death."

Veins can be made with blue darning wool. Ashton designed contact lenses with reversed tone values in some cases—white pupils with black backgrounds, or plain white lenses with pin-sized apertures to enable the wearer to see.

In 1966 Ashton created another magnificent monster for Hammer Films, *The Reptile*. In this film, set in a small Cornish village, as *Plague of the Zombies* was, Ashton proved again how very scary he can get.

A great deal of research went into the reptilian creation for this film. Ashton again consulted anatomical and zoological authorities, drew snakes many times, and constructed a model adapting the platelike reptilian form to the bones of the human head. Ashton made a basic structure from laminated paper over the head of the actress Jackie Pearce, from the nose to the back of the skull. He built hair into this to suggest a normal hairline.

For snakelike scales he took actual snakeskin and made a female mold of it in plaster. Into this he poured plastic skin, and it gave him a perfect snakeskin with all the real scales. Sections of this were fitted wherever it was appropriate, and upon application, head, cheeks, and neck took on a very real snakelike appearance.

The fangs were a complete plate that fitted over the teeth, from canine to canine, with extended points from which dripped the deadly venom—glycerine! This makeup took about two hours from start to finish. Ashton made the eyepieces with built-in lenses. These were separate from the main structure, and Ashton could put them in and take them out between takes.

Roy Ashton makes almost everything he needs for his monstrous creations by himself. He does not make contact lenses, however, as this is a very specialized field, and great care must be employed when working around or directly on the eyes. There is no question that this is the province of the optical technician. However, in making varied teeth appliances, Ashton explains that you first need an impression of the dental structure of the actor or actress involved.

This is simple to do. However, for those of you who do not know how to start, take a tiny tray that will overlap the teeth, fill it with a molding substance, press this over the teeth, wait for it to set (about five minutes usually), remove it, and there you have a female mold of the dental shape (or gums if the artist is toothless).

Into this mold pour dental plaster, which then hardens, giving you a replica of the inside of the actor's mouth. Dental technicians might smile to read such a simplified account, but it works nicely. In short, you model whatever changes you may wish to make in dental wax and make fresh casts of these, reproducing your modeled teeth in acrylic. Dental materials are freely available and are used for many purposes other than making teeth. You can create excellent bones from acrylic, too. But special dental appliances are best left to the dental profession. The design, however, should be in

For the violent aging process in the film *She*, star Ursula Andress could be used only for the early aging stages. Ashton employed numerous aging sketches to enable him to reach the concepts needed for his unusual makeup challenge. Here we have seven of his remarkable sketches. (*Hammer Films*)

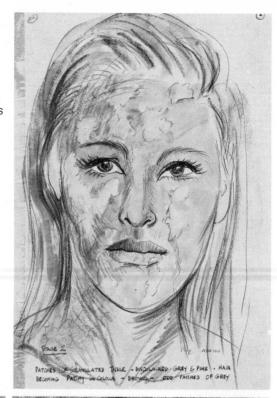

STAGE 2

PATCHES OF GRANULATED TISSUE - DISCOLOURED GREY & PINK - HAIR BECOMING PATCHY IN COLOUR - BROWN - ODD PATCHES OF GREY

STAGE 3

MOUTH BEGINNING TO DROOP

PATCHY SKIN - REDNESS ALMOST GONE - EYES BAGGING - LARGE CREASES - NECK CREASES APPEARING - HAIR ALMOST GREY - LANK & PATCHY

STAGE 4

UNEVEN SKIN - HOLLOWING EYES - COLOUR CHANGE IN IRIS(?) - GROOVED FACE - WITH DENTURES - SAGGING JAW LINE - PRONOUNCED TRACES OF MUSCLE UNDER JAW - HAIR LIFELESS - THINNING.

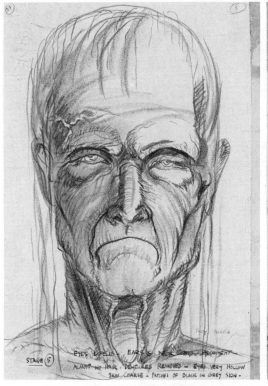

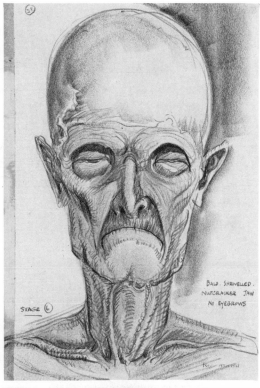

STAGE 5 — EYES EYELIDS — EARS & NECK CORDS PROMINENT —
ALMOST NO HAIR — DENTURES REMOVED — EYES VERY HOLLOW
SKIN COARSE — PATCHES OF BLACK IN GREY SKIN —

STAGE 6

BALD. SHRIVELLED.
NUTCRACKER JAW
NO EYEBROWS

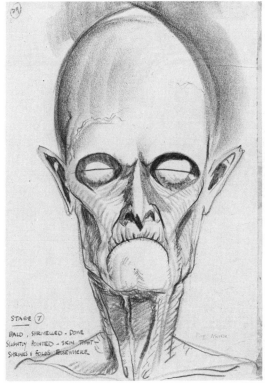

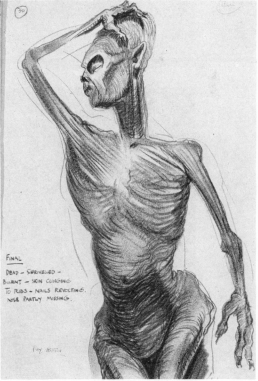

STAGE 7

BALD, SHRIVELLED — DOME
SLIGHTLY POINTED — SKIN TIGHT —
SHRINKS & FOLDS ELSEWHERE.

FINAL

DEAD — SHRIVELLED —
BURNT — SKIN CLINGING
TO RIBS — NAILS REVOLTING.
NOSE PARTLY MISSING.

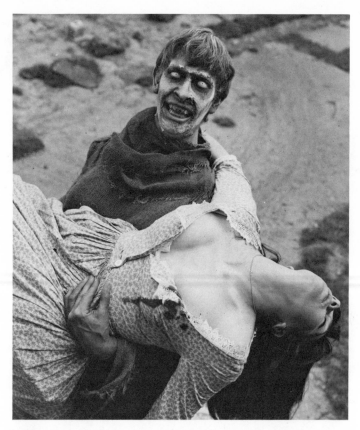
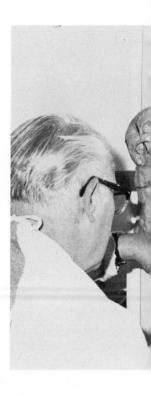

Ashton employed plain white lenses with pin-sized apertures to enable the actor to see in *Plague of the Zombies.* (*Hammer Films*)

Ashton created this swollen snake bite for *The Reptile.* (*Hammer Films*)

Ashton at work in his laboratory, surrounded by his various horrendous creations. (*Photo courtesy of Roy Ashton*)

A great deal of research went into the reptilian creation for *The Reptile*. Here, actress Jacqueline Pearce is terrified by Ashton's creation. (*Hammer Films*)

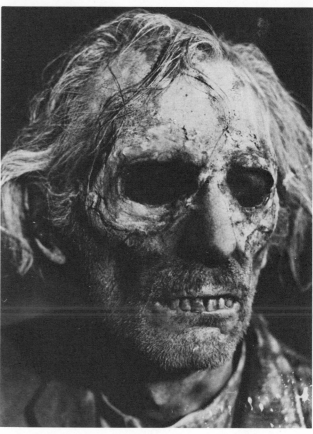

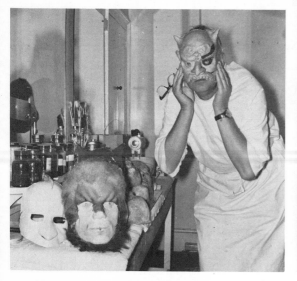

Ashton enjoys posing in his lab with one of his creations. Note the werewolf appliances on the workbench. (*Hammer Films*)

Ashton created a most startling makeup effect for Peter Cushing's role in *Tales from the Crypt*. Eye sockets were covered with opaque black material that would not register on the film. (*Amicus Films*)

consultation with the makeup artist for each particular project.

After working many years for Hammer Films, Ashton free-lanced and did many outstanding makeups for Amicus Films. One film that received high acclaim and a special award was *Tales from the Crypt* (1971), which starred Peter Cushing. In the scene where Cushing rises from his grave to avenge a heartless fellow, Cushing's face was shriveled and had hollow black sockets. Structures were made from laminated paper to suggest the severe wasting of features. The eye sockets were covered with opaque black material that would not register on the film. A slight growth of beard, combined with prominent discolored teeth,

and thinning and aging of the hair completed the desired effect. A spider who conveniently walked down the gravestone as the shot was taken duly returned to his starting position on take number two. Amicus Films gave Ashton some real headaches, but all were finally resolved. Making four or five men resemble zombies takes quite a bit of time to do when they have to be ready for early morning shooting.

Today Roy Ashton directs his makeup achievements to a less frightening genre of films, and one sees his makeup credits on such films as Blake Edwards' *Pink Panther* series, as well as such Disney films as *Candleshoe* (1978) and *Unidentified Flying Oddball* (1979).

Chapter 15

ROBERT SCHIFFER

Robert Schiffer, head of makeup and hairdressing at Walt Disney Productions, has had a varied history in makeup.

Schiffer started at RKO in 1934, working as an assistant makeup artist. Bill Phillips was the first to hire him. They worked on the film *Last Days of Pompeii* (1935), with Preston Foster and Basil Rathbone. In those days body makeup was actually a very heavy, gummy liquid that they would pour over the body, and it would last for a day. Schiffer says it was nearly impossible to wash off, and he remembers his introduction into the world of makeup artistry as a smelly room with anywhere from fifty to one hundred men having body makeup applied so they could go out and be fed to the lions.

Schiffer took a few steps up and worked with Barbara Stanwyck in *Annie Oakley* (1935). He then served an apprenticeship under the guidance of some of the senior makeup artists and worked on many of the Ginger Rogers-Fred Astaire films.

In 1935 RKO presented the first color film *Becky Sharp* with Miriam Hopkins. Schiffer describes the makeups used in those days as being "from outer space." They were green and blue, heavy and thick; and no one seemed to know in what direction they were going as far as makeup was concerned. Then Technicolor introduced the three-strip process that helped solve some of the makeup problems, and studios began to modify their makeups some, but still they were quite heavy and difficult.

Somewhere along the line, Schiffer garnered the reputation for being an expert with the ladies. "Whether my makeup had anything to do with it or not, I don't know." He made up such beauties as Joan Crawford in *The Gorgeous Hussy* (1936), Myrna Loy for *Test Pilot* (1938), Barbara Stanwyck in *Golden Boy* (1939), and Rita Hayworth for such films as *Cover Girl* (1944), *Gilda* (1946), and *The Lady from Shanghai* (1948).

Schiffer left MGM and went to Columbia in 1938. He began there on a film called *Arizona* (1940) with Jean Arthur and William Holden. He stayed at Columbia for about sixteen years and was under contract to Rita Hayworth and did all the Hayworth films, plus every other major feature that was made at Columbia.

When Schiffer made up Angela Lansbury for *The Picture of Dorian Gray* (1945), he used a heavy mascara on her lashes. In the more recent film *Bedknobs and Broomsticks* (1971), it wasn't necessary to do that, what with the improvement in cameras and lighting. The necessity for the emphasized features of the thirties and forties is gone. Because *Bedknobs and Broomsticks* was set in the forties, it was necessary for

Robert Schiffer and Burt Lancaster in the film *The Leopard*. Not only was Schiffer in charge of makeup on the production, but he also had a small role. (*Robert Schiffer*)

Schiffer to create that look without using the extremes so necessary in the forties for the film quality at that time. With the film stock used today, makeup has gone quite natural.

Schiffer left makeup to become a producer in the late fifties. Hecht-Lancaster made him head of their publicity department, and although Schiffer was an excellent makeup artist, he was the first to admit that he didn't know a thing about publicity. He enjoyed the affluence for a while, which included a barber, secretary, French manicurist, a big desk, and a green couch. Hecht-Lancaster folded before he knew it, and Schiffer was back in makeup, where he obviously belonged and was needed.

It wasn't until Schiffer went independent following the Hecht-Lancaster failure, that he really enjoyed himself. As an independent artist, he found he had greater flexibility than when working for a major studio. He could set up his own program in any manner he thought best. "You were the boss," he said, "and you did the hiring. You also took the blame. It was good experience and I enjoyed it."

Schiffer feels that until the late fifties, the makeup man was a servant who had to sneak up the backstairs, hide in dressing rooms, and give in to the whims of powerful stars over his better judgment.

"Makeup which is now taken for granted takes talent that required years to develop,"

Schiffer says. He is disappointed that all too often the only makeup that receives publicity or recognition has to be grotesque or a "specialty" number. He feels that the less obvious a makeup is, that when someone comes out of a theatre and doesn't mention the makeup, they are paying the greatest compliment that they can pay.

Of all the years he has worked in the makeup business, Schiffer thinks that the makeup for Burt Lancaster in *Birdman of Alcatraz* (1962) was one of his most successful. Lancaster has a very strong face and jaw, and Schiffer aged him from nineteen to eighty-five. He has always been proud of that makeup.

Schiffer had an opportunity to try his hand at acting in *The Leopard* (1963). His role was that of a friend to Burt Lancaster, who portrayed a prince. Schiffer did double duty on this film, as he was also in charge of makeup for the production. Schiffer's role required a beard, so Schiffer's own beard, with a little false hair added to it, filled the requirement. He also had his own hair curled for the role.

For the film *Camelot* (1967), Schiffer wanted to create a very unusual look for Laurence Naismith's portrayal of Merlin the Magician. He collaborated with Dr. Morton K. Greenspoon on the creation of mirrored lenses. The lenses were soaked in a solution that reacted to a black light. One partic-

Schiffer aged Burt Lancaster from nineteen to eighty-five in the film *Bird-man of Alcatraz*. (*Robert Schiffer*)

ularly impressive shot Schiffer recalled was of Merlin stepping out of a tree trunk with eyes aglow.

The last film Schiffer did independently was *The Gypsy Moths* (1969) with Burt Lancaster and Deborah Kerr. There are always unsuspected problems cropping up in film-making. Gene Hackman, who also starred in this film, had been having his hair dyed in Wichita, Kansas, and had apparently had it dyed too often. Hackman's hair began falling out, and in horror, he woke Schiffer in the middle of the night to tell him of his problem. The following morning, Schiffer took horsehair and laid it on Hackman's skull where his hair had fallen out. It was necessary for Schiffer to do this during the entire filming of *The Gypsy Moths*. A few years later, upon meeting Schiffer at the Academy Awards, Hackman told a friend with him that he could have been the biggest star in Hollywood if his hair hadn't fallen out from the dye job. It was obviously fortunate for Hackman that he had a man of Schiffer's expertise handy to fill in the gaps before filming.

Schiffer went to Walt Disney Productions as the head of the Makeup and Hairdressing Department in 1968. He was rather re-luctant at first. He all too readily remembered the thirties and the tremendous personality problems created by the "star system," the days of the Louis B. Mayer regime, then RKO. He lived in a sort of fright for years, never knowing whether the producer might suddenly decide he was no longer necessary. However, he had also been exposed to the cruel world of the film business, where he felt you had to hustle along to keep people from placing knives between your shoulders.

He went ahead and joined Walt Disney Productions and now tells us it has been a rewarding experience in his "twilight years" to finally be in a studio that shows such respect for what knowledge you have gained over the years and only demands what you give them—which is naturally your best when you are treated in such a respectful way. He regards Disney as a wonderful studio where everyone is sweet and means it and everyone says hello and means it.

When we asked Schiffer to describe his most unusual makeup, we were hardly prepared for his answer.

"I think it was dyeing a camel. They called me onto the back lot one day where

Schiffer begins the makeup transformation on Dean Jones for his role in *The Shaggy Dog D.A.* (© *Walt Disney Productions*)

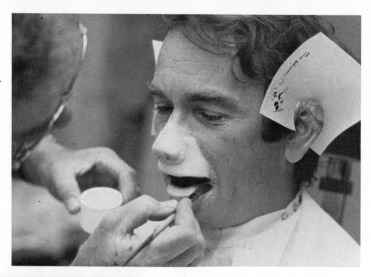

Gray streaks of hair have been added to Jones's own hair. (© *Walt Disney Productions*)

the camel they had been using in *One Little Indian* (1973) had become ill. They had brought in another camel, but the coloring was totally different. They had tried having the Paint Department paint it, but it wouldn't last, so I had to mix up actual hair dye, and dye a damn camel. Now, can you top that. I spent the whole four hours dyeing a camel and was four days getting the black coloring out of my fingers and off my clothes!''

Schiffer does feel that being the head of the Makeup Department has somewhat curtailed his artistic expression. He feels that he doesn't have that many films that are that demanding from a makeup standpoint. He did have a challenge when it came to the Vi-

Animal hair was progressively added to Jones's face. (© *Walt Disney Productions*)

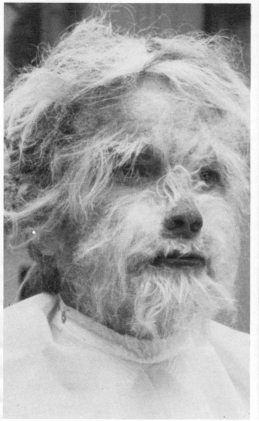

Jones is now almost unrecognizable. (© *Walt Disney Productions*)

Dean Jones in costume and makeup, with a real shaggy dog, Ali. (© *Walt Disney Productions*)

king film *Island at the Top of the World* (1975), when he had to create plastic contact lenses to turn the cast's eyes a beautiful blue. There being some danger in this procedure, Schiffer tested the lenses on himself first.

Island at the Top of the World required Schiffer to travel to England and Norway where the production was filmed. He was kept rather busy setting up beards and characters. To defray the cost of having hair lace beards made, Schiffer had his staff lay beards on false heads, then spray them with Krylon. The hair was then floated off with acetone. They were able to use the false beards three or four times. A great deal of hairwork was necessary for the Godi, who was portrayed by Norwegian actor Gunnar Ohlund.

In the film *The Shaggy D.A.* (1977) with Dean Jones, Schiffer found considerable challenge and satisfaction.

The plot of the film involves a ring, apparently from some Egyptian pharaoh, that when rubbed or picked up, turns Dean Jones into a shaggy dog at the most inopportune times.

Remembering the remarkable Dr. Jekyll and Mr. Hyde transformation scenes, Schiffer wanted to effect the same; however, he wanted his to be much smoother than the original transformation scene. He worked extremely closely with the cameraman setting up all sorts of camera angles and tying cameras off so that when he did the makeup changes, they would be very, very smooth.

The first step was to find a shaggy dog. He then took calipers and measured every inch of the dog's head so that when they modeled the dog, it would be the exact measurement of the head, including the tongue.

What Schiffer didn't know when he measured the dog, all calm and relaxed, was that when dogs are overheated or aggravated, the tongue becomes about an inch wider than when it is cool! So it became necessary to make four or five different tongues to match whatever condition the dog's tongue was in that day.

He prepared a regular cement epoxy and coated the hair around the mouth and nose, leaving a permanent shine. He found this worked very well and was impressive, giving the effect of the shiny nose and drooling mouth that dogs have. He also added some brown coloring around the hair by the mouth, as most dogs have brown hair there.

With all his care, he effected a very smooth transition, only to have the director make the decision that the audience would not want to stay with the transition for as long as it took, and cut from the dog to the people in the film. Needless to say, Schiffer was not too pleased with this after the many months of preparation. Schiffer, being the professional that he is, recognizes this as one of the many "crosses" artists must bear.

Besides his work at the Disney Studio, Schiffer lectures on makeup to students at the California Institute of the Arts, which is a Disney-sponsored university. Schiffer feels that if someone is interested in a makeup career today, he is faced with enormous hardships, as it is a difficult field to get into. Schiffer is the last department head to have an apprentice, mainly because there are only a few department heads left. His last apprentice turned out very well, and that was Stan Winston. He went on to do some great things with prosthetics, becoming very successful, and Schiffer is very pleased for him. "But who remembers Michelangelo's teacher, right?" Schiffer asked us. We're sure Stan Winston does.

The apprenticeship program at the Disney Studio selects ten prospective students and ten alternates from a list of perhaps three hundred that have sent in applications. These students will work for eighteen months at no cost to themselves, two nights a week for three hours. They are instructed by a makeup artist journeyman through the local. At the end of that period, they are given an examination, and if they pass it, they are allowed to go onto the Group Two roster group of the union.

Schiffer says his greatest fear now is that when "we all die off, there are really very few great names that have had the experience. You must remember that we used to have great programs that called for three years of apprenticeship. Today, they have to learn in eighteen months what they used to take three years to learn. The rest they hopefully learn on the set. You can understand my concern."

The Walt Disney production of *Pete's*

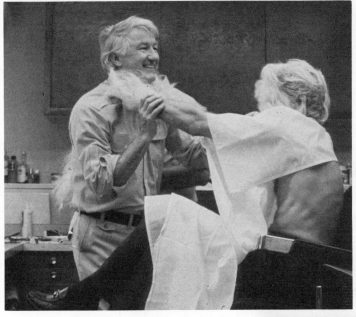

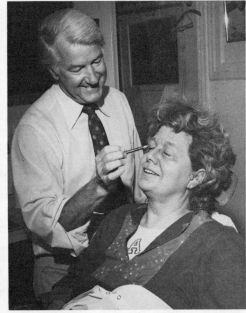

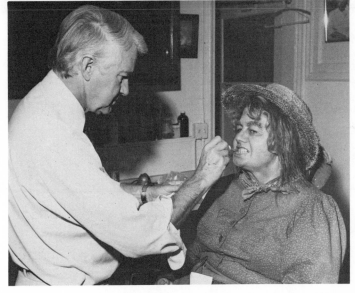

Above: A makeup artist has to be careful else a restless actor may try to turn the tables on him. Jones and Schiffer clown a bit. (© *Walt Disney Productions*)

Top right: Shelley Winters undergoes a transformation at Schiffer's hands for her role in *Pete's Dragon*. (© *Walt Disney Productions*)

Stained teeth add to Ms. Winters's character, and the wig and costume complete it.
(© *Walt Disney Productions*)

Dragon (1977) required Shelley Winters to undergo a transformation at the hands of Schiffer. Her makeup consisted of a gold tooth, false eyebrows, a gray wig, and a great deal of character makeup. Modern technology isn't always the rule, even in a studio such as Disney, and Schiffer ingeniously employed a simple piece of puffed wheat with a few hairs stuck in it to simulate a wart. Her teeth were appropriately stained and her hands made up.

One of Schiffer's most recent assignments was the film *Hot Lead, Cold Feet*, which has yet to be released. Jim Dale played three parts: an aged father of twin sons as well as the twins. One of the sons was a clean-cut missionary type, and the other, a rough and rugged "tough" in a small Western town. Schiffer employed prosthetics, as well as contact lenses to further the old-age look.

Schiffer continues to remain constantly busy with his position as head of the Makeup Department at Walt Disney Productions. One of the busiest studios in the country, Schiffer has little time to pause and reflect on the innumerable creations he has made during his career. With Disney's continuing role in the realm of fantasy, Schiffer will undoubtedly continue to be faced with makeup challenges for years to come.

Schiffer's pumpkin creation for Jonathan Winters for a Disney Halloween special in the fall of 1977. Latex was painted into the master mold and scotch foam used to fill in the area between Winters's head and the pumpkin area. (© *Walt Disney Productions*)

Every good pumpkin head should sport a proper stem. Schiffer tops off his creation with a little green paint. (© *Walt Disney Productions*)

Chapter 16

STUART FREEBORN

Stuart Freeborn became interested in makeup and organized a 16-mm *cine society*, for which he wrote scripts that included a great deal of "heavy" or character makeups. It took three years of trying to crash into the movie business before Freeborn got a break with the late Sir Alexander Korda in 1936. Born in 1914, Freeborn was twenty-one when he began his makeup career.

Among the many films Freeborn has worked on, he regards one of his most interesting to be David Lean's *Oliver Twist* (1948). The film was Alec Guinness's second; it was not released in the United States until 1951. Guinness's brilliant performance as Fagin was regarded as anti-Semitic and resulted in the film's withdrawal from circulation for a time.

Freeborn considers Guinness as having the ideal face for characterization. Guinness reported at five A.M. to Freeborn's makeup chair to become the evil Fagin. Makeup time took approximately three and a half hours to complete. After a monstrous nose and eye bags were secured to Guinness's face with spirit gum, Freeborn painted Guinness's face with a liquid adhesive which caused wrinkles when dried. Bushy eyebrows were laid, as well as a straggly beard, whose final appearance belied the meticulous care rendered by Freeborn. The overall makeup was startling and transformed the thirty-four-year-old Guinness into a cruel and ugly Fagin.

Another film favorite of Freeborn's was *The Bridge on the River Kwai* (1957) on which he again worked with Alec Guinness. Guinness won an Academy Award for his performance in this film.

When Freeborn created Peter Sellers as the President of the United States in *Dr. Strangelove, Or How I Learned to Stop Worrying and Love the Bomb* (1964), he employed a bald-cap technique he would successfully use in 1966 on Tony Randall in *The Alphabet Murders*. Director Stanley Kubrick gave Sellers three roles in *Dr. Strangelove*: that of Strangelove himself, and a wing commander, in addition to the American President.

Of the one hundred and twenty odd films Freeborn has been connected with, a number have required some very strange creatures. Some have been earthly, others extraterrestrial. Whatever was required, Freeborn endeavored to make them menacing by designing them to have a superior or supernatural intelligence, rather than simply being ugly. *2001: A Space Odyssey* (1968) was an exciting film for Freeborn.

"Undoubtedly," Freeborn commented, "*2001* was a most challenging project which called for as many as twenty-six actors each day wearing fully articulated

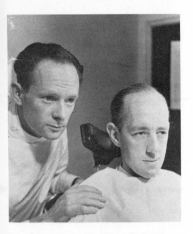

Freeborn regards Alec Guinness as having the ideal face to characterize. Here Freeborn prepares to make up Guinness as the evil Fagin in David Lean's *Oliver Twist*. (*Stuart Freeborn*)

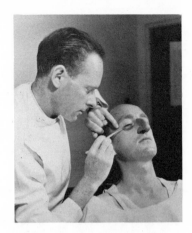

A monstrous nose and eye bags were secured with spirit gum. (*Photo courtesy of Stuart Freeborn*)

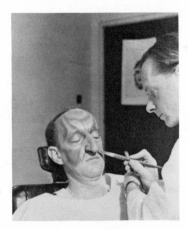

Wrinkles were added to Guinness's makeup with the use of a liquid adhesive. (*Stuart Freeborn*)

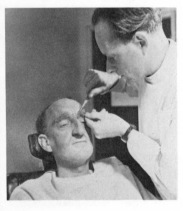

Once the wrinkled effect is achieved, Freeborn added bushy eyebrows. (*Stuart Freeborn*)

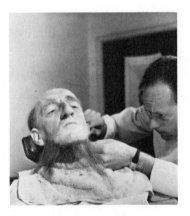

Freeborn lays a straggly beard whose final appearance belied the meticulous care he rendered. (*Stuart Freeborn*)

More hairwork as Freeborn lays a moustache. (*Stuart Freeborn*)

masks over a period of nearly three months.''

This too was a film directed by Stanley Kubrick, and Freeborn's task was made much more demanding by Kubrick's quest for realism. Apelike creatures were filmed for the dawn-of-man sequence, and Kubrick wanted to film close-ups of these creatures with their offspring in their arms, nursing from their breasts. It was impossible to life-cast human infants for the monkey babies, and because of the close-ups, fake creatures wouldn't do either.

The only solution was to use real infant chimpanzees and to make them up to look more like the apelike creatures and less like baby chimps. The chimps discovered they loved the taste of makeup and spirit gum, so it took a few days of application before they would stop licking their makeup off. However, this proved to be only a minor challenge. The real challenge was to get the chimps to appear to nurse from artificial breasts designed into the costumes which were worn by young boys.

Freeborn suggested that they put honey on the nipples, but Kubrick felt the chimps wouldn't remain nursing long enough, licking the honey off quickly. Kubrick decided that to have an effective and realistic shot,

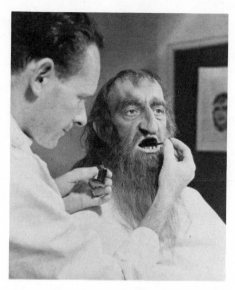

A washable black dye is painted on Guinness's teeth to give a rotted appearance. (*Stuart Freeborn*)

With expert care, thirty-four-year-old Alec Guinness is transformed into the cruel and ugly Fagin in *Oliver Twist*. (*Stuart Freeborn*)

the breasts really had to function.

"So I designed a breast as near as possible to the real thing, with five little holes in the teats and interchangeable milk bladders," Freeborn said.

Another problem was working out the consistency and taste of the milk. Not only did it have to be palatable to the chimps, it also had to be of the proper consistency to flow correctly through the nipples when the chimps nursed, yet not seep through otherwise. It took several days of trial and error in the makeup lab before they felt they had everything perfected.

"On the first day of shooting," Freeborn explained, "after the boys had been on the set for a while, running and jumping about in the hot lights, the milk must have become thin, as it suddenly started to squirt from the breasts every time they moved. This caused a bit of an uproar, and Kubrick was not pleased at all."

A quick trip back to the Makeup Department resulted in the milk being thickened to the proper consistency, and all worked out fine.

To create a character that requires appliances, the first thing Freeborn does is to draw in the character over a photograph of the actor. He then shows this conception to the actor and the director. If the design meets with their approval, his next step is to take a life-cast of the actor. From the life-cast, he makes a positive head in plaster on which he models in clay the prosthetic pieces. He then covers these in plaster, forming the molds in which to put the foam rubber mix prior to curing in the oven.

Freeborn has a complex filing system that he has built up over the years. It covers just about everything imaginable: different ways to age, beauty fashions over the years, famous and notorious people, kings and queens, animals, strange creatures, tattoos, native war paint, anatomy, bears, and so on.

"I find all types of makeup fascinating. I really have no preference. To me, beauty makeups need just as much thought and attention as the most complicated appliance or intricately articulated mask. It is a question of using judicially your artistic and mechanical aptitudes, which often go together in many professions. Every now and again, the other makeup artists come up with something very interesting and make me

Freeborn adds a few finishing touches to Peter Sellers's makeup as the Wing Commander in *Dr. Strangelove, Or How I Learned to Stop Worrying and Love the Bomb*. (*Columbia Pictures*)

Freeborn used a bald-cap technique on Peter Sellers as the American president in *Dr. Strangelove*. (*Columbia Pictures*)

envious that I didn't think of it myself."

Freeborn worked with Tony Randall, who played Hercule Poirot in *The Alphabet Murders,* a film which was shot in England. Randall had definite ideas on how Poirot should look which were taken from an artist's rendition in an early Agatha Christie novel in which she had quite accurately described her character. Before the cast and crew left for England, Bill Tuttle, director of makeup at MGM at the time, and director Frank Tashland went to New York where Tuttle made up Randall as Hercule Poirot. Once they achieved the desired look, Tuttle photographed the makeup. He removed the mortician's wax nose he had added to Randall's own, taking it back to Hollywood where Charles Schram cast it. Batches of the nose were then mailed off to England when filming began.

The makeup required a bald cap, and Randall had never used one that he felt satisfied with, that is, until he met Stuart Freeborn.

"Stuart Freeborn had his own way of making a bald cap," Randall confided. "I didn't have to shave my head, and it was the best I've ever known. It wouldn't work for the whole head, just for a pate on top."

A cast was made of Randall's head, upon which Freeborn painted a thin layer of vinyl exactly where he wanted the baldness to be. As the vinyl dried, he continued to paint layer upon layer of the vinyl on the cast, leaving the leading edge quite thick. As Freeborn built the vinyl up, he also added a few pockmarks and a vein here and there,

creating a realistic looking bald head.

When he reached the thickness of about one-eighth of an inch, the pate, which now resembled a broken eggshell, was ready. Freeborn placed the bald pate on Randall's head, dissolving the leading edge on the forehead and covering this dissolved edge with makeup. A fringed wig was then added around the bald pate. Whenever he removed the pate, he would dissolve the leading edge with a small amount of alcohol and use it again the following day. Randall believes there were three bald pates in all, which they rotated. He liked it so well that he kept one of the pates, feeling that he might use it again someday.

"I never knew anyone else to have that technique," Randall commented. "Freeborn is a master makeup artist."

A makeup artist seems constantly to face a different set of challenges for each film he devotes himself to. *Murder on the Orient Express* (1974), based on the Agatha Christie novel of the same name, was no exception. In this instance, it was Wendy Hiller, winner of the Academy Award for supporting actress in *Separate Tables* (1958), who presented Freeborn with an unusual challenge.

Ms. Hiller's role as Princess Dragomiroff required an aging makeup, which is normally done by stretching the skin and applying latex rubber. However, Ms. Hiller has extremely delicate skin, and the results of a previous aging makeup had disastrous enough side effects to require Hiller to carry a note from her doctor that explained that in his opinion there was no way this type of makeup effect could be achieved on Ms. Hiller's skin without ill effects.

In discussions with Freeborn about the problem, Hiller related that she always used a medical cream on her face which served as a barrier before applying any type of makeup. Freeborn had an idea, and Hiller had the courage to allow him to try it. Using some of the medical cream, Freeborn discovered a way of mixing it with the rubber latex. He then applied the mixture to her face in thin strips, thereby allowing the skin to breathe through the gaps in between. Not only did Freeborn achieve an excellent wrinkling effect, the makeup was easily removed with a mild skin lotion. Despite the fact that the aging makeup had to be applied many days in succession to Hiller's face, there was absolutely no ill effect to her skin from using Freeborn's formula.

From a nice little Agatha Christie mystery, Freeborn then plunged in with devils and demons in the production of *The Omen* (1976). When during the course of the film ferocious dogs attack the film's star, Gregory Peck, and hang from their teeth, it was Freeborn who was asked to bring realism to this scene without any calamitous results.

Freeborn created articulated fiberglass and foam rubber dogs covered with synthetic fur. The dogs were made to bite, showing their fangs with their lips drawing

One of Freeborn's most challenging films was *2001: A Space Odyssey*. Here Freeborn touches up a simian's head appliance. (*MGM*)

back, and as they bit, spittle and blood, which was pumped through tubes, would splash from their mouths. Freeborn created the fangs from a soft plastic; otherwise they could have been as lethal as real ones. Impressions were taken from tranquilized dogs.

There were numerous "blood and gore" effects for Freeborn to achieve in *The Omen*. When Gregory Peck plunged a knife into the cheek of the devil woman, Mrs. Baylock, this convincing effect was achieved also by Freeborn. The knife was to cut into the face at the cheekbone level, then be drawn down and left to hang until the victim grabbed it and pulled it free. Once it was free, blood would spurt forth from her face. Freeborn made a false cheek from foam rubber with a tube that ran under it and over her ear. The wig and costume aided in covering the tube, which continued past camera range where Freeborn pulsated the blood using a pump.

The makeup effect was filmed twice, once full face, and again with the stabbed side of the face away from the camera. Freeborn's creation was so successful and realistic that the producers chose the profile version as they believed the full-face version to be too grotesque to ever pass the censors.

It came as no surprise that Freeborn was chosen to do makeup for the phenomenally successful *Star Wars* (1977), which exploded onto the screen and brought millions into the coffers of Twentieth Century-Fox. As exciting as it is to watch *Star Wars*, it was

Peter Sellers in Stuart Freeborn's *Dr. Strangelove* makeup. Sellers played three roles in *Dr. Strangelove*. (*Columbia Pictures*)

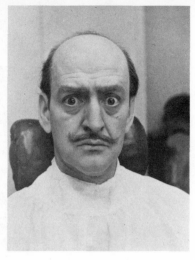

Tony Randall in Stuart Freeborn's Hercule Poirot makeup design. (*Stuart Freeborn*)

"Stuart Freeborn had his own way of making a bald cap," Randall confided. "I didn't have to shave my head and it was the best I've ever known." (*Stuart Freeborn*)

also thrilling to be a part of its making.

Freeborn was in his laboratory, knee-deep in gore for *The Omen* when director George Lucas stopped by to quiz him on his previous creatures. Freeborn's portfolio is full of them, and Lucas knew he had the man he needed to create those space oddities for the cantina sequence. One of Freeborn's creations is also the favorite of many *Star Wars* fans, that overgrown, somewhat ferocious, yet lovable Teddy bear Chewbacca, also known as Chewie.

Peter Mayhew, an over seven-foot-tall London porter, was enlisted to play Chewbacca. As if seven feet of height was not convincing enough, Freeborn added lifts to raise Chewie to eight feet. Leaning heavily on his techniques for the ape creations in *2001: A Space Odyssey*, Freeborn also created an enormous built-up head mask for Mayhew to add even more to his height.

Lucas had a rough sketch of his concept for Chewbacca, but Freeborn had to expand on the design to accommodate the necessary mechanics. An entirely different concept was employed to control Chewie's facial expression. It did not resemble the cable system combined with different masks used for *King Kong* (1976). Unfortunately, at this writing, it remains a trade secret.

Freeborn designed Chewbacca to appear friendly in repose, yet ferocious when his teeth were bared. Freeborn made the teeth in dental acrylic. Mayhew found little diffi-culty in maneuvering about in the suit, which is actually quite light and flexible. Chewbacca's fingers were Mayhew's own. In a throwback to Frankenstein, his nails were also blackened. It took Freeborn three weeks to create Chewie and a half minute for Mayhew to don the head. The costume takes a bit longer.

Freeborn also created some of the infamous cantina creatures, including a favorite of Lucas's, Greedo—Jabba's hit man. However, Freeborn's extremely exhausting schedule finally forced him into the hospital during production. A vacation would have been preferable, but at least it was restful. Although at the time of his hospitalization Freeborn had many of the cantina creatures at least three-quarters of the way done, Lucas returned to Hollywood and employed Rick Baker to finish up. Baker, who was also extremely busy at the time, gathered a crew and supervised their making of slip rubber masks of the remaining aliens.

Early in 1977 Freeborn spent five weeks with the Star Trek Company modeling reptilian creatures for the television film *Spectre*. He had to create a huge skull of reptilian shape for this film. The skull was designed with quite large facial holes. Freeborn created it from fiberglass, molding it in the usual way, as it was too complicated to be vacuum-formed.

An object cannot be vacuum-formed when it has undercuts or deep shapes close together. A sheet of plastic is laid over the

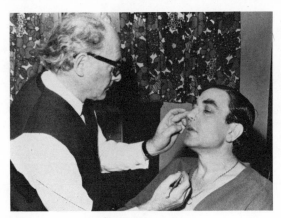

Albert Finney undergoes a makeup transformation for his role as Hercule Poirot in *Murder on the Orient Express*. (*Stuart Freeborn*)

Freeborn declined to repeat the makeup on Finney he had created on Randall, who played Hercule Poirot in an earlier film. He based his design on Finney's approach to the character personality-wise. (*Stuart Freeborn*)

model which has had small holes drilled in it. The plastic is then softened by heat and sucked down over the model by a vacuum pressure applied through the small holes. If the plastic is stretched very far, it becomes too thin and breaks. The plastic also tends to web across two high points that are close.

The skull had to be covered with the thinnest possible foam latex ''skin'' Freeborn could create. Because the reptile's skin surface was composed of scales and bumps, Freeborn knew he would have many bubble traps. This proved true on his first try, although it had cooked perfectly in four hours. Freeborn tried a different approach on his second try.

He added a very thin layer of slush latex to the mold before adding the foam latex, and he cooked the mold for four hours. Before he removed it from the oven, he pinched the flash (excess foam rubber which has squeezed out between the mold) from the lowest hole before opening it. It took another three hours of cooking before it was cured, or finished, probably because the mold was much wetter because of the slush. It was well worth the wait, however, as the final results were perfect.

Early in 1977 Freeborn joined the director of *The Omen,* Richard Donner, and became a part of an amazing challenge, to make two films simultaneously. Referred to as *Superman I* and *II,* nearly half of *Superman II* was completed before *Superman I* was finished in September of 1978. During filming Free-

Wendy Hiller's role in *Murder on the Orient Express* required an aging effect which her sensitive skin could not tolerate. Freeborn was able to overcome the difficulty, and the effect, as seen here, is most convincing. (*Stuart Freeborn*)

Freeborn and son Graham at work in Freeborn's lab on some of the creatures for *Spectre*. The film starred Robert Culp, Gig Young, John Hurt, and Gordon Jackson, and was rated as the best television show of 1977. (*Stuart Freeborn*)

Kathy Freeborn, an excellent makeup artist in her own right, helps to emphasize Chewbacca's height as she struggles with a last-minute touch-up. (*Copyright © 1977 Twentieth Century-Fox Film Corporation*)

born traveled extensively. Filming was done in Calgary and Banff, Alberta, Canada; New York; and New Mexico.

Returning to England in the summer of 1978, Freeborn completed his work on *Superman I* in September, only to begin on the second *Star Wars* feature in October. In 1979 Freeborn will be back on the second Superman feature.

Freeborn's wife, Kathy, is also an excellent makeup artist, very often heading the Makeup Department on her films. Son Graham, too, is in the makeup field and often assists his father. The Freeborns have two other sons in the film industry, though not in makeup.

The United Kingdom is most fortunate in having one of the most talented, inventive, and energetic men in the makeup field today as their own. Although we've only skimmed the surface of Freeborn's immense knowledge, we know there is much to be explored.

Freeborn is most pleased with his creation Chewbacca from *Star Wars*. Peter Mayhew played the giant Wookie in *Star Wars*, as well as in the sequel. (*Copyright © 1977 Twentieth Century-Fox Film Corporation*)

Chapter 17

DICK SMITH

Dick Smith began with television when it was in its infancy. He was hired by NBC in 1945 as the first staff makeup artist in television. Smith had picked up a little experience with theatrical makeup while at Yale University.

Television and Dick Smith grew up together. From 1945 to 1950 Smith not only developed materials and techniques for use on black-and-white television but added and trained a staff of twenty makeup artists. Smith invented quick-change techniques for live television dramas, pioneered the use of plastics and foam latex in television, and developed the makeup shades for color television.

When Claire Bloom starred in *Victoria Regina* in 1957, it was an hour and a half *live* drama of the life of Queen Victoria from a young woman to an old queen. It was Smith's quick-change masterpiece. In the first act Claire, in her twenties, wore a light-brown wig over her own black hair. Between Acts One and Two, she had three minutes and forty seconds to change to a plump age forty. She ran from one set to another and stood while wardrobe ladies quickly altered her costume by removing tacked-on panels. Then hair stylist Virginia Darcy had thirty seconds to work the bun which was high on the wig to a low-neck position. Bloom sat at the desk where she

would begin Act Two and posed while Smith and his assistant stood beside her applying foam-rubber jowls and neck. A third makeup artist applied adhesive to the appliances and handed them to Smith while counting off the seconds allowed. A rubber nose was also applied. Smith used cigarette girl-type trays on which they had the necessary tools and makeup. They had little more than two minutes for a job which would normally take an hour and a half. They made it.

The next change required Claire Bloom to age to sixty but allowed only one minute and twenty seconds. The costume change was simply a rubber dowager's hump in a shawl thrown over her shoulders. Darcy then performed the "miracle" of putting a gray wig over the brown wig without it looking "wiggy." Smith popped on foam-latex bags, eyelids, a little lip and chinpiece, more makeup, and *printed* lines on her forehead with a special rubber stamp.

The last scene called for the queen to be eighty, sitting in her wheelchair on her balcony while the people cheered below. Smith talked the director into a "cheat," using a double with a complete entire face mask designed to look like a continuation of the previous makeups. The queen's lines were spoken as voice-overs. The show and the makeups were a triumph. Only one thing went wrong. Time ran out and the makeup credit never reached the screen!

After fourteen years with New York's NBC-TV, Dick has designed and executed makeup for hundreds of their biggest shows, including "Kraft Television Theatre," "Robert Montgomery Presents," "Producers' Showcase," "Hallmark Hall of Fame," "The NBC Opera," *Cyrano de Bergerac* with José Ferrer, *Peter Pan* with Mary Martin, *The Little Foxes* with Greer Garson, *The Barretts of Wimpole Street* with Katharine Cornell, *Victoria Regina* with Claire Bloom, *Mayerling* with Audrey Hepburn, *The Taming of the Shrew* and *Twelfth Night* with Maurice Evans, and *The Moon and Sixpence* with Sir Laurence Olivier.

Smith believes his executions on Sir Laurence Olivier for *The Moon and Sixpence* were one of his favorite creations to date. The story ends with Olivier becoming leprous, and the makeup went beautifully, drawing the supreme compliment from Olivier that the makeup would be acting for him.

Smith resigned from NBC-TV in 1959 and went to work for David Susskind's Talent Associates, where he designed makeup for such notable programs as *Medea* with Dame Judith Anderson, *Don Quixote* with Lee J. Cobb, *Oliver Twist* with Eric Portman, *Ethan Frome* with Sterling Hayden, *The Dachet Diamonds* with Rex Harrison, *The Scarlet Pimpernel* with Michael Rennie, and *The Heiress* with Julie Harris. Other productions included *The Power and the Glory*, again with Sir Laurence Olivier, *The Devil and Dan'l Webster* with Edward G. Robinson and David Wayne, "Dupont Show of the Month," and "Breck Family Classics." He also designed makeup for the first series dealing with the macabre, "Way Out."

In 1961 Smith created the makeup for Anthony Quinn in David Susskind's film production *Requiem for a Heavyweight* (1962). Then Smith faced a very difficult challenge. Stanley Kramer brought him to Hollywood where he was to create about a dozen masks for stunt men in *It's a Mad, Mad, Mad, Mad World* (1963). When he arrived

Opposite: Smith removed the jaw from a plaster skull, readjusted it in an awkward position, and using Plastolain, melted wax, and a phony eye, created this horrendous creature for *The Picture of Dorian Gray*, a television film produced by David Susskind. (*Dick Smith*)

Jack Palance as Jekyll and as Hyde in the 1967 televison production of *The Strange Case of Dr. Jekyll and Mr. Hyde.* Palance's nose has been lengthened for the character of Mr. Hyde. A more jutting chin has been added, along with thicker lips and longer earlobes. A lower hairpiece and jutting eyebrows add to the character's air of evil. (*Dick Smith*)

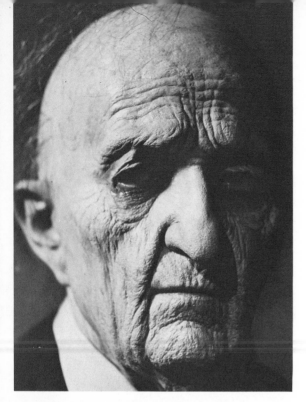

Smith aged Jonathan Frid to a hundred-and-fifty-year-old vampire for ''House of Dark Shadows'' by use of a foam-latex mask. (*Dick Smith*)

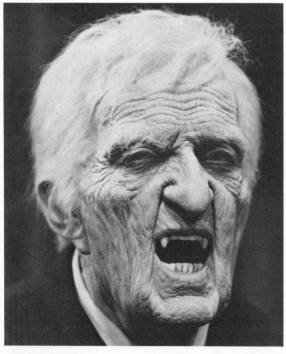

The vampire of television's ''House of Dark Shadows,'' Jonathan Frid, in Smith's old-age makeup. (*Dick Smith*)

Dick Smith begins the makeup process that will turn the thirty-two-year-old Dustin Hoffman into a one-hundred-twenty-year-old Indian for *Little Big Man*. (*Dick Smith*)

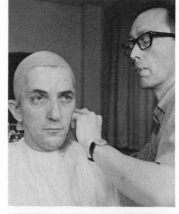

Smith delicately glues the nose appliance into place. (*Dick Smith*)

The upper lip appliance is attached. (*Dick Smith*)

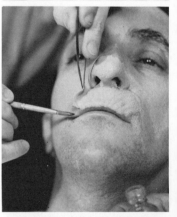

One of Smith's innovations was movable eyelids. (*Dick Smith*)

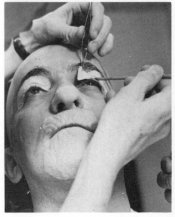

The forehead appliance is attached. (*Dick Smith*)

A one-piece appliance including cheeks and neck is secured. (*Dick Smith*)

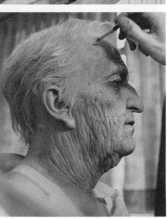

Liver spots were carefully painted in to add to the realistic makeup effect. (*Dick Smith*)

Dustin Hoffman in *Little Big Man* wearing twelve overlapping foam-latex appliances on head and shoulders to effect the appearance of a one-hundred-and-twenty-year-old Indian. (*Dick Smith*)

there, Smith discovered that he had a three-week deadline for a job that would normally have taken almost three months of hard work.

Smith was determined to meet this challenge. Kramer wanted fleshlike masks for the thirteen stunt men to make them look like the stars for whom they were doubling. It was no easy assignment with the time element involved, and Smith virtually worked night and day, existing on only one hour of sleep each night in order to complete the assignment. "Now, that was when I was forty and obviously very healthy," Dick commented.

Later in 1962, Smith worked on such films as *All the Way Home* (1963) with Jean Simmons and Robert Preston, Otto Preminger's *The Cardinal* (1963), and *The World of Henry Orient* (1963) with Peter Sellers.

Oriental makeups were designed for Anthony Quinn as Kublai Khan and Robert Hossein as his son in *Marco the Magnificent* (1965) filmed during 1964 in Yugoslavia.

Returning to television in the winter of 1966–67, Smith created makeup for *The Diary of Anne Frank* and Hallmark's *Soldier in Love*, a story about Sir Winston Churchill's ancestor, the Duke of Marlborough.

The latter required effecting old-age masks for the beautiful Jean Simmons, Claire Bloom, and Keith Michell.

In 1967 Smith created one of his favorite makeups when he made Hal Holbrook up for the television production of *Mark Twain Tonight!* The application required five hours, and Smith was rewarded for his diligence when he received an Emmy for his creation.

Smith then became involved with Jack Palance in *The Strange Case of Dr. Jekyll and Mr. Hyde.* This makeup was nominated for an Emmy. Changing Palance's face was quite a challenge because Palance has an enormous face. Since in makeup you can only add appliances, not take away, the problem Smith faced was where could he possibly add.

He became inspired by a little ivory carving of a satyr which he had in his art collection. The sculpture had retained a rather flat, half-cylinder form to it which reminded Smith of Palance's facial structure, flat and broad. It occurred to Smith how appropriate for this particular script, which was a rather modern Freudian thing, that Mr. Hyde should be a satyr.

Because Palance has a small bashed-in nose, Smith straightened out his nose to make it look a little handsomer for Dr. Jekyll, and then gave him a satyr-type nose for Mr. Hyde. He even gave him a bigger chin, though Palance certainly isn't deficient in that area; however, he wanted to create a more jutting chin. Palance has very thin lips, so Smith gave him a thick, sensual lower lip and fattened up his upper lip and the tissue at the corner of the mouth. He gave him a low Neanderthal-type brow structure and little bags or crinkles under the eyes. At Palance's suggestion, Smith changed his ears by simply lengthening his earlobes. They also used a hairpiece that lowered his entire hairline, but in a rather attractive way.

When Palance was all dressed up in his tails, he looked quite handsome, and it became very believable that "Mr. Hyde" could live in society and be accepted as a rather unusual-looking individual, but nothing so totally bestial as to cause anyone to call the police.

"I therefore think it is a much more believable rendition than earlier versions of Mr. Hyde," Smith went on to explain. "As far as the makeup is concerned, there's nothing remarkable about the execution of it. I've done foam-latex lips before, and by using modern adhesives like Medico or Secure Liquid, even a very large lip can be held on quite securely. The rest was fairly straightforward."

It was in 1967 that Smith did a makeup for the "House of Dark Shadows" television series, creating a one-hundred-and-fifty-year-old makeup for Jonathan Frid who played the vampire Barnabas Collins.

Because there was little time and a low budget, this job was hurriedly done, but it was important to Smith as a testing ground for techniques which he would later use for *Little Big Man* (1970).

The chance to do a truly big makeup on a star does not come along often in films. In 1969 Smith was given one of those rare opportunities which was to make Dustin Hoffman one hundred and twenty-one years old for *Little Big Man.* This was the type of job that Smith likes best. A single makeup into which he could pour all his knowledge and art to create a character that was completely realistic. Smith spent three months creating this makeup and the others that Hoffman wore in the film. Since Hoffman was only thirty-two at the time, making him appear to be one hundred and twenty-one meant a complete masking of his head down to his shoulders. Usually a makeup of this kind is done with a one-piece mask covering the face, like the one used on Agnes Moorehead for the *Lost Moment* (1947). However, Smith prefers to cover the same area with a number of smaller overlapping appliances because he is able to fit and glue them on more precisely. This method does involve more preparation time because of the number of molds and intricacies of designing the overlapping appliances. The *Little Big Man* appliances covered the following areas and were applied in the order listed: the eyelids, nose and upper lip, lower lip and chin, the ears, sides of face and front half of neck, shoulder hump, bald head consisting of front and back overlapping pieces glued together before application, and the eye bags. Finally, appliances on the back of the hands.

There were several innovations in this makeup. In the past, fake eyelids, whether for old age or Orientals, were fit slightly in front of the actor's own lids. They did not move, and if the actor looked down, his own lid appeared, unnaturally, from behind the false one. It was on "Dark Shadows" that Smith experimented with making a foam-latex lid that would actually fold and unfold naturally. This required a delicate and involved mold. The usual gypsum materials were too fragile, but Smith found that he could use U.S. Gypsum's Epoxical 405 for the eyelids and other appliances requiring delicate detail. The eyelids he made for "House of Dark Shadows" were a partial success, but they pointed the way to the perfectly movable lids Dustin Hoffman wore. Ironically, after all that care, Hoffman does not blink in any of the close-ups used in the film.

Another innovation for this type of makeup was to prepaint it with special colors—not makeup—before application. This saved a great deal of makeup time and gave more subtle coloration. All of the veins on the bald head were airbrushed and each liver spot carefully painted. The bald head was enormously effective because it was made in foam latex instead of the usual plastic cap material. Plastic caps are smooth and featureless. With foam latex, every anatomical detail can be three-dimensional, but one cannot make a whole bald head in a two-piece mold. Stuart Freeborn solved the problem in *2001: A Space Odyssey* when aging Keir Dullea. He made his bald head in two pieces, front and back with gently overlapping edges so that there was no apparent seam. Smith elaborated Freeborn's innovation. After the bald head was assembled and painted, individual white hairs were punched into it to provide a fringe around the ears, and eyebrows that appeared to be really growing.

In spite of all the prepainting, it still took five hours to apply the makeup to Hoffman. Foam latex appliances are made so soft and flexible that gluing them on requires great care. The eyelids alone took over half an hour. The process started at six A.M., so Hoffman could start filming at eleven. Smith was ably assisted, especially with the hand appliances, by Irving Pringle.

It took an hour to clean off Hoffman's face. All appliances are destroyed when removed, which means one must have duplicates for each day's filming. Fortunately, the scene of Hoffman at one hundred and twenty-one took only three days to shoot. Smith considers the *Little Big Man* makeup his best individual creation and has warm affection for Hoffman. When Smith did the film *House of Dark Shadows* (1970), he used some of the same facial pieces, but he did resculpt the forehead piece as he hadn't been too pleased with the modeling of the first one.

This film was done after Smith did the *Little Big Man* makeup. Again, it was a low-budget situation, and he couldn't do an elaborate foam-latex bald head as he had done for Dustin Hoffman, so he improvised. He attached the back half of the bald head from the *Little Big Man* makeup to the back of Jonathan Frid's plaster head. Then he sprayed bald-cap plastic over the front of the plaster head and around onto the back over the foam-latex appliance. The result was a smooth plastic bald cap in front, with a wrinkled foam-latex back attached. After it was on, most of the smooth front was covered with the foam-latex forehead appliance. It worked very well and was much more effective than the white wig which had been used for the television version.

The small but intriguing problem on the *House of Dark Shadows* film was the request by the director, Dan Curtis, to produce truly realistic vampire bites. He didn't want just two little holes in the neck, he wanted a whole big bite, as though all of the teeth had chewed into the neck. Smith tried to sculpt teeth bites but found they just didn't look right. They looked sculptured, not bitten.

That evening while observing his wife preparing veal cutlets, he was seized by an inspiration and requested she save him a raw veal cutlet. After supper he bit into the raw meat very deliberately, and then carefully made a mold of the bitten area. From this, he was able to make a wax duplicate, and by very slightly opening the wax duplicate by deepening the holes made by the canine teeth, he achieved exactly what was needed—a very realistic bite of a vampire. This model was made into a foam-latex mold from which the foam-latex appliances of the vampire bites were made.

In 1971 Smith was sent to England to talk with Marlon Brando about *The Godfather* (1971) makeup. Brando was reluctant to use foam-latex appliances so it was decided to try to age him with old-age stipple, also called "stretch latex." Brando was forty-four at the time, and two coats of latex stipple over his face and neck added ten years of texture. Shadows and liver spots made it real, but his jawline remained too young. A dental plumper was made by Dr. Henry Dwork. This device was a light silver band around his lower teeth. In the jowl area, dental plastic was formed and attached to make the jowls protrude. Brando's light hair was dyed, and then gray streaks were added in front. His eyebrows and moustache were also grayed. Finally, his teeth were stained. The entire makeup took an hour and a quarter. When "The Don" was supposed to be ten years older, Smith used four coats of stipple, more shadows, and gray hair.

The Godfather was the beginning for Smith of what he regards as special makeup effects. The director, Francis Coppola, wanted the bullet hits to be very realistic, especially when Al Pacino shoots police captain Sterling Hayden in the forehead. Smith devised a method. A one-sixteenth squib, which is a small explosive, was glued to a small, thin, metal disc. The disc was glued to the center of Hayden's forehead. The wires from the squib were run through the actor's hair. Then a thin foam-latex appliance which duplicated the appearance of Hayden's forehead was glued over the entire area, except for a small circular area surrounding the squib. After makeup was applied, blood was injected through the appliance into the air pocket around the squib with a hypodermic needle. The special effects man, A. D. Flowers, hooked up the squib and, at the moment of shooting, detonated the squib, blowing a hole in the latex forehead and allowing the blood to stream out in a very realistic way.

In 1972 Dick became involved in the horrifying thriller *The Exorcist* (1972). Dick faced some incredible makeup challenges in this film of a young girl's demonic possession. Long months and hours of conferences resulted in the decision to show a subtle and natural transformation designed to keep the audience guessing as to whether the young girl was sick—or possessed! Thirteen-year-old Linda Blair gave an excellent portrayal as the possessed "Regan."

Eight-to-ten small foam-latex appliances

Smith aged Marlon Brando for his role in *The Godfather* by using old-age stipple, a dental plumper, and dying his light hair. Gray streaks were then added to the front area of his hair. (*Dick Smith*)

were used to simulate cuts which progressed to uglier wounds. These wounds began to alter her mouth and eyebrows. Contact lenses were used, and jaundice and black-and-blue discolorations. Her hair was matted and her teeth tinted. Smith credits much of the effectiveness of the makeup to the great skill of Owen Roizman, who was the director of photography.

One of the more difficult effects was to create the appearance of the girl's neck blowing up. Smith first made a rubber bladder about two inches in diameter and connected it to a narrow polyethylene tube. A foam-rubber normal neck appliance was used to cover the bladder. However, the bladder turned out to be too bulky and the appliance wrinkled when Blair turned her head. The next approach was to glue a circular piece of rubber from a prophylactic with Medico adhesive to the polyethylene tube under one edge. In order to ensure an airtight seal under the membrane edges, the tube was first embedded in a small flat piece of foam. As the foam neck was glued on, it was stretched considerably to keep it smooth no matter what the head position. The membrane was then blown up by mouth.

When faced with the difficulty of Blair's head spinning completely around, the only logical solution was to make a complete dummy as realistic as possible. In a "sitting-up-in-bed" position, Linda's entire body was molded in sections using fast-setting plaster bandages. Plaster positives were cast and refined, then hydrocal molds were made from the casts.

When Blair's head was molded, Smith glued the appliance on, put in her teeth and scleral contacts, and using dental alginate timed to set in two and a half minutes, Blair was able to keep her eyes and mouth open and smile. The results were perfect.

It was necessary to make the head and chest of the dummy of polyester resin as that supported the installation of an axle for rotating the head. However, the remainder was of a soft polyurethane foam with a rubber skin. Armatures were used in the arms and legs to allow for any slight adjustment of her position.

The chief special effects man, Marcel Vercoutere, is credited by Smith with having done a marvelous job with the mechanics. A remote-control device was used for moving the eyeballs in the head, and piping was installed through the axle for steam so the dummy's "breath" would condense in the studio the same as the live actor's did.

In *The Exorcist*, anyone who walks into Regan's room becomes very cold. The characters didn't have to "act" at this when they entered the set. It was decided to refrigerate the room to about zero.

In order to effect the illusion of lettering rising on Linda's stomach, Dick found that when he used trichloroethane on foam latex, it puffed up the latex but then evaporated quickly without leaving a blemish. He created a quarter-inch-thick foam-latex appliance to cover Linda from neck to hips, modeling in the illusion of gaunt ribs. The film was reversed in the camera and the camera run at a slow speed. Linda's pajamas were stiffened and pinned so they would not move; and the letters were produced by painted-on trichloroethane. They were then dried with hot air from a flameless heat gun, and when the lettering was almost faded, the camera zoomed back from its tight shot. When this was projected normally, the letters appear as though they are growing larger, spelling out "Help me."

Trying to effect projectile vomiting from Linda's mouth was no easy task either. Director William Friedkin wanted to do a full-face shot. By using the flameless heat gun again, Smith formed thin plexiglass sheets over plaster forms of Linda's cheeks with mouth corners retracted. From the plastic sheets Smith then made very flat tubes of about three-sixteenths of an inch thick and one and a quarter inches wide with a passage of one-sixteenth inch by about an inch. At the mouth corners, these became round tubing that connected almost like a horse's bit, with a nozzle opening on the front side. The back ends passed under the ears and then connected with rubber tubes to a pump. The pump forced hot pea soup through the tubes and out Linda's mouth. A wig, makeup, and a partial mask concealed everything.

Max Von Sydow's old-age makeup was one of the most difficult Smith ever created. The temperature range created unique problems during the filming in Iraq. Smith was pleased with the opportunity for testing the makeups that this film required, as they were able to achieve a degree of perfection almost impossible today.

Foam-latex pieces were necessary for Von Sydow, as he was only forty-four at the time, and for dramatic reasons as well, since many close-ups were planned which required the makeup to be executed with infinite care and attention to detail.

In the heat, Smith discovered that the stipple on the neck and hands sweated off quite quickly, and in the cold some of the latex stipple became a bit brittle. They found that Allen Arthur Inc. Secure Liquid was superior to Medico for foam-latex appliances near the mouth, and after much experimentation developed an old-age stipple latex that was impervious to the heat.

Max Von Sydow's makeup took three hours to apply. The facial coloring required eleven shades of base and stipple colors. Although the "demon" makeup is what everyone thinks about in regard to *The Exorcist*, Smith feels that his best work in the film was Von Sydow's makeup, because it was filmed extremely close, with no diffusion whatsoever over the lens; yet most people who have seen the film are unaware that Von Sydow is wearing an extremely heavy and elaborate makeup. Smith was superbly assisted on the production by makeup artists Bob Laden and Reg Tackley and hair stylist Bill Farley.

In 1975 Smith created an old-age makeup for Walter Matthau in *The Sunshine Boys* (1975), which had one interesting facet about it. Walter has a good face for aging with old-age stipple, but his hair is impossible. He has thick black hair with a low hairline, and it wouldn't have been feasible to gray his hair or put a wig on it. So Smith suggested something rather drastic which was to make Matthau nearly bald. Smith employed a process he had created for a character in *The Godfather II* (1974).

Smith spent about four hours going all over the top of Walter's head with tiny little scissors that surgeons use for iris operations on the eye. Dick would part Walter's hair and would cut right down to the scalp, cutting out little clumps of hair. He had to do it in a very precisely scattered pattern all over his head until he had reduced the hair on the top of his head to about 15 percent of its original growth, leaving thin hair, mostly in the middle. In order to keep them from growing out again, the electric razor with a fine screen is used right over the long hairs that remain. It will not cut the long hairs, but it will cut the ones that have been thinned out to the scalp. Provided, of course, that you don't let them grow out too long. Should the actor be off for a week, he has to shave it himself at least every other day so that the hairs don't grow too long.

The stubble had to be covered with an opaque makeup and the dark hair grayed. Being as black as it was, it couldn't be done

perfectly, but the general effect was certainly convincing. Matthau's face was then made up with old-age stipple latex.

Smith had more special makeup effects in the film *Taxi Driver* (1975). There is one memorable scene where an actor has his hand shot off. The problem Smith faced was that the action was to be shot on location on a staircase in a narrow hallway in a real building. The first suggestion that comes to mind is to have the hand yanked off with a wire or a monofilament, but because of its being shot in an actual hallway, there was no place to pull the hand off out of camera range without its looking like a hand suddenly traveling through the air.

It occurred to Smith to make the hand actually blow up. He made molds of the actor's right hand in two positions: one a normal, relaxed position and the other mold in a doubled-up fist position. Using these, he constructed a stump made out of latex rubber, reinforced at the stump with rigid plastic. This stump was designed to fit over the actor's fist. The stump, of course, is more than just a stump. It is about four inches longer than what it would normally be, but that isn't too much, and with a longer sleeve, it becomes a reasonable extension.

Usually, the more hand you try to remove, the more ridiculous the remaining arm looks. If you remove ten inches of hand and wrist, the stump that is left looks much too long. Dick worked on the premise of leaving as much there as possible, so the stump represented the thumb and half of the palm.

Inside the stump were tubes through which the blood could spout after the hand was blown off. Once the stump was constructed, Dick used the mold of the open hand and made another mold from which he could construct a wax hand which would eventually be the hand that is blown off. This was like a wax glove of four fingers with most of the palm hollow. It would then slip over the stump and fit very nicely, and with a minimum of mortician's wax applied around the edges, it could be blended in and appear as though it were a whole hand.

An unusual technique was employed by Smith to thin Walter Matthau's own sumptuously thick hair for his part in *The Sunshine Boys*. Matthau's face was made up with old-age stipple. (*Dick Smith*)

The wax had to be formulated so that it was strong enough to take a small amount of abuse in handling, yet at the same time, be brittle enough to fracture as it exploded. Dick created several wax hands, and inside each he made a wax chamber that went along the base of the four fingers in the upper part of the palm. Two squibs were placed into the chamber, which was filled with "blood" and sealed.

The wires that would explode the squibs were fed through the stump. The hand was painted with artists' acrylic paint. When the squibs were detonated, it literally blew the wax part off and into a million pieces, and the blood went flying all over. The special effects people would pump the blood, which came spurting out of the stump. It was a very gory effect. So gory in fact that the final scenes in *Taxi Driver* toned down all the bloody parts by printing the scenes darker and printing the reds in a browner shade—and by very fast editing.

Smith was faced with another "hand problem" in *Marathon Man* (1976). Roy Scheider has a fight with a thug who throws a wire around Scheider's neck in an attempt to strangle him. Roy puts his hand up and catches the wire, and the wire wraps around the outside of his right hand, cutting into the flesh and causing it to bleed.

The only material that Smith could find that would allow the wire to cut into it, without cutting the actor's hand, was gelatin. Smith formulated gelatin and glycerine to create an appliance that would be soft enough. On the inside of the appliance were passageways to pump the blood through. Picture wire was used because it is a woven wire and isn't as sharp as a thin piano wire would be.

The difficulties came in trying to glue the gelatin appliance on without the blood leaking through and ruining the shot. The solution was to line the gelatin appliance with a flexible plastic to which adhesive would stick. It was a tricky procedure, which took an hour to prepare before filming. On the first try, the seal was perfect—too good, because there was no way for the air to get out as the blood was pumped in. The pressure ruptured the seal and ruined the first take. On the second try, Smith left an escape vent for the air. The blood filled the passages properly and spurted when the wire cut through.

In another scene in *Marathon Man*, Laurence Olivier turns around and cuts the throat of a man with a blade concealed in his arm. Smith created this effect with a device he had developed for *Godfather II* but which was edited out of that picture because the film was so long.

He used a foam-latex neck appliance, behind which was attached a tube to pump the blood. The neck is cut and then stuck together with Karo syrup blood. When the action takes place, the knife is passed across the actor's throat, he jerks his head back as one normally would react, and this breaks the seal of the cut. The slit in the rubber neck opens up, and behind it the skin is painted the color of blood. At the same time, the blood is pumped out. It looks very realistic.

Smith's major activity for 1976 was as a consultant on two films. He didn't work on the entire film but ran in and out doing special chores. *The Sentinel* (1977) was one, and *The Heretic* (1977) the other.

The Sentinel made *Taxi Driver* look tame, with all the bloody things in it. Fred Stuthman, who had his throat cut in *Marathon Man*, plays the father of the leading lady, Cristina Raines. In the film, he dies and comes back in a macabre scene as an apparition. This apparition chases the girl until he finally corners her. The girl, in desperation, stabs the apparition with a kitchen knife.

Director Michael Lerner wanted this scene to be tremendously gory. He wanted to show close-up insert shots of each stab that the girl makes into the actor, who is dressed only in shorts and made up in a deadly gray tone. The first stab is in his left shoulder, which leaves a five-inch gash. The next is into his naked chest, right to the hilt of the knife. She then stabs him over the left eye down through the eyeball, and then she cuts the tip of his nose off.

Several duplicates were made of the kitchen knife, plus the real one, and one having a retractable blade. This one was used for the shoulder stabbing. Smith made a soft plastic appliance that covered from the shoulder down to the elbow on the front side of the arm. This plastic appliance had a five-inch gash in it, and the piece of plastic that was cut out for the gash was saved, attached to the monofilament fishing line, then replaced, sealed with mortician's wax, and made up. The appliance had a hollow slot which led to the gash. On the other end, buried in the appliance and coming out the back side, was a tube which would be attached to pump the blood.

Smith's own hand was used for these effects, since they were close-ups and only the hand would show. Even though it was supposed to be the girl's hand, it happened so fast, one can't really tell the character of it, and Smith knew better than the actress how to make the effects work.

Holding the monofilament line in his left hand and the knife in his right, he had to plunge the knife so that the blade retracted right at the shoulder, alongside the gash. He plunged the knife into the shoulder, then dragged it down the length of the cut and pulled it away. As he did this, his left hand ripped out the plug very quickly. At the same time, someone pumped blood so that the minute the knife is withdrawn and the plug drawn away, blood is pouring out of this five-inch gash.

The chest stabbing was simulated in this way. Smith made a mold of the actor's chest and shoulders, and then made a number of Styrofoam reproductions of the chest. About a half inch behind the center of the chest he made a cavity into which blood could be pumped. Instead of using the original kitchen knife, they used another knife which had a much thicker blade, so that when it plunged into the Styrofoam, it would leave a wider hole than the kitchen knife's blade would have left.

Because the blood was under pressure, all they had to do was plunge the knife into the Styrofoam chest, and when it was withdrawn, the blood would immediately pour out. This was the second effect and perhaps the easiest, although there was a lot of work to making the chests and painting them. A number of chests were made because they could use one only once.

The most difficult effect to achieve was the stabbing through the eyeball. Naturally, there is no way to do this on a man's face and have it appear realistic. Smith made a life mask of the actor's face in a lifelike grimace. To do this, he cast the actor's head and face with his eyes open. Scleral contacts were used to protect the eyes, and the eyeballs were anesthetized. The actor's mouth was opened with his face in a rather shocked expression.

Smith reproduced a head made out of polyester resin (like fiberglass) with a large oval hollowed-out area that went from above the man's left eyebrow down to his cheekbone. He made a reproduction of the missing area in a soft colorful material. The tip of the nose was also made out of this material. He designed the head this way so that he could repair it if the shot didn't work.

This involved some very complicated molding, calling for a number of stages, but Smith achieved the effect that he wanted. He had a mold which would make him a perfect plug to go into the missing place and also a mold to reproduce the missing tip of the nose.

These plugs had to be made out of a material that could be cut through, and Smith wound up using a mixture of gelatin, glycerine, and, of all things, bread crumbs! The bread crumbs were most important because they stiffened the gelatin mixture so that it wouldn't be bouncy or rubbery but also kept it weak so it could be cut through easily. He could have made a firmer gelatin/glycerine mixture, but that wouldn't have been difficult to cut—or a weak gelatin mixture that would have cut easily but would have been too soft, like a dessert mixture.

The eyeball was done separately, involving another mold. A perfect eyeball was needed to fit into the socket that was made from the second mold. The eyeball was made out of a thin skin of plastic filled with ordinary gelatin and hot water, which gelled when it was chilled.

On the back side of the gelatin and breadcrumb mold there was a passage that would conduct blood in through tubes through the inside of the head. Where the knife was going to plunge into the gelatin just above the eyeball, the blood passage was expanded so that it was very close to the surface of the gelatin skin, thus making it easy to cut. The knife then sliced through the eyeball, which was equally soft, and down through the lower lid. This was all made very thin, and the passages that carried the blood were very close to the surface, so it was easy to cut through.

One of the big problems Smith faced was finding a way to glue the gelatin plug into the plastic head so the blood wouldn't leak through prematurely. He used Glop Type 8, which he found in a hardware store. After it was glued in, the edges were sealed with mortician's wax. A sealer was painted over the wax, and then acrylic paints were used to blend everything in. A wig was added, and the other eyeball was made to match the actor's own.

The nose was relatively simple. The tip was gelatin, and the area that remains after the tip is cut off was prepainted red with little holes in it to bleed so that it would look like the stump of a nose after the tip had been cut off.

The knife used for the actual cutting was a real kitchen knife. The first time they did the shot, a plugged bloodline fouled things up, but the second shot went beautifully. As the knife went down and passed through the eyeball, the eyeball turned over and came halfway out of the socket and, of course, bled profusely. The nose came off well, too.

Smith was rather surprised that they were able to show it on the screen, but he thinks one of the reasons was because it was not being done to a human being. The victim is actually a "monster," a dead person, a ghoul, and that way one can accept what is happening. He feels that if the audience saw it being done to an actual human being, it would make them sick.

At the end of *The Sentinel* some of the demons are supposed to punish themselves for their failure by scratching the skin off their faces. In developing this trick, Smith made a new material. This was a paste made of methyl cellulose that can be spread on the skin and can be made reasonably smooth. It can also be modeled in some other form. It stays on reasonably well and is flexible, unlike mortician's wax or putty. Smith did one face of an extra who was supposed to have a completely scarred face and found that the material stayed on beautifully. After the material was applied, a sealer was put over it because it had a lot of water in it.

This material can be made in a "blood-red" color, applied to the skin, sealed, and then made up so that the skin looks normal. Anytime this material is cut into with a dull knife or other instrument, it actually appears as though you've cut into flesh. It makes a very realistic effect.

When Chris Sarandon revealed that he was damned, cracks appeared in his face. These were done by taking a fine silk gauze, painting it with unplasticized bald-cap material, which made it very tough and thin. Connecting cracks were then drawn on. Each crack is one-eighth of an inch long. The pattern was cut out with scissors and a piece of monofilament line was tied to one end of the pattern. Sticky blood was applied on the underside of the gauze, and then it was stuck to the skin. Soft melted mortician's wax was then spread thinly over this pattern, burying it. The forehead was then made up to look normal.

On a close-up of the actor, the monofilament is raised, lifting the pattern off the forehead. As it comes through the wax, it leaves openings the exact size and shape of the gauze pattern.

There were far less makeup problems on *Exorcist II: The Heretic* (1977). Linda Blair's contract relieved her of wearing the demon makeup again, so it was applied to two doubles. Some of the same appliances could be used; some had to be made over. Max Von Sydow appeared briefly in his old-age

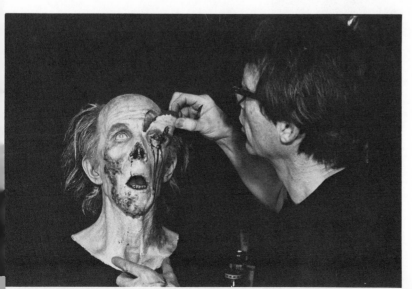

Smith carefully inserts an eye plug made from gelatin, glycerine, and bread crumbs in the eye socket of this gory apparition appearing in the film *The Sentinel*. (*Photo courtesy of Dick Smith*)

makeup and also as the character at a younger age. "Now," Smith says, "the audience will see how much Von Sydow was changed by the makeup."

There was only one new makeup. An African boy becomes possessed. The Linda Blair type of makeup would not have been appropriate, so Smith designed facial distortions that were based on a form of leprosy. A similar makeup had been tested, along with many others, on Blair for *The Exorcist*, and rejected, but on Joey Green it worked well, as did the demon contact lenses like the ones Blair wore.

Smith is not happy with the trend in films to more and more realistic blood and gore, but he does enjoy inventing solutions to the problems. Although his first hero was Jack Pierce, and his early fascination was for monster makeup, Smith prefers creating character makeup to gory effects. By "character makeup" Smith means a makeup using appliances.

"There is something absolutely magical about making up an actor with appliances," Smith commented. "When you paint over the appliances with the first layer of flesh color, all that rubber suddenly becomes a part of the actor's face. Actually it is no longer the actor's face but a new human being that you have created—like Dr. Frankenstein. It's a creative thrill that I never tire of. Many of these characters that I have created are as real to me as people I have known. I try to make my makeups as realistic and believable on the screen as possible and am constantly searching for better materials and techniques to reach that goal."

Smith turned Hal Holbrook into Mark Twain in the television production of *Mark Twain Tonight!* A variety of foam-latex appliances were employed in this makeup. (*Dick Smith*)

Chapter 18

CHRISTOPHER TUCKER

Christopher Tucker began his career creating prosthetics in a humble garret apartment in England. Tucker was already enjoying a fairly successful career as an opera singer when he developed a keen interest in makeup. He became extremely curious as to how false noses and the like were created.

He decided to buy a couple of books on the subject. Tucker's wife recoiled in horror when her husband spent two pounds on a gallon of latex. They weren't terribly prosperous, and she felt this an enormous waste of money.

Tucker decided to cast his own face, and knowing nothing about alginate, he used plaster. He did think to grease his eyebrows and eyelashes, but some of the plaster worked its way into his ungreased hairline, and he recalls "roaring like a bull in pain" when he and his wife attempted to remove the plaster cast from his face. He never used plaster again. After that he always used alginate.

He began by building up quite a collection of nose molds, about twenty or thirty different ones. He kept adding new shapes and new designs, but he made them for his own use only.

Then Tucker and his wife went through a period of financial hardship. Tucker wasn't doing as much singing as before, and money was scarce. They were forced to try selling the prosthetic noses he had created to the various wigmakers and theatrical costume houses. Nathan Wigs bought quite a few, as did Charles H. Fox Ltd. This saved the day for the Tuckers, but more than that it kicked off a career for Tucker that he truly enjoys.

Tucker found that his prosthetic business began to escalate. He started supplying companies with rubber noses, and the number of his nose molds grew to about a hundred different shapes and sizes. Tucker added bald caps and other prosthetics to his new "line."

He continued his career of opera singer, but he began to get jobs in the makeup area. He did a plastic cap for British actor Donny Atkinson, who would later play the first Quasimodo hunchback creation Tucker would do. This cap was for a small film which was more or less a semiamateur production.

Then a television commercial company contacted Tucker and asked him if he could do a bald cap for an actor who wasn't in England at the time. Tucker, who wasn't even a member of the Film Makeup Artists Union, agreed to it. The fact that he'd never made a plastic cap for an unknown person before was quite immaterial to him. Nor for that matter did he have a mold or any cap plastic. However, he scurried around and found

Stuart Wilson as Johann Strauss, Jr., for ITV's presentation of *The Strauss Family*. (© *ITV*)

Stuart Wilson in the second stage of aging. (© *ITV*)

all the necessary supplies, and with one or two rather vague measurements they telephoned him from Germany, he began making the bald cap. The company then asked Tucker if he could do the actor's makeup, too, and when Tucker agreed to that, they asked if he couldn't handle the other actors as well. Tucker assured them he could—he'd bring along his wife.

One thing led to another, and someone suggested to Tucker that he apply for membership in the Film Makeup Artists Union. He applied and was accepted. Gradually, he found himself working on feature films and leaving his singing career behind. Still only in his early thirties, he is now extremely busy and has expanded enormously into the prosthetics field because this is where his main interest lies.

Many of Tucker's original life-casts were done in his flat. Sometimes it was even necessary for the actor to lie on the bed in the small apartment. Tucker recalls Richard Greene, who played Robin Hood in the original British television film, lying on the bed while the cast was taken. And when other actors came around to their garret apartment with its sloping roof, it was quite a revelation to them. Toward the end of their stay the Tuckers found it became a challenge just to get in the door, much less across the room. The time had come for Tucker to find more suitable premises. He located a large Georgian house at 1 Trafalgar Avenue in London, which has become the Christopher Tucker Studios. He has a large basement and a laboratory as well.

Tucker has expanded in all directions within the prosthetic field. He has developed his own plastic material to take the place of foam latex. He was doing prosthetics for the ITV special *The Strauss Family*, when he developed this material to use in an aging process. The material is basically acrylic, very flexible, and soft. It looks and feels like real flesh. It is actually possible to apply the material to the face and to make up the prosthetic to match the skin, which is impossible to do with foam latex.

Once Tucker had invented the material, the immediate problem was to make it work in a mold. This proved far more difficult. He began by trying to process it in the normal foam-latex mold, but then the two halves, positive and negative, cemented themselves so hard after they had been baked in the oven that when he tried to separate them, the mold shattered. He had to de-

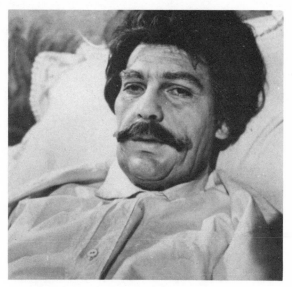

The television production insisted on being historically accurate. Because Strauss dyed his hair as he aged, Tucker wasn't able to use a gray wig to help depict age. (© *ITV*)

Fortunately for Tucker, Strauss did shave his beard in later life so that eventually one could see there was an aging process going on. (© *ITV*)

velop an entirely new molding technique for the process. This proved to be very sophisticated and time-consuming, and he doesn't use the technique too much.

Tucker began to expand into dental appliances. He bought books on dentistry, chemistry, physics, and engineering. There are times when he feels he spends most of his evenings immersed in textbooks. Keeping current on the latest industrial processes and techniques, Tucker then tried to apply these techniques to his field.

Tucker has found an enormous field for his creations from television commercials to the world of opera. He has created an incredible number of pieces for the British Broadcasting Corporation, ITV network, Southern Television, and Thames Television companies. India, Egypt, and Australia have been added to the list of regular overseas customers, and Tucker continues to work on films all over the world.

During the summer of 1976 Tucker was busy creating pieces for the British Broadcasting Corporation's production of *I, Claudius.* This involved aging five leading British actors in several stages over thirteen one-hour episodes. Simultaneously, Tucker conceived and created the makeup for the

BBC/NBC coproduction of *The Hunchback of Notre Dame.* While this was going on, he also designed the stylized prosthetics for the Glyndebourne production of Verdi's opera *Falstaff*, which was televised by Southern Television.

Next Tucker became involved in the Yorkshire Television production of *Raffles*, based on the character by E. W. Hornung. This was another series of twelve one-hour episodes necessitating innumerable disguises.

With *I, Claudius* and *The Hunchback of Notre Dame* finished, Tucker seemed to be busier than ever. He was involved in another television film version of Shakespeare and Harry Nilsson's musical fantasy *The Point*. Tucker had to create thirteen pointed heads for this production. He also completed appliances and full dentures for the BBC's production of Dickens's *Nicholas Nickleby*; and did some old-age makeup for a Belgian Television production about the life of Rubens.

I, Claudius was certainly one of the most ambitious aging sequences that had been done in British television. The film won several British Academy of Film and Television Arts awards as well as one or two interna-

Brian Blessed and Sian Phillips in the BBC's production of *I, Claudius*. (© *BBC*)

Derek Jacobi was only one of five leading British actors Tucker had to age in several stages over thirteen one-hour episodes. (© *BBC*)

tional awards. Even the makeup girl in charge on the production received an award. The film starred Derek Jacobi as Claudius; Sian Phillips as Livia, wife of Augustus; Brian Blessed as Augustus; George Baker as Tiberius; and Margaret Tyzack as Antonia, the mother of Claudius.

Each episode was made within two weeks, which gave Tucker considerably less than two weeks to make each set of prosthetics for the various characters. The five characters had to age in stages so that in each episode they would be slightly older. The modeling and mold making was an endless job for Tucker. In this type of television film where there is a significant time span between episodes, Tucker stresses that if the aging makeup is too subtle, it will look as though nothing has gone on at all. If an actor has to age ten years, you may have to age them fifteen or twenty years in order to make the proper impression.

Derek Jacobi had an extensive appliance, as did most of the actors. This was because of the briefness of the Roman costumes. Most of the actors had to have prosthetic necks down to their collarbones, which is unusual for most aging sequences. There was no time for preparation on *I, Claudius* and Tucker was doing the original life-cast for Derek Jacobi and one or two other members of the cast while he was working on *Star Wars*. Tucker explained that he would prepare these in the evening when he got back from the studio. There was no preproduction time at all, and they found they were making designs up as they went along.

Tucker explained his style of preparing an old-age life-cast:

''I usually do two life-casts of the actor, having him in two different positions. One position is on an angle, and one requires sitting straight up. This is to judge the difference in the face when it is being dragged downward. I believe that the weight of the alginate and plaster bandages placed on top of the face tends to distort the face ever so slightly. If you have the actor sitting up, this will tend to drag the flesh downward. Of course, this is what tends to happen anyway to an old person, so that can help up to a point.

Derek Jacobi minus aging makeup. (© *BBC*)

"I also, very often, take what I call a precision cast. This is a technique that I evolved fairly recently, just prior to *I, Claudius*. As a matter of fact, Phil Leakey was my guinea pig.

"For this type of cast, I use a special medical sealastic material which I paint on very thinly. It sets quickly, so one has to move very fast. The application is extremely difficult. I then put on one or possibly two layers of plaster bandage. This I allow to set, and then I jiggle the plaster bandage free from the sealastic material. The sealastic material is then peeled off. This is almost like peeling off skin because the sealastic material is so very thin. It doesn't shrink or distort in any way.

"I then fill this up with plaster in the normal way. Using this technique, I get almost photographic reproduction. It reproduces skin texture in a way that has to be seen to be believed. It's a very good technique, but it is extremely expensive, costing roughly about one hundred dollars per face, so it's not cheap by any standard."

Because of the sheer volume of the work on *I, Claudius*, it would have been impossi-ble to use Tucker's special plastic. It is very difficult to apply, and many of the makeup artists working on the production wouldn't have had the experience in applying prosthetics, anyway.

One of Tucker's specialties is the hunchback look. The first hunchback that he created was made of foam latex. The eye was made out of latex with cap plastic to make it shiny. He added a bit of makeup, and there it was. He feels it was rather rudimentary and is unable to recall for whom it was done.

The next hunchback he created was for the film *Barry McKenzie Holds His Own*. Donald Pleasence starred in the film, and Robert Gillespie was the hunchback. The script called for a one-eyed hunchback named Dorothy. Barry Humphries wrote the script and played the remarkable character Dame Edna Everage.

Tucker created this hunchback in his own plastic. He received the ultimate accolade for his makeup when the accountant on the nearly all-Australian crew went up to the director and said, "Awfully nice fellow that Robert Gillespie. Very nice chap—but isn't it

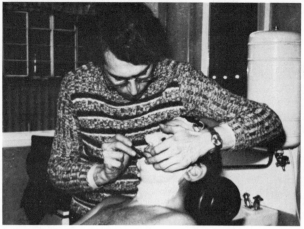

Tucker applies prosthetic appliances to Donny Atkinson for Tucker's first Quasimodo hunchback. (© BBC)

Donny Atkinson as Quasimodo wearing a fully articulated eye mechanism. (© BBC)

a pity about his face?'' The poor man thought the makeup was real.

Tucker created another hunchback for a Panasonic color television commercial. Not only did they want a hunchback with a deformed eye, but they wanted the eye to wink! Tucker had about two weeks to conjure up this minor miracle. It was quite a complicated procedure to make a mechanical eye, and one needed to be almost a jeweler to do so.

However, Tucker succeeded in creating the hunchback, winking eye and all, only to have the Independent Broadcasting Authority, who censors all television commercials, deem Tucker's creation a little too horrific. They didn't reshoot the commercial, though, but instead went back through every bit of footage shot and eventually managed to cut together a highly censored version.

Tucker created still another hunchback for the BBC/NBC coproduction of *The Hunchback of Notre Dame*. It was created on Warren Clark, and Tucker never cared for the design.

Although Tucker recognizes sketches and drawings as helpful, he prefers to make his rough model directly on the cast. If one has the skill to draw, one can probably draw almost anything, but the difficulty lies in trying to superimpose the drawing onto the actor's face. One may create many subtle differences, perhaps making the nose appear

thinner and so forth, but it is not such a simple matter to transfer this from a flat sheet of sketch paper onto a live face. And because he will end up modeling the sketch onto the face anyway, Tucker prefers doing so in the first place. He will, of course, get rough ideas from drawings done on a scrap of paper, but seldom will he go in for too much in the way of drawing.

Although he had made humps before, Tucker had never studied the anatomical design. It is actually a deformity of the spine which alters the entire rib cage. Tucker modeled the hump to look like what a real hunchback would look like, and this added quite a lot to his character. But the Wardrobe Department insisted on having a sort of sacklike costume, which tended to disguise the hump more than anything else. Although there was the scene where he was stripped to the waist and flogged, the cameras didn't linger very long on the scene.

Tucker also made deformed hands for this same hunchback. Unfortunately, they were never used. It took about two hours to make up the face and position the hump. Each hand would have added an hour to the total makeup time. He also created a set of discolored upper teeth to distort the upper jaw.

For a television commercial for a well-known lager beer, Tucker was hired to create a Frankenstein monster. Tucker created

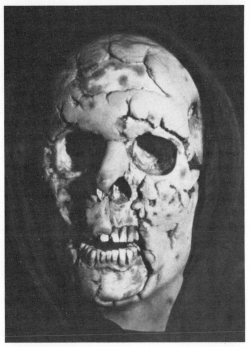

Tucker effected this experimental witch makeup on a twenty-year-old girl. (© *BBC*)

A gruesome trial makeup Tucker experimented with for a horror film. (© *BBC*)

the monster in his special plastic material, but the director insisted on the lipstick and conventional neck bolts, and Tucker wasn't all that pleased with the creature. He found Pierce's original creation of Karloff as Frankenstein unique, but the Frankensteins created thereafter tended to become a bit more exaggerated.

This monster was another one of Tucker's commercial creations that was originally banned by the Independent Broadcasting Authority. The voice-over by Victor Borge proclaimed this beer to be the beer that refreshes parts that other beers cannot reach. The IBA finally agreed to screen it once after the ten o'clock news. They found that no one complained, and it has been showing ever since.

Reflecting on the past, Tucker feels he's never had it easy, always being thrown in at the deep end and experiencing hard going all the way. This he feels was especially true of the first major feature film he was involved in entitled *Julius Caesar* (1970). Tucker did this with makeup artist Cliff Sharpe, who was a fairly old man by then. They had great difficulty at the time because there were many films in production, and it was difficult to get any additional help when they needed it.

The film starred such notables as Charlton Heston, Jason Robards, Richard Chamberlain, Robert Vaughn, Sir John Gielgud, and Christopher Lee, just to name a few. It was to be an epic production, but Tucker didn't feel it was ever very successful. They seemed to have nearly every star they could get squeezed into it.

It became a rather traumatic production for Tucker because they fell behind schedule and ended up working very long days. At one point they had a lot of naked girls in it that were dreamed up mainly in connection with a publicity stunt with a Playboy Club. Twelve naked girls came into makeup to have their bikini marks removed, but Tucker says, "I suppose this was rather enjoyable in many respects. However, when one had something like eight or nine major actors onstage on one set and a publicity stunt going on on another, attempting to cope with both simultaneously became rather difficult, to say the least."

Almost everything that can happen to a makeup artist, Tucker feels, has happened to him. He feels it has certainly proved a colorful career to date, and that he seems to attract all the odd, extraordinary jobs.

When Tucker was involved in aging Stuart Wilson (Johann Strauss, Jr.) for ITV's *The*

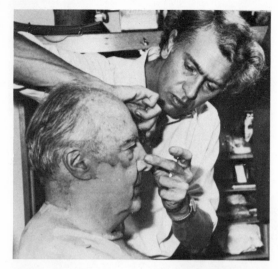

John Houseman is made up
by Tucker as Churchill for
David Susskind's production
of the Potsdam conference.
(*Chris Tucker*)

Lee Remick as Jenny
Churchill for Thames
Television's *Jenny*.
(© *Thames Television, Ltd.*)

Strauss Family, ironically it was Strauss himself who made Tucker's job more difficult. The Makeup Department at the studio insisted on making Strauss do what he did historically. As the real Strauss aged, he decided to dye his gray hair black, to grow whiskers, and, in effect, try to cover up the aging process as best he could. As Tucker was attempting to create prosthetics to achieve an aging makeup, the studio Makeup Department was applying a jet black wig to Wilson. "Fortunately," Tucker puts it, "Strauss had the decency to shave his beard off before he died, so we could see that there was some aging going on."

Tucker created various pieces for the ITV "Father Brown" detective series. He created a severed head which was quite effective. He did a life-cast of the actor, then made the various molds, and came out with a very good head. He created it in his special life-like material, so it not only looked real but felt it too. Then he filled it with plastic entrails and considerable blood. He sent it off in a box with a note that read if it was still bleeding when it arrived, stand it up on end and let it drain for a while.

On the David Susskind production of the Potsdam conference, Tucker's time was mainly occupied in making up Truman. Dick Smith made the prosthetics for Stalin, Truman, and Churchill. There were an enormous number of historical characters portrayed, and Tucker made a few prosthetics

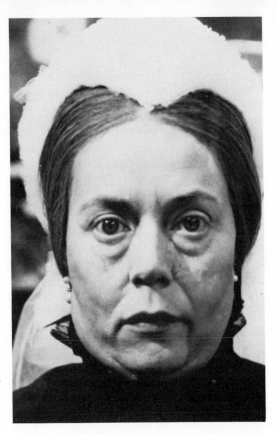

Annette Crosbie won a major award for her performance as Queen Victoria in ITV's production of *Edward VII*. (© *ITV*)

for the English members of the cast. Truman's makeup took two and a half hours—two hours for prosthetics and about a half hour to do the toupee.

For Hal Wallis's *A Bequest to the Nation*, Tucker had to create false breasts for Glenda Jackson, who portrayed the rather well-endowed Emma Hamilton. One of the problems Tucker encountered in this endeavor was to create loose, full breasts for beneath Jackson's negligee in the "bedroom scene" and then to model another set to look supported and restrained beneath a very tight dress.

One remarkable aging makeup Tucker created was for Lee Remick as the mother of Sir Winston Churchill in *Jenny*. This was done for Thames Television. He also aged Janet Suzman in *Florence Nightingale* for Southern Television.

Despite Annette Crosbie's winning a major award for her performance as Queen Victoria in ITV's production of *Edward VII*, Tucker was never pleased with her makeup. Originally turning the job down, Tucker was somehow eventually persuaded to take it on. Unfortunately, they were already into the sixth episode when Tucker began, and they had already shaved Annette Crosbie's hairline back three inches, which Tucker feels

didn't make his job any easier. It made it impossible for him to make her look anything like Queen Victoria, so all he did do was to make her look older and a bit plumper.

The Private Lives of Alice was a Granada Television production for which an enormous amount of work had to be redone in practically no time at all. Tucker had something like two weeks, and they had about ten or twelve characters to create for this production, which was more or less a takeoff on *Alice in Wonderland*. Tucker created lizards, dormice, the Queen of Hearts, the Gryphon, and the White Rabbit. When he did the life-casts, they brought the actors all at once, and for the entire day he did life-casts. At the end of the day he felt like a mobile cement mixer, just mixing out plaster.

More recently, Tucker did *The Picture of Dorian Gray* for the BBC. This starred Peter Firth as Dorian Gray, and Sir John Gielgud as Lord Henry Wotton. Tucker also created heads and other appliances for *The Romantic Englishwoman* and took a life-cast of Helmut Berger.

One interesting feature of Tucker's makeup expertise is his use of a video camera. He will record a whole sequence of movements of the face in close-up, profile, and three-quarter views. He will also vary the lighting to bring out the various facial muscles. The idea is to show as much of the facial movements as possible. In this way, he can gauge where the stress marks are so he can make the edges of the appliance fit accordingly and not cross the lines of stress. Otherwise, the edges tend to lift more readily than they are inclined to anyway, particularly around the mouth area.

"The great thing is, you mustn't lose identity. Anybody can cover an actor's face in foam latex and make all sorts of wrinkles, lines, and sagging jowls; but unless they conform anatomically to the actor's own face, there is no way it will ever resemble the actor, so you lose identity. This is particularly so on a television series when an actor is going from youth to old age. It's certainly essential to retain the identity of the actor, otherwise the audience doesn't know where they are. They're suddenly confronted with a strange character that they haven't seen before or don't think they've seen before because they don't recognize the actor.

"Whatever else, the actor must be recognizably the same actor. This is very difficult. The aging process, as I understand it, requires that the actor age naturally. This is something the makeup artist must assess with care. Different faces age in different ways. Some portions of the face may tend to go to fat; some portions of the face may go thin. An aged face isn't necessarily one that is covered with lines. It's very often just sagging flesh. The muscles tend to sag. They're not as taut as they were in youth, making the jawline in particular sag in places. There are certain characteristics of aging that are common to all faces, certain aspects, for example, of an aging neck or jowl; but even so, one must be careful not to become stereotyped in doing the same thing on another face when it doesn't belong there.

"I've developed my own techniques. I suppose every makeup artist does. Mine vary slightly from Stuart Freeborn's, and they vary slightly from Dick Smith's. To quote individual peculiarities in one's technique is really fairly immaterial, since individual people always do things their own way. I'm very often searching for different ways to do almost everything. I think that perhaps like Dick Smith or Stuart Freeborn, every time I do a job I vary at least one or two parts of the procedure just to see if I can get a better result.

"The eyes are very revealing. Youthful eyes and long eyelashes are a nightmare. They always have been and always will be. There's not an awful lot one can do about this. I have tried using full contact lenses that cover just the sclera, but I find that they are not particularly helpful in that they do tend to make the eyelids bulge out farther than ever, whereas old eyes tend to recede into the skull, so this doesn't really help. Wigs and hairpieces, of course, are essential in nine cases out of ten. I get wigmakers to make those.

"If it's a case where the actor has to age in various stages, it's often a good idea to age them as far as you can and then try to work backward, so to speak. On *I, Claudius*, I'm afraid we didn't have time to do even that. It had to be a case of adding on a bit each week."

Another photographic technique Tucker employs is that of printing large transparencies through which one can view the original cast. This way he can locate any inaccuracies in the cast. His transparency will be about six and a half inches by eight and a half inches, or ten inches by eight inches. He will then superimpose this transparency of the actor over a cast of the actor's face taken from the same position, either straight or profile.

"In starting an old-age makeup using straight makeup," Tucker explained to us, "it's a matter of using highlight and then shading, as one does in all makeup. Makeup is based on the illusion of highlight and shadow, in the same way as a portrait painter creates an illusion of three dimensions on a flat canvas. At least a makeup artist has a three-dimensional surface to start off with. Granted, the optical illusions that are involved with the human face are enormous and cause all sorts of problems. I believe a makeup artist should undergo some training program. The BBC does have their own makeup training school, but as it only runs for three months, it obviously is only rudimentary.

"What I feel is absolutely mandatory for the makeup artist is to be given a system of facial analysis. I hit upon this by chance. I did a great deal of work for a man called Jacques Henri who created the photo-fit police identification system that is used world-

Tucker had approximately two weeks in which to create ten or twelve characters for the television production of *The Private Lives of Alice*. Three of his many characters are shown here. (*Chris Tucker*)

wide now. This consists of building up a face from various sections: foreheads, chins, noses, mouths, and eyes. We did considerable research into the human face. At the time, I was teaching a normal straight makeup, which I still do from time to time, and I was trying to work out some methods to explain to my students how to analyze a face. How to discover what is 'wrong' with a face, or what is 'right' with it, or what is, in fact, going on. I achieved my own system of facial analysis, and it's been invaluable ever since.''

Tucker has specialized mainly in prosthetic work and has become known mainly for that. He has done an incredible amount of work in a very short time. He has created at least seven hundred or more life-casts of the face alone, which has resulted in an extremely large collection of faces. He has created many bodies; life-casting torsos, arms, legs; to say nothing of all the aging sequences he has done.

"Makeup cosmetics have undergone very little basic change in the last ten years. I notice that in British and Canadian television many makeup artists are now using 'day' cosmetics as opposed to 'theatrical' ones. I'm not quite sure of the reasoning behind that. I think perhaps they feel they are being more 'with it' or something, but there is certainly nothing to be gained by it. A 'theatrical' cosmetic is designed so that it can be repaired during the day. It's basically made to stay there all day, while the 'day' cosmetic isn't. It's intended for either street or evening wear and is not built to last for an entire day. Nor are the colors very predictable from one batch to another batch.

"As far as my own work in prosthetics goes, I would like to develop all sorts of techniques in the future, mainly to make life simpler for myself in the making of these things. It would be nice to develop equipment or techniques whereby prosthetics could be greatly simplified or made quicker and more reliable. My imagination has carried me to extensive realms sometimes. I would love to invent a machine that could take a three-dimensional photograph of an actor's face. This could then be processed or developed into a three-dimensional form which could then be recast, giving you one hundred percent accuracy. But I think the complications involved in a machine like this would be simply monumental. However, I've been giving it serious thought, but at the moment I'm afraid the only ideas I come up with are very expensive ideas and hopelessly impractical in many respects."

Tucker's love for invention and innovation, combined with his love of ambitious concepts and far-reaching ideas, will certainly lead him in interesting directions in the future.

Christopher Tucker's laboratory looks a bit akin to that of most mad scientists. (*Photo courtesy of Chris Tucker*)

At times Tucker uses a magnifying glass to be certain of his accuracy. Here he is at work on the life-cast of Lee Remick. (*Chris Tucker*)

Chapter 19

JOHN CHAMBERS

With a unanimous vote of the board of governors the Academy of Motion Picture Arts and Sciences presented John Chambers with an Oscar in 1969. The Oscar had been presented only once before to a makeup artist in the Academy's forty-year history.

As most of us have discovered, nothing comes from nothing, and Chambers was no exception. His route to the Oscar was long and tedious and began many years before Ben Nye, Sr., contacted him in Europe where he was busy on the "I Spy" television series, to discuss the possibility of Chambers working on the soon-to-be-made *Planet of the Apes.* It was for Chambers's incredible work in transforming Roddy McDowall, Kim Hunter, Maurice Evans, and many others into orangutans, chimpanzees, and gorillas for this film that he received the Oscar.

After high school Chambers designed jewelry and then carpeting, and then he joined the army. He became a dental technician, and, oddly enough, this led to Hollywood.

A gifted sculptor and artist, Chambers found himself able to experiment with various forms of plastics, and he was able to develop new adhesives and rubber compounds. Some of his experience came from working in the army's Fitzsimmons General Hospital in Denver, Colorado, and then later in Santa Maria, California, where he spent three years creating prosthetic devices such as artificial noses and ears for wounded soldiers.

Chambers eventually found his way to the Hines Veterans Hospital. He was in charge of prosthetic devices. He would follow surgeons into the operating rooms, making anatomical notations.

Using these, he would create in plastic the parts necessary for reconstructive surgery. He created a palate, allowing patients who were unable to form words to speak again. He replaced shoulders which had been blown away in battle and created artificial breasts for WACs and nurses who had been wounded. He was able to improve techniques for painting artificial eyes, perfectly duplicating the coloring and even the texture of the patient's existing eye. He would create full orbital appliances which consist of the eyelid and lashes, as well as the eyeball. He was able to create artificial plastic thyroid glands for use in cadaver research. On one occasion Chambers did a full-face restoration on a young soldier after the jeep in which he was riding hit a land mine and the metal floor of the jeep sliced off his entire face.

At one time during his film career he heard of a woman who had had her nose removed due to a severe facial malignancy.

Robert Culp, star of the television series "I Spy," prepares to be made up as a warlord. (*John Chambers*)

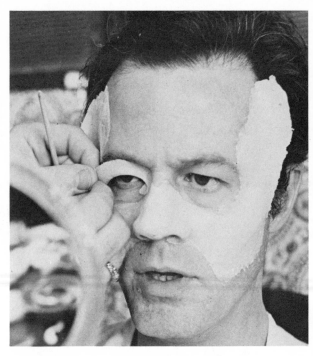

Eyepieces will aid in the Oriental appearance needed by Culp for this particular role. (*John Chambers*)

John had her come to his lab where he created a plastic nose which fitted perfectly. Showing her how to put it on and cover it with makeup which blended into her complexion, he did it so beautifully that no one could suspect the slightest imperfection in her features.

"It just makes me feel good to know I can help people," Chambers replies. Looking down at his hands, he adds, "God put it there, and it comes easy."

In 1953 television was just starting to grow. Chambers began to notice that what he was doing in his realm was a far superior job to what he saw come out of television. Chambers's talent was sorely needed. The golden aura of Hollywood, compared to the morbid work he was involved in, appealed to John. Since he was a creative artist, there was the anticipation that in Hollywood there would be only the world's greatest minds and talents. Of course, Chambers found that

as in many realms, there is genius, but there is also mediocrity.

Chambers wrote NBC offering his services, and when he had heard nothing from them for nine months, he left Chicago for Hollywood anyway. The day he left, a letter from NBC arrived, offering him a job.

He brought to Hollywood scientific techniques that no one was familiar with. The studios had worked only with smatterings from the plaster shop, or they might have a cousin or a friend who was a dentist and could teach them how to make a set of fang teeth. He found that very few technicians ever went deeply into the art and science of the materials.

There were, of course, real artists who, despite crude, old techniques and old types of plaster and hydrocal stones, were doing marvelous creative makeups.

Chambers disguised Charlton Heston as the beast in a Shirley Temple Storybook

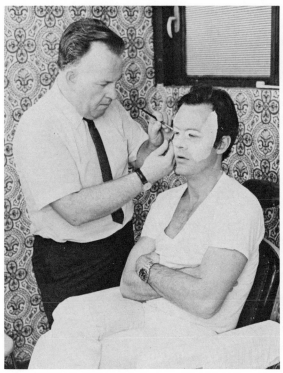

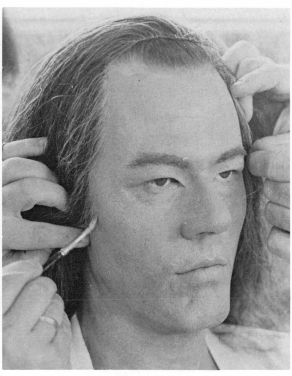

Chambers secures the facial appliances. (*John Chambers*)

A wig is added to complete the transformation. (*John Chambers*)

production of *Beauty and the Beast*. He also created and handled the makeup for Paul Newman in *The Battler*, Hemingway's story of a boxer. Newman had to appear unscarred in one scene and badly beaten up in the following scene. These scenes were live and only seconds apart, but Chambers and a well-trained makeup crew achieved the required effect. He was also involved on assignments for "Matinee Theatre" and "Lux Video Theater." He enjoyed the experience and excitement generated by "live" television.

After six years, Chambers went to Universal where he worked on *The Ugly American* (1962) and *Bedtime Story* (1964), fashioning a complete upper set of veneer teeth for Brando in order to effect a toothier appearance.

But Chambers's first real love was the vehicle that brought him to film prominence, *The List of Adrian Messenger* (1963). In this film he helped create as many as ten dis-

guises for Kirk Douglas from a young farmer to an elderly cleric. He even turned handsome Burt Lancaster into a horse-faced woman and Frank Sinatra into a gypsy.

He experienced many disappointments on the film. Bud Westmore was the "main man," the department head. Chambers ran the laboratory and solved the problems. Westmore demanded that the picture be black and white, while Chambers felt that it should have been in color. Then it would have been a classic. Westmore feared that the appliances wouldn't look right in color. "So we went to black and white and modified a fine picture," John lamented.

Chambers created teeth appliances for Marlon Brando in *The Chase* (1966). Chambers has a certain notoriety for being able to keep five or six makeup artists busy at the same time, fitting the appliances he creates for them. He has a laboratory in his garage where he creates thousands of appliances for good money, but without screen credit.

Chambers in his studio with many of the molds and impressions used for the film that brought him to prominence, *The List of Adrian Messenger*. Bud Westmore was makeup director on this film. (© *Universal*)

He created the head of the man seen in the water in *Jaws* (1975). For a scene in *True Grit* (1969) he prepared fingers so that John Wayne could chop them off a fellow cowpoke.

When an Egyptian peasant's ear was cut off in *Justine* (1969), it was one of Chambers's creations. He made all of the appliances for Ross Martin in "The Wild, Wild West" television series. And "trekkies" will be glad to know that Mr. Spock's ears were made by John Chambers.

Chambers also worked on the first "Mission: Impossible" pilot and did some episodes for "The Outer Limits," "Lost in Space," and "Night Gallery."

Many of these television programs had to exist on low budgets despite high ratings and the need for creative staff. Chambers would turn out two and three monsters a

week. He made scores of vampire-type teeth. For "The Outer Limits," he created a domed head for David McCallum in "The Sixth Finger."

One of Chambers's favorite creations is the Pickman's Model from the television series "Night Gallery." The story concerns a young artist in whose studio there was a trapdoor that led to the sewers of Boston. Legend had it that every so often a creature who lived in the sewers would emerge, take a woman captive, and return below. The young artist painted the creature (which he actually saw) and won acclaim for such "creative" work.

Pickman's Model was another low-budget creature. Comprehensive sketches were made of the concept. Chambers worked in collaboration with sketch artist Tom Wright. Wright did all the "Night Gallery" portraitures.

Actor Jan Merlin in five makeup tests of disguises created for Kirk Douglas in *The List of Adrian Messenger*. (© *Universal*)

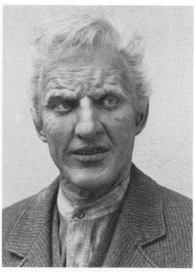

It was necessary to come up with sketches in only a day or two on such programs, instead of the two or three weeks they would normally have on a better-budgeted feature. The creature itself would have to be completed in a week and a half at most.

Robert Prohaska wore the Model's suit. It was made from bits and pieces. They made the head, then cut and hand-carved the lump. Chambers took a mold of a tremendous snake and made a tail out of it. Sheepskins were bought and stripped so that they would be flexible. There was no time to make molds. They hand-cut the skins and fit them on leotards. Chambers made red full-scleral contact lenses for Prohaska for the tight shots.

Chambers's most well-known work, of course, was for *Planet of the Apes.* Eventually, Chambers and Dan Striekpeke would be together on *Apes,* but in the beginning, it was Chambers alone under Ben Nye, Sr. No one seemed to have any real concept of what they wanted, only of what they didn't want. Chambers would try this and that and the other thing, only to receive negative comments from everyone.

Bill Creber, the art director, was his biggest help. Creber had the propmen bring into the lab all the old, stuffed, falling-apart monkeys, chimps, and orangutans they

Martin Landau in costume and makeup for his role as a military figure in the first "Mission: Impossible" series. (*John Chambers*)

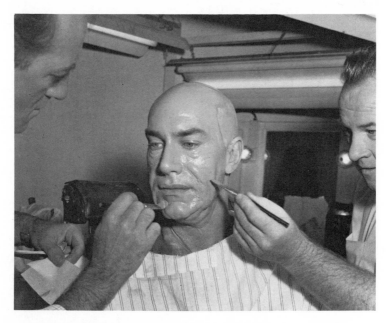

Martin Landau gets a new face for his role in the first "Mission: Impossible" television series. (*John Chambers*)

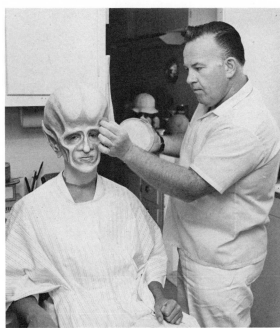

Chambers created this makeup, which was worn by David McCallum in "The Sixth Finger" segment of the television series "Outer Limits." (© *ABC*)

Leonard Nimoy's Dr. Spock ears were a product of John Chambers's expertise. (© *NBC*)

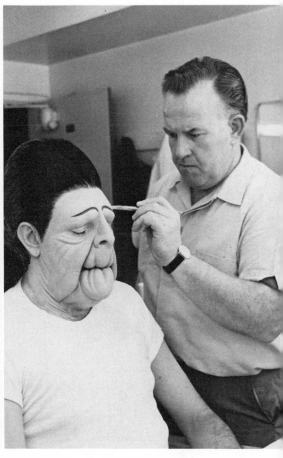

The incredible Prune Face for an NBC *Dick Tracy* pilot. (© *NBC*)

could find. Chambers had them hanging all over, as they gave him sketch ideas. He was alone. The budget at that time wouldn't allow for him to hire any help. Sometimes Ben Nye would pull Tom Burman or Werner Kempler off some other project and allow them to help, but basically, in the beginning, Chambers was alone.

The first sculptures Chambers did were of a gorilla and a chimp. The chimp had a very natural appearance, and when they tested it, they found that the slits of the nose were just too ugly. After much discussion, they came up with a modified "button" nose for the chimpanzees.

Although they toyed with the concept of a Neanderthal type, this wouldn't work. They needed the strength of the animal face, but without the grotesqueness. They also had to find a way for the actors to project their voices for sound recording without it seeming as though it were coming from a cavern deep within the ape's body. The actor's lips

also had to be synchronized with the ape lips so that when they spoke, the ape lips would form the words visually. It was known from experience that heavy foam-rubber appliances would absorb the sound. It became necessary to invent makeup that would allow the dialogue to sound natural.

After the first film test it was necessary to eliminate some wrinkles around the eyes to permit greater expression. Sometimes the actors' own teeth could be seen behind the ape teeth. They had the help of the camera people and lighting experts in this area, who selected angles to minimize the problem. They would also black out the actors' teeth so they would not reflect the light.

The actors had trouble with the noses and couldn't breathe through them. A passage was designed through the ape's upper lip, and this made it easier for the actors to breathe.

Chambers also wanted color conformity. Because eventually there were so many

The Pickman's Model was a low-budget creature Chambers helped create for a "Night Gallery" segment. (© NBC)

Several molds ready for the ovens. (© NBC)

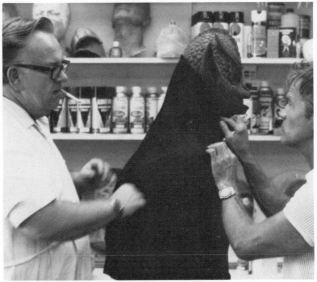

The rubber skin is removed from the mold as Chambers concentrates on the head appliance for the model. (© *NBC*)

Janos Prohaska and Chambers fit the completed head appliance to a dummy and adjust the body shirt to which sheepskin will be added. (© *NBC*)

Once the makeup is completed, the sheepskin is glued in place, one layer at a time, on the neck section which will blend the head appliance in with the humped back. (© *NBC*)

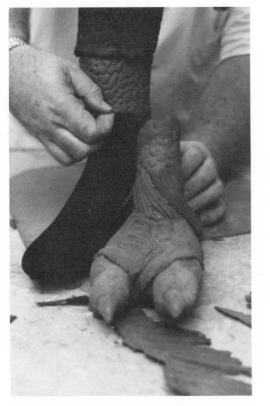

The Pickman's Model's foot. (© *NBC*)

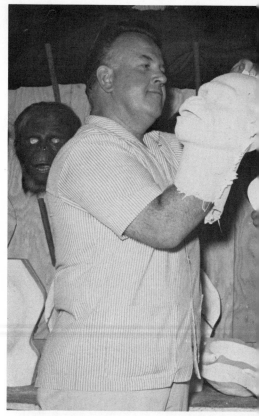

An early ape concept by Ben Nye, Sr., for *Planet of the Apes*. Edward G. Robinson appears as Dr. Zaius, the role Maurice Evans would eventually make famous. Owing to a heart condition, Robinson declined the role because shooting was to be done at a high altitude.
(© *Apjac Productions, Inc. and Twentieth Century-Fox Film Corporation*)

Chambers and Tom Burman mixing impression material.

Burman and Chambers inject foam latex into the ape appliance molds. These will be baked at high temperatures in ovens.
(© *Apjac Productions, Inc. and Twentieth Century-Fox Film Corporation*)

Rubber masks were worn by many of the extras in *Planet of the Apes*. Chambers closely examines an unfinished mask. (© Apjac Productions, Inc. and Twentieth Century-Fox Film Corporation)

Each foam-latex appliance had to be carefully identified as to which actor would wear it. Some of the appliances could be reused. (© Apjac Productions, Inc. and Twentieth Century-Fox Film Corporation)

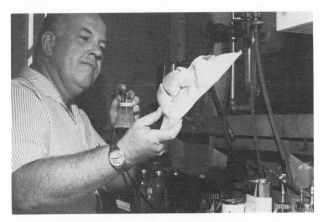

Chambers sprays makeup onto an orangutan appliance which will be used by Maurice Evans. (© Apjac Productions, Inc. and Twentieth Century-Fox Film Corporation)

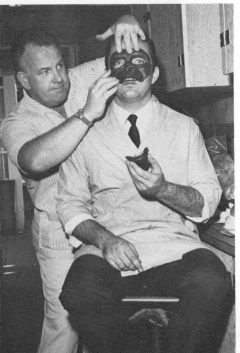

Apprentice Burman willingly allows Chambers to test a gorilla appliance on his face. Note Burman's own mouth below the gorilla muzzle. (© Apjac Productions, Inc. and Twentieth Century-Fox Film Corporation)

Chambers and Ben Nye examine two of the many masks. (© Apjac Productions, Inc. and Twentieth Century Fox Film Corporation)

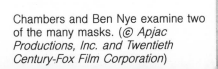

Kim Hunter, who won the Academy
Award for Best Supporting Actress
for her performance in *A Streetcar
Named Desire*, poses with and
without makeup and costume for
her role in *Planet of the Apes*.
(© *Apjac Productions, Inc. and
Twentieth Century-Fox Film
Corporation*)

Lou Wagner finds himself
transformed under Chambers's
skillful hands. (© *Apjac
Productions, Inc. and Twentieth
Century-Fox Film Corporation*)

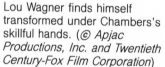

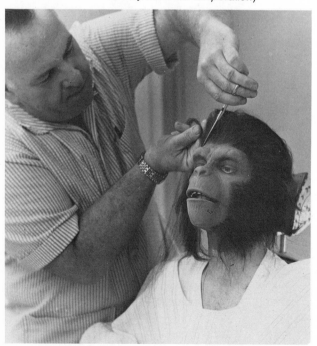

If Maurice Evans wanted to catch up on his
reading during a break in shooting, he didn't let
his Dr. Zaius makeup stop him. (© *Apjac
Productions, Inc. and Twentieth Century-Fox
Film Corporation*)

Chambers poses with (*left to right*) an orangutan, a chimp, and a gorilla. (*Photo courtesy of John Chambers*)

makeup artists working—at one time there were as many as eighty—it was a real problem. He achieved uniform coloration by premaking up the appliances. He had the appliances presprayed with new rubbers. They used rubber adhesives, glues, and paints that no one had ever used before. No one had ever premade up before, either. It took nearly five hours for each actor to be made up, and this had to be cut down. Extras were hired simply for makeup tests.

There was no commercial product designed for premakeup, so it became necessary to create a special paint. Prepainting saved about forty-five minutes of labor in the chair for each actor. It also allowed the makeup men to paint large numbers of appliances at the same time with the same batch of paint, thus maintaining color consistency. The edges were blended in after attachment to the face, but the basic color was already there for the makeup artist.

It was also necessary to develop a paint that would allow the actor's skin to breathe. In the beginning, sweat would make the appliance come loose, and the new paint also prevented this. It had a plastic base that allowed it to be sprayed at low air pressure.

Small particles of paint stuck to the rubber but never completely joined each other, leaving small breathing areas not visible to the human eye. This, in conjunction with the open-cell foam rubber that was developed, allowed the body sweat to be transmitted through the substance, so that when the ape's face was bathed in sweat, it was the actor's own.

Another product developed was a spirit gum that, unlike the existing product, would not have a sheen to it. A special sealer was devised to protect the rubber from the effect of a mineral-based oil. This also had a sheen to it, but they were able to flatten it. Using a research grant from a rubber company, a foam rubber was developed that had a high degree of softness, cutting down the heavy bulk of the muzzle and chin.

It was necessary for the actors to learn to eat correctly too. In the beginning, although they could open their mouths, they had to use a mirror to see where to place the food. Often they would resort to feeding each other, and that was an amusing sight to see. They found it easiest to chew solids that had been cut small. Of course, there were always those who didn't respect the makeup.

They'd fill up on greasy foods, and after lunch their chins would be hanging off. Food would be caught in the foam-rubber lips, and the actors would go to Makeup for repair.

Drinking was done through straws, and smoking through long cigarette holders. James Whitmore had to find a long stem for his pipe.

Some of the appliances could be reused. It was necessary to remove them without using any solvents or mineral oils. The appliances were rewashed in a mixture of acetone and alcohol, the edges were cleaned and sterilized, and then put through a refinishing process so that they could be used as often as three or four times. It all depended on the makeup man and the actor who wore it. Because there were so many appliances used, some were interchangeable. All were named and numbered.

For example, Woody Parfrey played one of the wise orangutan judges, along with James Whitmore and Maurice Evans in the "see no evil, hear no evil, speak no evil" parody for Heston's trial sequence. Parfrey had a fairly large nose and bone structure. His appliances were large enough to be reused on other actors and would look as though they were custom-made. When an actor was being fitted, they would refer to the appliances that might work on him as being a "Woody Parfrey" or a "Roddy McDowall."

For one day's shooting, the entire makeup ran about $700 to $800, but reuse would bring that figure down. The makeup artists themselves were earning from $1,200 to $1,400 a week.

Josephine Turner did all the hairwork for the film. Chambers describes her as a genius of a lady. Her work was all hand-ventilated onto the finest lace. She is the grande dame of wigmaking in Hollywood.

The mutants in *Beneath the Planet of the Apes* (1969) wore full-head appliances of foam rubber. Over this, a thin skin of clear silicone was painted to give the effect of depth, as though looking through transparent skin. The wardrobe designer designed a hood that could be pulled off. Chambers had several exceptional makeup artists and sculptors working on the likenesses of the overmasks, creating them to look human. These were worn over the mutant full-head appliance. The mutants flipped off these

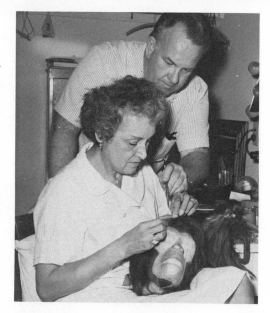

Josephine Turner did all the hairwork for *Planet of the Apes*. Hair was ventilated onto the finest of lace. Turner is regarded as the grande dame of wigmaking in Hollywood. © Apjac Productions, Inc. and Twentieth Century-Fox Film Corporation)

covers when they worshiped the atomic bomb that adorned their altar.

This was a difficult effect because it had to be done rapidly. The mutants had to look as though they had a natural human face, which was actually the hood, and when this was removed, the mutant head remained. It cost thousands of dollars to create this effect, which lasted for about three seconds on the screen. However, it worked.

Working with the actors in ape costume could be quite amusing. Chambers recalls Maurice Evans in full ape regalia, wearing his own eyeglasses and reading his newspaper, as he sat in a car on the Ventura Freeway returning from shooting out at the Fox ranch. Other drivers on the Freeway would nearly put their cars in a ditch viewing such a sight. The first time they were out filming on location and had to drive one of the actors in full makeup into town for something, the local people were stunned to see this "animal creature" ordering things from a luncheonette counter.

Chambers himself, though he knew the actors beneath all the makeup and had worked with them many times before, began to think of them as being ape creatures. He found that he would forget that it was Kim Hunter, Roddy McDowall, or Maurice Evans, and he would actually begin to think of them as the characters they were playing.

It seemed only fitting to those behind the
Academy Awards that John Chambers be
presented with an Oscar by a simian for his
outstanding achievements in makeup for
Planet of the Apes. Walter Matthau was given
the dubious honor of controlling the chimp.
(© *Academy of Motion Picture Arts and
Sciences*)

It was a strange feeling.

Chambers and Dan Striekpeke have recently finished *The Island of Dr. Moreau*
(1977), which was filmed in the Virgin Islands. Chambers's involvement in this film
began nearly two years earlier. Striekpeke
was first approached to do the film and
agreed if Chambers would, too.

The two men recognized that the makeup
would lie somewhere between the *Primal
Man* concept and the *Planet of the Apes*
concept. The mechanics had already been
licked in these previous films, but the concept would take some doing. They worked
with Sandy Howard in developing the creatures. Although they studied the original film
version of *The Island of Dr. Moreau*, which
was titled *Island of Lost Souls* (1933), they
felt that they could offer much more than
could have been done in 1933.

Originally they had wanted less hair on
the faces, giving a more human aspect, but
this was changed, and more hairwork was
added to the face. Haircloth was used because of the tropical climate. Normal hair
just would not stand up to the humidity.

Striekpeke went to the Islands first, doing
makeup on Burt Lancaster and Michael
York and others. Chambers remained back

at the lab with his crew preparing enough
appliances. The requirements changed continually up until the last moment.

The first makeup on Michael York was
created by Dan Striekpeke. He created a
sunburnt, blistered, dehydrated look
brought about from the shipwreck Michael
survives. York becomes the first specimen
that Dr. Moreau attempts to transform from
human to animal, the norm being from animal to human.

Chambers had created appliances so that
he could subtly transform York into a wolf
without the audience realizing it. However,
York, taking "dramatic license," wanted to
do the part dramatically and physically
rather than with appliances. Striekpeke did
a beautiful job in creating an effective
makeup using highlights and shadows and
a little hair. The makeup, combined with
York's performance, achieved the effect
very successfully.

One scene called for the Bullman to be attacked by a real Bengal tiger, and
Striekpeke created a fiberglass helmet from
a mold of Bob Ozman's head. It was outfit-
ted with straps and a protective covering.
The production staff had been advised that
when an animal attacks—provided he does

become "wild" enough to do so—he could snap at a head or neck in an attempt to crush the skull. Because they were going to train the tiger to bite one of the Bullman's horns off anyway, they felt every possible precaution should be exercised.

The tiger did try to bite Bob Ozman, who was playing the Bullman, on the back of the neck, and another time a fang just grazed his eyes. Both times the helmet was the life-saving factor. Striekpeke had to repair it after the first encounter, which is some indication of how severe the attack was. At other times, the tiger would slash at a hand, tearing off a foam-rubber glove.

Makeup calls varied from three A.M. to four A.M. It took four hours per person to make them into a Humanimal, mainly because there were so many appliances involved. The Wardrobe Department helped a great deal with other parts of the costumes such as fur jackets. Although the makeup could probably have been completed in three and a half hours, Chambers and Striekpeke insisted on an allowance of at least four, and the cameras were never held up.

Chambers did anticipate problems with the appliances and the moisture, particularly because some of the action required fighting scenes in the water. Special adhesives were used, and the problem never arose.

Chambers was quite proud of the teeth he designed and created. They were veneer and tamped right in. Despite the fighting with the actual animals, there were no broken real teeth, and the actors could talk with them, too.

Chambers has found that a surprising number of young people are interested in makeup as a hobby. They are very creative, and both the talented and untalented have the same enthusiasm. It is out of this group that our future makeup artists will come. Chambers tries very hard to answer letters he receives from these fans. One of the first things he tells them is to be honest with themselves as to whether they are artists. The mechanics of the profession can be taught, but without the creativity, they will remain mechanics, never to become anything greater.

If they are good artists, Chambers recommends that they go to school and get a college degree in one of the sciences or go to art school. There is no easy way to make it today.

Although Chambers has realized his element in television and movies, he is still connected to the medical field. He is prosthetic consultant to Los Angeles County General Hospital and makes many of the appliances required by the veterans there and at San Diego Naval Hospital.

Chambers was the only makeup artist for years to operate a commercial makeup lab. He worked mainly as a lab man, doing makeup creations and appliances for other makeup artists for good fees but no film credit. His studio is the John Chambers Stu-

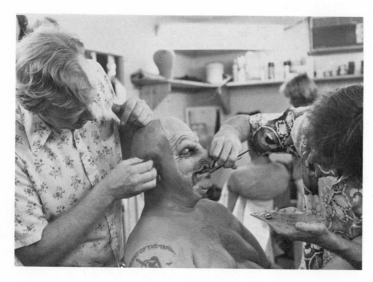

John L. Sullivan is transformed into the Boarman in *The Island of Dr. Moreau*. (© American-International)

Sullivan in complete Boarman makeup. (© American-International)

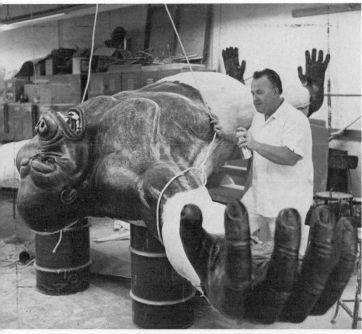

Another project of Chambers was to construct this cuddly gorilla for a Canadian wax museum. (*Photo by Gerald Smith*)

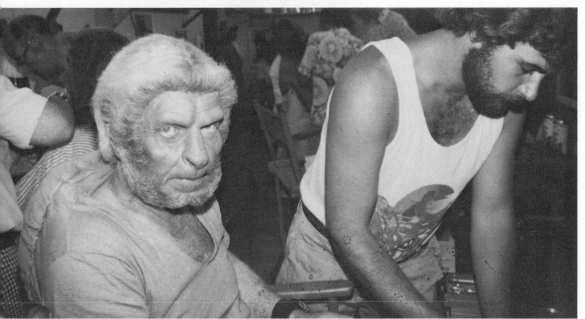

Richard Basehart, as the Sayer of the Laws, during makeup. Ed Henriques applies Basehart's makeup. (© *American-International*)

dio at 330 South Myers Street, Burbank, California.

Chambers is the first and only makeup artist to possess both the Oscar and the Emmy for outstanding creative achievement in both the motion picture and television industries. He has trained many of today's successful makeup lab men and remains extremely proud of them. In 1978 he was elected president of the Society of Makeup Artists and was also selected by the Hollywood Chamber of Commerce to become the first motion picture makeup artist to be honored by them with a star in Hollywood's well-known Walk of Fame. Chambers has contributed an enormous amount to the progression of the makeup industry.

Chapter 20

FRED BLAU

Fred Blau was born in 1939 in Los Angeles. He became interested in makeup during a theatre arts course at Los Angeles Valley College. He had been a professional actor in movies since 1956, and when taking a makeup class in his theatre arts course, he found that as a result of his acting experience he was soon showing his instructor techniques never heard of before. That seemed to be the crucial factor in deciding his future.

Blau served an apprenticeship of three years with Warner Brothers. After his graduation, his first assignment was on the film *Cool Hand Luke* (1967), and since then his career has continued to develop. Some of his movie credits are *Finian's Rainbow* (1968), *Winning* (1969), *Bite the Bullet* (1975), and *Sparkle* (1976).

In 1967 another milestone in makeup history occurred when John Chambers of Twentieth Century-Fox began the laborious task of creating the now-familiar simian creatures for *Planet of the Apes*. John Chambers won an Oscar, and the incredibly successful movie spawned four sequels and a television series.

It was Fred Blau's daily assignment at Twentieth Century-Fox to make up the series' star, Roddy McDowall. McDowall was the only actor to have played three different ape roles: Cornelius in *Planet of the Apes*, and *Escape from the Planet of the Apes* (1971), and Caesar in *Conquest of the Planet of the Apes* (1972), and *Battle for the Planet of the Apes* (1974), and Galen in the television series. With all these feature films under McDowall's belt, Blau readily admits that McDowall could tell him more about makeup than he could tell McDowall.

The heat on the Twentieth Century-Fox ranch in Malibu Canyon, where most of the exterior shots were filmed, didn't offer the most pleasant working conditions. Skin divers use neoprene suits for insulation against cold water—depending on body heat trapped by the rubber to keep them warm. Latex has the same effect and is used for appliances because it moves with the skin. One can well imagine the strain of wearing a rubber appliance for fourteen hours under the 110-degree temperatures at the Malibu ranch.

The first step in Roddy McDowall's transformation was his hair. Sheral Ross, hair stylist on the series, began by taking small bunches of McDowall's hair and securing them tightly with rubber bands. When Ms. Ross had completed that task, she covered the entire area with a black stocking cap. The bunches of hair would give appropriate anchor points needed later when the wig had to be secured.

After this had been done, Blau would begin. He first took a small pallet knife and

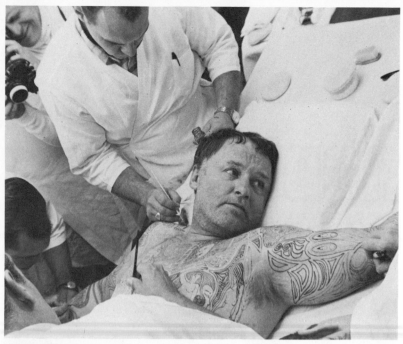

Fred Blau was one of nine makeup artists who worked under the direction of Gordon Bau to create the intricate and beautiful pattern on Rod Steiger in *The Illustrated Man*. (© *Warner Bros.*)

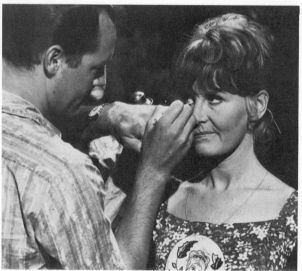

Blau adds a little eye-liner as Petula Clark makes a face to aid him in his work on the set of *Finian's Rainbow*. (*Fred Blau*)

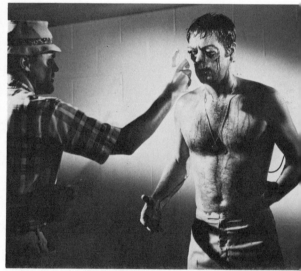

Robert Wagner, star of *Winning*, gets a touch-up from Blau for a bloody scene. Note the "blood" tubes taped to his arms. (*Fred Blau*)

painted McDowall's eyebrows and side-burns with Dumold—a wax that prevented the adhesives used later from adhering to McDowall's real hair. If this step was missed, McDowall's appliances, when removed after the day's shooting, would undoubtedly pull sideburns and eyebrows off with it.

Using a small makeup brush, Blau would then paint the inside of the appliance that covered McDowall's nose with a rubber ad-

hesive; then the same adhesive was used on McDowall's nose. With an adequate amount of adhesive on the appliance and face, Blau then would press the muzzle firmly over McDowall's nose and upper lip, securing it. Now that the appliance had an anchor point, Blau would go on to glue down the eyebrows and cheek sections in the same manner. Using a tweezer, he got under the very thin edges of the appliance, smoothing them down at the same time. If this wasn't done, the edges might have bunched up and become lumpy, hampering the total illusion.

The drying of the adhesive was speeded up by using a hand-held dryer. Then Blau used more adhesive to thicken and build up the edges of the appliance so that it would fit snugly to the contours of McDowall's face.

After the upper half of the appliance is secured, Blau used a small stipple sponge and darkened McDowall's neck and the still-exposed portions of his forehead and cheeks with castor grease. Castor grease has been around as long as rubber appliances. It is used exclusively on rubber because it will not affect the rubber as normal makeup greases and oils will.

The ears were applied next. They were constructed of hard rubber rather than foam latex like the other appliances. The only problem with these ears, which were used on the chimpanzees, was that they created difficulty in hearing.

After the appliances were secure, a wig was applied to McDowall's head. Next Blau painted McDowall's teeth with black enamel, so that they would not show through the teeth attached to the appliance for the simian makeup. Blau then used rubber adhesive again, first on McDowall's chin, and then on the inside of the chin appliance, which was secured and again carefully smoothed out and dried.

The hairpieces were then attached. Four facial hairpieces and a wig were used on the apes. The hairpieces were made of human hair. The actual hairpieces used on the apes were ventilated onto lace, the same way a hairlace wig or beard is made. Every strand of hair was hand-tied onto this lace and shaped according to the needs of the actors.

In the case of the ape hair the wigs were made to look like the hair on a chimpanzee, gorilla, or orangutan. Those pieces were used over and over. They did take a lot of rough use. Blau added the side pieces, which looked like muttonchops, and the frontal piece to the forehead to blend into the wig. Then the chinpiece was added. This was like a small goatee.

The forehead hairpieces were then applied. First McDowall's skin area and then the inside of the hairpiece were painted with spirit gum and pressed onto McDowall's forehead, then dried. Rubber adhesive was used on McDowall's face because it is less irritating to the skin than spirit gum and holds appliances better. The sides and beard were then glued on in the same manner.

After the facial pieces were in place, Blau used human hair and a crepe wool mixture to overlay the lace and create the look that hair was actually growing out of the skin. Ideally, human hair was preferred, but the cost was prohibitive. Wool was used with the hair to serve as a filler, and it also made the hair easier to handle. Besides the intricate work on the appliance, the hair overlay was probably the most important job. The overlay could actually have made or destroyed the authenticity of the makeup because after it was laid by hand and glued onto the face, it then had to be picked up by a hot curling iron to give it the appearance of growing out of the skin. It was this procedure that put the finishing touches on the simian makeup, overlaying the individual hairs, giving the impression of a natural-looking unevenness.

Once the facial appliances and hairpieces were attached, Blau would then apply castor grease to McDowall's eyelids and the uncovered facial sections, blending the coloring until it was impossible to tell where flesh ended and appliance began. The grease was then dusted with powder to seal it and prevent running. McDowall's hands were then prepared simply by slipping on a pair of nylon gloves with hair and fingernails attached.

When John Chambers created the makeup for the original films, he used foam latex because, though firm, it is soft and flexible, permitting the actors a good range of expression with minor discomfort. However, for some, the discomfort wasn't minor enough. Three stars selected for the roles, Edward G. Robinson as Dr. Zaius, Julie Harris as Zira, and Rock Hudson as Cornelius, gave them up because they could not tolerate the makeup for various reasons. McDowall's perseverance is admirable.

There were over twenty makeup and hair personnel working at one time on the *Apes* television series. The series was shot at one of the most active times in the industry, and Blau says good appliance help was scarce. There were times when he made up three apes in one day, approximately nine hours

It was Fred Blau's daily assignment to turn Roddy McDowall into Galen, the chimpanzee star of the popular television series ''Planet of the Apes.'' (© *Twentieth Century-Fox Film Corporation*)

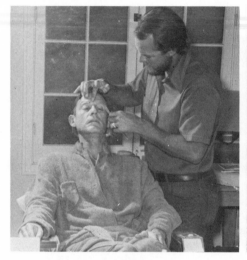

Using a small pallet knife, Blau painted McDowall's eyebrows and sideburns with Dumold to prevent adhesive from adhering to McDowall's facial hair. (© *Twentieth Century-Fox Film Corporation*)

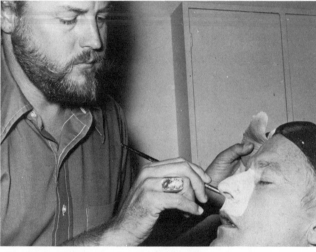

Adhesive was painted on McDowall's nose, as well as the inside of the appliance, to secure the appliance to his face. (© *Twentieth Century-Fox Film Corporation*)

of straight makeup. Fortunately, Blau's philosophy is that when he is doing such an assignment, it must become a labor of love. He feels he could make up the apes all day long and never stop.

There are always comical occurrences when working on projects of this magnitude. Once Blau accidentally glued another actor's chinpiece onto McDowall's face, and McDowall had to play his scenes with his lower lip tucked under. Fortunately, that didn't happen twice.

Blau became involved in research and experimentation when he developed a crea-

ture for *Super Beasts* (1975). It was the first big appliance project he had been asked to do, so he chose to consult with John Chambers.

Super Beasts is a film about a mad scientist who takes a drug which causes a Jekyll-and-Hyde regression on him. Blau and Chambers decided on a Neanderthal-type of creature and made appliances quite similar to the ape appliance. However, instead of a two-piece appliance, which consisted of the upper part which went from the upper lip to the forehead, and the second piece which was just a chin, they con-

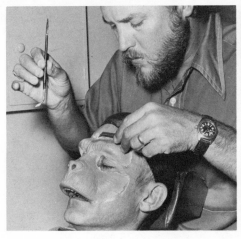

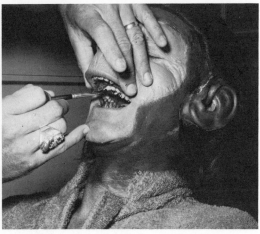

Being extremely careful not to tear the thin edges of the appliance, Blau gently glues the edges down while smoothing them out at the same time. (© *Twentieth Century-Fox Film Corporation*)

McDowall's teeth were painted with a black enamel so that they would not show through the teeth attached to the appliance for the simian makeup or reflect the camera lighting. (©*Twentieth Century-Fox Film Corporation*)

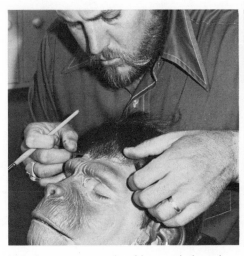

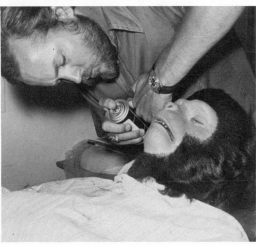

Hairpieces were made of human hair and ventilated onto lace. Four facial hairpieces and a wig were used on the Apes. (© *Twentieth Century-Fox Film Corporation*)

A frontal hairpiece was added and blended into the wig, as well as side pieces, which looked like muttonchops, and a chinpiece. (© *Twentieth Century-Fox Film Corporation*)

structed the appliance in one full piece. With this appliance they had to create three stages of regression. After Blau and Chambers made the three stages, Blau managed to use them to create two more regressions by cutting the foreheads off some and matching them with more or less advanced stages of the lower part of the face.

These appliances were used on actor Craig Littler, who played the mad doctor. The film was produced in the Philippines. Blau fit the appliances to the Filipino actors, whose faces were smaller than Littler's. This was done by taking a pie-shaped cut out of

the sides of the appliances and squeezing them down. The spaces were filled in with cotton.

A horse race took place in *Bite the Bullet,* which was set at the turn of the century. Mario Arteaga's character suffers from an exposed abscessed tooth, the pain of which is averted by a drug in pill form. He runs out of the pain-killer during the race, and at one of the checkpoints in the race, fellow actor Gene Hackman fits a .38-caliber bullet shell over Arteaga's right lower bicuspid. Blau turned to John Chambers for assistance on this unusual situation. Chambers not only

An unsuspecting Antoinette Bower daydreams as Craig Littler transforms into a Super Beast. (*Fred Blau*)

Blau with two of his Super Beast creations. (*Fred Blau*)

had the necessary equipment to make the full upper and lower impressions of the teeth this assignment required, but his splendid track record speaks for itself. Producer Richard Brooks expected nothing short of the best result, and that's what he got. Viewers actually saw Hackman fit the bullet on Arteaga's tooth.

Blau recalls one of his most demanding assignments, involving six makeups on one actor, for Richard Brooks's *Bite the Bullet.* Blau had a stunt man who doubled for two different actors and one actress, then played three different parts in the picture—and all was achieved through aging and facial hair. None of Blau's fellow makeup artist friends ever seemed to suspect that he had accomplished such a feat, so he assumed it went over well.

On the film *Barquero*, Blau had to create the illusion of a bullet hit right in the middle of an actor's forehead. Any time special effects makeup is done, it is referred to as a gag. The "gag" was to have a full shot of the actor with a bullet hole exploding in his head.

Blau and the special effects man rigged a squib—which is very much like a firecracker electrically ignited—over a blood bag. A blood bag is a plastic pouch of theatrical blood. This was placed on the actor's fore-

head, and about forty minutes were spent creating a new forehead to cover the blood bag and the protruding portions of the bag itself.

In the blood bag, Blau had a flat plastic tube rigged which he wove through the actor's hair until it was no longer visible. The tube went down the back of his neck, through his clothes, and out his pants leg, and was connected to a 60-cc syringe loaded and primed with more theatrical blood.

The "victim," who is wading from a barge to the pier, is shot by another man who is on the pier, so Blau went into the water and hid near the pier out of the camera frame. When the special effects man set the charge off, Fred depressed the syringe and caused the wound to bleed. The shot went splendidly except for one thing—the tube that was connected to the syringe broke loose because of the pressure and managed to douse the whole crew with blood. The shot worked, but everyone had to clean up a bloody mess.

Blau describes another extremely interesting project he was involved in. "Danny Striekpeke brought me in on the film he was producing entitled *SSSSSSS* to help out on one of the big appliance jobs. John Chambers was working on the transformation of a

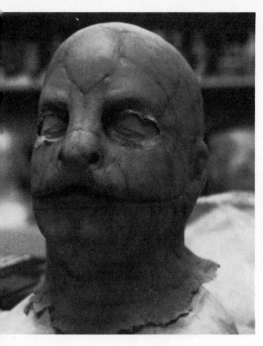

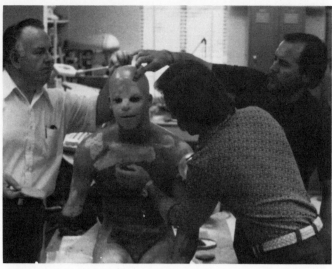

John Chambers *(left)*, Fred Blau *(right)*, and an unknown makeup artist *(foreground)* work to accomplish the *SSSSSSS* creature, which was Chambers's creation. (© *Universal*)

Dan Striekpeke brought Fred Blau in on the film *SSSSSSS* to help on one of the big appliance jobs. Here is a model of the serpentlike creature they were to prepare. (© *Universal*)

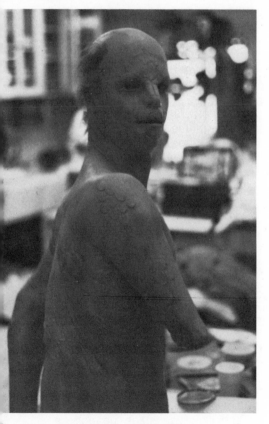

The actor who played the serpentlike creature was an amputee who was without his legs and one of his arms. (© *Universal*)

man into a snake. Strother Martin played the mad doctor whose specialty was reptiles. He had a serpentarium and hired aides, whom he then experimented on. One of the actors was an amputee who was without his legs and one of his arms. He portrayed the specimen who was a by-product of the drug that Strother Martin injected into his aides. He was entered as a freak in a sideshow.

Another makeup assignment given Blau was on a project for Disneyland called *Fantasy on Parade*. He did this for five seasons during Christmas and New Year's.

Blau created elaborate butterfly masks for the Butterfly Girls who hatched out of a caterpillar. He painted the masks on each of the seven girls with sequins and iridescent makeup. The painted masks covered their faces completely—forehead to chin. Then Mary Poppins, Snow White, Santa Claus, and many other characters all had to be completed in three hours. Blau had to teach the varied makeup steps to the young people themselves because the lack of time prevented him from doing every character each day himself. Blau did, however, have to make up all the main characters.

We asked Blau what procedure he would recommend to anyone who might be interested in becoming a makeup artist.

"There are many ways of becoming a makeup artist—all very different and difficult. Most of the major studios don't have apprenticeship programs anymore. It's a matter of contacting the various unions and finding out from them if there are any positions available. Or you can, perhaps by chance, get picked up as an auxiliary. By this I mean you make yourself available, and when all the makeup artists in the union are all working, then there's a possible chance that they can start you working at one of the studios.

"If this happens, you put in one hundred twenty days under the various labor acts, then you're eligible to take an examination. From then on you can move up in status in the makeup program. Then again you could apply at television studios. The pay is less, but you can apply the same way as an auxiliary. When you take your examination, you will become a Television Makeup Artist. After that, you can take another examination to become a regular Motion Picture Makeup Artist. There is a difference in the status of television and motion picture makeup artists, but they both require the same amount of knowledge."

Describing an average day on the job, Blau told us it begins by getting out of bed at four-thirty A.M. to make a six-thirty A.M. makeup call. Depending on the cast and its size, the actors and actresses are normally made up prior to eight or nine A.M. The actresses come in earlier because their makeup is a bit more involved than the actors. After everyone reaches the set, the makeup men attend to the actors and actresses, who are called principals, and make sure throughout the day's shooting that the makeups match from scene to scene. A TV day consists of twelve to fourteen hours. A motion picture day, because of larger budgets, is somewhat less at times.

One of the most challenging projects Blau has had was *Apocalypse Now* (1979), which was filmed in the Philippines. It is a Francis Ford Coppola Production. The film goes to great lengths to re-create scenes from the Vietnam War.

Ifugao tribesmen were brought from Banaue to Pagsanjan to play the part of Cambodian Montagnards. A practical village was constructed for them which was also to be used as a major set in the picture. The hair and makeup work for the Ifugao called for bowl-type haircuts and various camouflage war paint—some crude and others styled.

One demanding experience Blau faced on *Apocalypse Now* was the director's request for Blau to effect the gag of an actor's leg blown off at the knee with blood pulsating from the raw wound after stepping on a booby trap.

Although it normally would have taken four or five days to prepare the foam-latex appliance and create the effect in the usual way, Coppola advised Blau that he wished to shoot the scene that same day. Blau knew that meant he could not rely on the conventional rubber appliances but would have to fall back on old techniques.

Beginning at three that afternoon, Blau had the actor sit in the same position his leg would be in when the scene was shot. Using cotton and plastic sealer, Blau began creating the wound on the actor's knee to look as though there was a jagged piece of bone protruding from it.

Plastic sealer, which has a methyl ethyl ketone base, is very quick drying; however, a layer is added one at a time, it being necessary for each layer to dry completely before another is added. Despite working as quickly as possible, the shooting ended for the day before Blau's gag was prepared.

The following day Blau was ready. He ran a plastic bleeding tube up the actor's pants leg, and he had made overflaps to appear as though the skin had been torn off. Blau used about thirty feet of tubing, which he ran under the camera dolly and hid. He allowed one beat per half second for the pulsating blood flow to appear as though the "casualty's" heart rate was accelerated. Blau also had to keep careful watch on the camera and use the blood in his syringe only when the camera was actually shooting the leg, as the syringe held only a certain amount of blood.

Blau is an avid bass fisherman and utilizes his makeup experience in his hobby by making molds for his lures and plastic worms—pouring a hot-melt, cold-cure plastic into the molds. He has traded the blood and gore of the Vietnam War era for the charms of angels—"Charlie's Angels," to be more specific. Blau made up actress Kate Jackson for her role in this popular television series.

Chapter 21

THOMAS BURMAN

Tom Burman owns a laboratory that is unlike any other in the world. The Burman's Studio, Inc., of Van Nuys, California, sports a vacuum form machine, a large walk-in oven for curing rubber, spray-painting booths, and other tools needed in the art of creating some of the most incredible makeups of today.

Burman was born in 1940 in Santa Monica, California. When he was three, his parents moved to a house next door to Warner Brothers Studios, where they lived until he was eight. Burman's mother wanted him to be a doctor, but it was his father who had the greatest influence upon his son's career. The senior Burman was an inventor, sculptor, and artist. He had his own business making masks and props. During his childhood, Tom got a taste of working with rubber, plastics, and other materials.

Burman was fortunate enough to begin an apprenticeship at Twentieth Century-Fox Studios under Ben Nye, Sr., in 1966. Approximately one year later, Dan Striekpeke took over as department head, and Burman worked almost entirely with John Chambers, who came to Fox to do *Planet of the Apes*. Except for Chambers, Burman feels that he worked in more areas and facets of *Planet of the Apes* than anyone else. Burman considers working with John Chambers and having Chambers receive an Os-

car for *Planet of the Apes* as one of the high points of his career.

Chambers chose Burman as his assistant to work as a department head on the set of the film *The Ardry Papers*. This film related modern man to primitive man from his earliest beginning. The film was never released, but it was decided that the creations were much too good to leave on the cutting-room floor, so a documentary-style series was developed for television and titled *Primal Man*. The series depicted man's primitive activities, such as hunting and locating shelter, and dealt with territorial instincts and the discovery of fire.

The television series was reshot, using the same makeup artists and the same creations they had used for *The Ardry Papers*. This time, however, Burman was in full charge. Because John Chambers had prior commitments he was unable to be involved. Burman had fourteen makeup artists working twelve weeks to achieve the look they wanted.

For the third series Burman received a Special Emmy Award for Outstanding Achievement in Any Area of Creative Technical Crafts. As Chambers had done a good share of the original creations with Burman for *The Ardry Papers*, he too received an Emmy. During the filming of the last show there was a tragic plane crash, and Burman and Chambers lost some very dear friends

Burman was chosen by John Chambers to be his assistant and work as a department head on the set of the film *The Ardry Papers*, which was never released. This is stunt man Janos Prohaska who, along with many makeup artists, lost his life in a fatal plane crash during the filming of the subsequent television series. (*Wolper Productions/Tom Burman*)

The Ardry Papers was later reshot for television as *Primal Man*. Burman was in charge of makeup on the production. (*Wolper Productions/Tom Burman*)

and the industry lost some very talented craftsmen.

Many of the films Burman has worked on have been extremely challenging, calling for considerable experimentation. There were problems that had to be solved and no one to look to for a precedent in solving them. Some of these problem films were *A Man Called Horse* (1970), *The Man Who Fell to Earth* (1976), *Demon Seed* (1977), and *Close Encounters of the Third Kind* (1977).

In *The Devil's Rain* (1975) with Ernest Borgnine, it was necessary to create the effect of people melting, and the challenge was to bring them down to nothing without using stop-motion. Tom's ever-present objective when working on such a film is to fool the audience and have them ask, "How the heck did he do it?"

The makeup team went into this picture rather blindly, and after a lot of brainstorming, it was decided to use inflatable figures. A vacuum was used to draw the figures down to nothing. At the same time, liquid and smoke were pumped into the figures. The effect of breathing was created by injecting air into the dummy, drawing it out, injecting it in, drawing it out; but each time drawing out a little more so that it would start to sag, at the same time, pumping more smoke and fluid. Three different colors

of fluid were used, and the effect of a person melting into the ground was achieved.

In the beginning of the melting process the people would have, as Tom describes it, "goop" running off their arms and hands. This would accumulate and smolder until their faces appeared to slowly melt away.

Ernest Borgnine played the grotesque Goat Demon. Foam appliances were used on all the melting faces, similar to those made for *Planet of the Apes* (1968). A wig covered a fiberglass helmet that had the goat horns attached to it. Tubes went into the appliances so that it would spill the "melting fluid" out through small holes.

William Shatner, who also starred in *The Devil's Rain,* described the ordeal he and the others faced with the makeup demanded for their roles.

"We were fitted for a mask which covered the cheekbones and forehead. The eye-holes were covered with a gauzelike material that allowed us to see but gave the appearance that we had no eyes. Actually, we were practically blinded. This went on for days. When the time came to "melt," liquid was injected into tubes and poured out of the eye-holes. This gave us the feeling of drowning because the liquid first filled the mask, filling our noses before pouring out the eye-holes."

The many faces of William Shatner by Tom Burman for the television series "The Barbary Coast." (*ABC*)

Shatner had the opportunity of working with Burman again in the short-lived television series "The Barbary Coast." Time was extremely sparse on this series, and Shatner, Burman, and the wardrobe man were given only a bare outline of the character involved each week to work from. The three of them would confer as to what their ideas on the character were, then separate to do their individual jobs. Much to his surprise, Shatner discovered that once the makeup was applied and the costume donned, he could look into a mirror and become the character whose lines he'd memorized. The wardrobe and makeup would suggest to him that special gait or voice so necessary to bring forth the character he was to portray.

There were days on "The Barbary Coast" that Shatner had to have three extensive makeups applied in one day. Several days he spent as much as nine hours in the makeup chair. With nearly twenty-seven different characterizations, none of which were even similar, Shatner recalls "The Barbary Coast" as a physically punishing show but considers Burman a genius in his field.

The Food of the Gods (1976), which starred Ida Lupino, Pamela Franklin, Marjoe Gortner, and John Cypher, had its problems, too. With only thirty days to tackle the task of creating and building fifteen giant rats, two giant chickens, ten giant worms, and eight giant wasps, plus the various makeup appliances, there was no time for preliminary sketches nor for trial and error construction.

Seven of the giant rats had to be animated, and their heads had to be removable for close-up inserts. The chickens and the

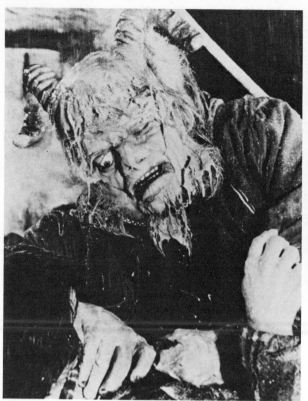

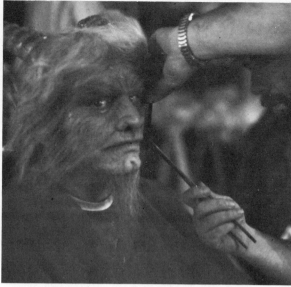

Burman lays whiskers on Ernest Borgnine. (*Bryanston Pictures*)

Ernest Borgnine played a grotesque Goat Demon in *The Devil's Rain*, who was destined to melt, with a little help from Tom Burman. (*Bryanston Pictures*)

The insects in *The Food of the Gods* were cast in neoprene and the wings were vacuum formed in clear vinyl plastic. (*American International*)

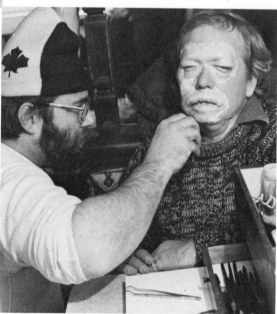

The victim of a bee sting is given a realistic makeup by Burman. (*American International*)

Three of the rats were suits. Burman's son, Barney, would crawl inside the suit and operate it when they wanted the rat leaping toward the camera or onto someone. (*American International*)

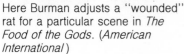

Here Burman adjusts a "wounded" rat for a particular scene in *The Food of the Gods*. (*American International*)

Burman supports one of the vicious rats he created for *The Food of the Gods* as Ida Lupino prepares to slay it. (*American International*)

worms also had to be animated. The picture was filmed on a tiny island in Vancouver, Canada, and the production unit found it very uncomfortable, with the weather cold and wet. If it didn't rain, it snowed.

The rats were built from neoprene—the heads cast in neoprene and the bodies modeled in clay. Hard neoprene was used because of its durability, enabling the crew to mount the mechanics inside the neoprene without risk. The feet, ears, and tails were cast in latex, and the bodies were covered with scotch foam and synthetic hair (fun fur).

The mechanical heads were used as inserts, appearing at the edge of the picture, from left or right, when they were devouring people. They had one handle with which to hold the head and another handle to operate the mouth and pull back the lips. The rooster head was operated in the same way.

Three of the rats were suits. Burman's son, Barney, would crawl inside the suit and operate it when they wanted the rat leaping toward the camera or onto someone's back. The other five rats were complete dummies, over nine feet long.

The insects were cast in neoprene, and the wings were vacuum formed in clear vinyl plastic. The worms were built out of

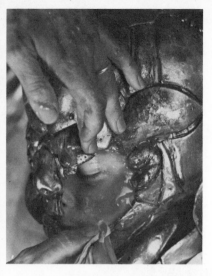

The structure of the suit used in *Demon Seed* was difficult for Burman to work out, as the scales overlapped each other, allowing flexibility. (*MGM*)

Within the skeletal frame there exists a human child with all the knowledge of his computer father, Proteus IV. (*MGM*)

The Demon Seed being helped into his birthplace. (*MGM*)

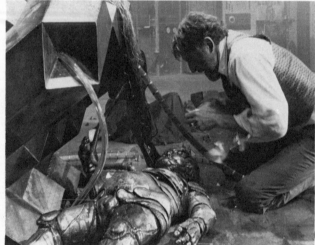

Fritz Weaver portrays computer scientist Alex Harris, the inventor of Proteus IV. (*MGM*)

foam rubber, using monofilament inside so they could be animated. To animate them, Tom put a small hole in the top of a table, and by pulling underneath the table, the worm would coil up. When the monofilament was released, the worm would straighten out. When the worms wrapped themselves around Ida Lupino, the effect was most realistic indeed.

The rooster was made with neoprene, and the inside of its mouth was foam rubber. The combs were foam rubber so that when the rooster went from side to side, they would flop like a real rooster's would. The eye was vacuum formed and hand-painted. The body was made from scotch foam, covered with "tricky feathers" that were dyed individually to match the actual

rooster that was used for the matte shots. A matte shot is a technique of blending actors filmed in the studio with trick scenes or scenes done on location. The actor is filmed against a nonreflective background such as blue velvet. A high-contrast negative of this image is then combined with the desired background.

Plagued by the unpleasant weather, and being on a fifteen-by-three-mile-wide island with only one small store for supplies, the production team had their share of accidents. They constructed a large rooster wing, and then it was left out in the snow. It

Opposite: Burman found himself facing another difficult task when he created the spacesuit for David Bowie for his role in *The Man Who Fell to Earth*. (© *Cinema Five*)

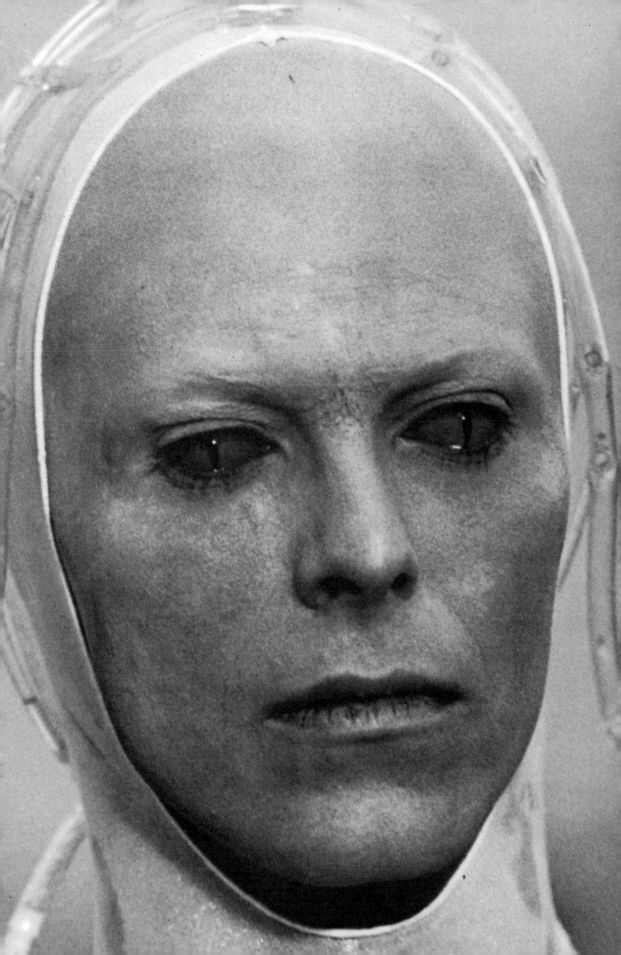

had to be dried and almost rebuilt right there on the island.

Another incident that was extremely frightening to Burman occurred when they were doing a scene where gasoline was supposedly thrown on a wasp nest, which was then set on fire. The propman mistakenly used real gasoline, and the wasp nest held the fumes. When the match was lit, the gasoline exploded, throwing people down and nearly destroying the set. Burman's children were standing about fifteen feet from the explosion, so he was badly shaken. There were no fire extinguishers on the set. Fortunately, no one was seriously injured, although two special effects men received glass fibers in their eyes.

In making up the men who were stung by the giant wasps, Burman made a series of foam-latex appliances and the camera was made to move back and forth from one actor to another. Each time that the audience would see the actor, his face was a little more swollen. Burman used about five stages of swollen face, laying the actor down in place, putting one appliance on, coloring him, taking it off while the camera was on the other actor, then putting on a more swollen face for the next shot.

In *Demon Seed* (1976), a supercomputer, complete with the power to reason, produces a child through artificial insemination.

A complete body cast of a midget was taken for the Demon Seed and over that the entire suit was sculptured. Plaster molds were made, then cast in neoprene, then recast in rubber. Each one of the segments of neoprene was cut apart, polished, painted, and then stuck back onto the thin rubber suit. They were all formed together so that the midget could actually get inside. The arms, legs, head, and body were all separate pieces, and it was put on much the same as a suit of armor would be put on. It was a very difficult structure to work out, as the scales were overlapping so that one scale could fold within another, allowing the man to move freely.

When Gerrit Graham attempts to shut the computer down, his efforts are foiled. Graham is decapitated with a device the computer has manufactured for its protection.

A separate head was done for Gerrit Graham. An impression of his entire head was taken, then a plaster cast was made

In 1977 Burman assisted John Chambers and Dan Striekpeke on *The Island of Dr. Moreau* and considers the Bullman one of his most successful Humanimal® creations. (*American International*)

from that impression. Burman carved the eyes open, did a mold over that, cast it in rubber, filled it with polyurethane, and put the glass eyes in it. Later on wigs were made for it.

A mannequin head was done in *Black Sunday* (1976) for Clyde Kosatsu. It was done in the same way as the head in *Demon Seed*. The head was used in the scene where Clyde Kosatsu picks up the phone and speaks into it, his voice triggering a bomb that blows his head off.

The space suit that was created for *The Man Who Fell to Earth* (1976) was another difficult task. The use of radiator tubing made David Bowie appear as if he had to wear a cooling suit on the planet he came from. The suit had to be totally self-contained. Burman had to have compressed air bottles concealed inside a special backpack. The compressed air was metered through regulators and flow valves and injected into a suit that was filled with liquid so the air bubbles would pass through and give the effect of liquid in motion. Although Burman played around with this for months,

A stand-in for Brooke Adams tries out Burman's design for pod transformation in *Invasion of the Body Snatchers*. (*United Artists*)

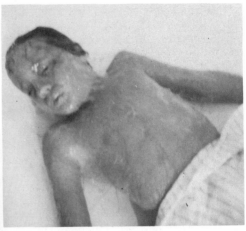

Barney Burman becomes a willing subject when it comes to helping his father out on his many projects. (*Photo courtesy of Tom Burman*)

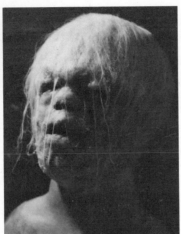

Joe Gibb, who is a midget, portrayed the second-sized fetus in a pod transformation sequence. (*United Artists*)

trying to perfect it, it was just a moment in the picture.

In *A Man Called Horse,* actor Richard Harris suffers the Indian Mandan Sun Val Ceremony, whereby he is hung by bones piercing his chest. This effect was achieved by building a false chest, using foam rubber and having pockets in them filled with blood so that when cut into, the blood would flow out. This ceremony had to be researched so that it would be done as accurately as possible.

Burman does most of his work in foam latex when dealing with appliances or prosthetics that go on the face or any part of the body, feeling that it's been a most convincing material. He precolors and prepaints almost all of his work. He also manufactures his own makeup that goes on rubber, explaining that you can't use just any makeup on rubber, as it has a tendency to react chemically with the rubber.

A Bigfoot creature was created for a Wolper documentary called *Man—Myth or Legend*. Burman purchased every publication he could get on Bigfoot to come up with

his concept. The appliances were foam rubber; the teeth were made of acrylic. All of the hairpads were glued directly onto the actor's skin. Feet were made for him but not hands. The man stood seven feet three and a half inches high. The makeup took three hours for the face and two hours for the body—five hours of makeup!

Burman spent part of the winter of 1977 in the Virgin Islands where work was in progress on *The Island of Dr. Moreau*. Burman's creative input came not in the concept but in the detailing of the Humanimals, the name given the half animal, half human beasts. By employing his expertise in the realm of synthetic or "fun fur" and scotch foam, Burman was able to create the illusion of furry bodies, particularly with the Bullman. Burman considers the Bullman as one of his most successful Humanimal creations, likening his pathetic looks to an almost Frankenstein quality.

In June of 1977 Burman met with director Philip Kaufman and producer Bob Sole to begin discussion of concepts for their latest undertaking, a remake of the fifties science-fiction sleeper which became a classic, *Invasion of the Body Snatchers*. This version, filmed in color as opposed to the original black and white, was to be a remake more than a sequel. Although the story line remained similar to the original, it was also to be updated. The film starred Donald Sutherland, Brooke Adams, Jeff Goldblum, and Leonard Nimoy. Kevin McCarthy, who played the film's hero Dr. Miles Bennell in the original version, does a guest appearance.

Invasion of the Body Snatchers is extremely vivid, and Tom Burman, along with his partner in this project and longtime good friend Ed Henriques, began in September of 1977 to create the special makeup effects needed for the film. Burman was faced with the problem of creating a pulsating pod which would split open and from which a fetus would emerge. The fetus would then begin to grow into one of the actors. Seedpods were created in various scaled sizes, with the first fetus designed to about the actual size of a real infant. This infant was mechanically animated.

Joe Gibb, an actor who is also a midget, portrayed the second-sized fetus. Gibb was covered with foam-latex appliances to effectively portray the second-sized fetus. The third, and full-sized pod person, was covered with a clear plastic silicone material, had nylon "tendrils" inserted in the material, giving an almost corn-silk appearance over his body.

Throughout the film, a dilapidated beggar is seen on the streets with his dog, a boxer. Donald Sutherland comes across the sleeping beggar in one sequence and sees one of the frightening pods (which are the body snatchers) forming next to the beggar's body. Angered, Sutherland kicks the pod. Later, Sutherland and Adams, behaving as though their bodies have already been snatched by the pods, are discovered by the beggar's dog, who now has the face of the beggar. In order to achieve this makeup effect, a cast was taken of the beggar's face and also of the dog's face. Burman then fit the beggar's face to the dog's and the results were stupendous.

In the film's finale, Brooke Adams collapses as though she is drying up. This was achieved by making an inflatable skull. A foam-latex appliance of Adams's face covered the skull. A vacuum pump, hooked to the skull, drew the face into the skull first, and then the skull deflates.

When asked his opinion on the future of the makeup industry, Burman tells us that he feels the surface has only been scratched. We know that with his expertise and his unique studio, Tom Burman will be a large part of that future.

For the 1978 remake of the classic *Invasion of the Body Snatchers*, Burman created a face appliance of a beggar to fit over the face of a dog. (*United Artists*)

Chapter 22

KEN CHASE

Ken Chase was accepted into Make-up Artists and Hair Stylists Local 706 in 1967 after gaining experience on two television series, "The Long Hot Summer" and "Time Tunnel."

His first experience in the application of prosthetic appliances came when he worked on *Planet of the Apes,* where he was assigned the job of making up Maurice Evans as an orangutan. He also did this in the sequel. In the final picture he made up singer Paul Williams as an orangutan.

After making up Paul Williams one morning, Chase felt it might be fun to go out to lunch with Williams in "full dress." They strolled into a rather nice Mexican restaurant in Century City, amazing fellow diners. One can easily imagine the astonishment as Williams, playing his role to the hilt, ordered—of all things—a banana daiquiri with a straw!

After the *Apes,* Chase did makeup on the television series "Wild, Wild West." This presented him with the challenge of creating weekly disguises for costar Ross Martin. Many appliances were used on this series, and it was an invaluable experience.

They had a set stock of appliances on the series that were made by John Chambers for Ross Martin. Among these were about six different noses. Because there was not always the time to prepare prosthetics for the other actors, Chase found himself using Martin's stock noses now and then, usually very successfully.

Time is always of the essence on a weekly show, and the time factor was sometimes responsible for some tragicomic crises. When Ross Martin, in full makeup as an old man complete with wig, moustache, and rubber face, fell during a scene and broke his leg, Chase had to run along beside Ross's stretcher, peeling off the outer layer of skin, wig, and moustache. Despite the fact that Ross was in a great deal of pain, the "show must go on," and Ken needed those articles to make up another actor to appear to be Ross Martin in disguise to finish one remaining scene in the show.

"Wild, Wild West" employed a stock company of stunt men that were easily recognizable by the audience. It became standard procedure, show after show, to try to make the stunt men appear different and unrecognizable with the help of moustaches, beards, and other devices.

Soon after "Wild, Wild West," Chase worked on *Little Big Man* applying makeup on Martin Balsam under the supervision of makeup artist Dick Smith.

Marty Balsam played a bizarre character in the film, who was continually having runins with the Indians. During the course of the film he lost a leg, an arm, and an ear and was finally scalped! Dick Smith designed the makeup that Chase applied each day.

Ross Martin displays an array of makeup from the television series "Wild, Wild West." (*Ken Chase*)

He found it a valuable opportunity to work with Smith because there was so much information to glean from Smith's abundant talent and profuse experience.

In the film *Jeremiah Johnson* (1972), starring Robert Redford, there were many character makeups that made it a challenging film for Chase. The mountain man in particular was interesting because of the scar closing up his eye, a very large obvious moustache, and a shaved head. Chase used spirit gum and colors to dull down the actor's teeth to make them stained and rather ugly.

The actor, Stefan Gierasch, wore contact lenses, so it was always necessary to be sure these were in place before the application of the scar.

One scene called for Gierasch to be buried up to his neck in the sand by the Indians who had left him to die. Robert Redford rides up and discovers Gierasch with live buzzards hovering above.

It was a beautiful, calm desert day when they went out to shoot this sequence. Gierasch had recently arrived from New York, and his head was freshly shaved. He was a little nervous about the buzzards being so near and the hot sun beating down upon his shaved head.

The crew had finally finished burying him up to his neck when suddenly the desert winds sprang up at about forty miles an hour, and everyone ran, covering their eyes and throwing blankets over the cameras to protect the lenses. Suddenly Chase noticed Gierasch's bald head sticking out of the sand, yelling, and fortunately some kind person finally threw a blanket over him.

Other films Chase worked on include *Summer of '42* (1971), *Prime Cut* (1972), *99 & 44/100% Dead* (1974), *At Long Last Love* (1977), *Nickelodeon* (1977), *Day of the Locust* (1977), *Heroes* (1977), *The One and Only* (1978), and *The Stunt Man* (1978).

Chase indicated that makeup on *Prime Cut* and *Summer of '42* were basically simple. In *Prime Cut* there is one scene where a girl is beaten up. Chase put a prosthetic eye on her and effected burns. He describes it as a gruesome makeup but nothing monumental.

The show that Chase believes gave him his first real exposure to lab work was the Wolper series on the evolution of man, which became the television special *Primal Man*. Chase worked for over two months on the preparation for this series under John Chambers and Tom Burman, whom he describes as two of the best lab technicians in the business.

There were three or four stages of the evolution of man, and Chase did the makeup on one of the principal actors, who was actually a stunt man, through each phase of the cycles. Some of the makeups took about five hours to execute. They wore full-face appliances, and in some of the stages the actors wore a body stocking with hair sewn into it in the same manner that hair is sewn into a wig.

Chase has worked on many movies for television, including NBC-TV's *The Entertainer* (1976) with Jack Lemmon, and *Helter Skelter*, which he considers a makeup artist's dream, creating the many faces of Charles Manson and effecting shaved

Ruth White in character makeup for her role as Mrs. Dubose in the film that won two Academy Awards, *To Kill a Mockingbird*. (© *Universal*)

Stephen Railsback in character makeup as Charles Manson for the television film *Helter Skelter*. (*Ken Chase*)

heads for many of the female members of the Manson cult.

The actor who played Manson, Stephen Railsback, bore a close resemblance to Manson and had his own beard. Chase felt the beard just wasn't right, so they shaved it and laid a new beard on him. The hairdresser added a wig, and they were amazed at how much he took on the look of Manson. There was very little preparation time for the film so everything was done very quickly. However, they were extremely pleased with the results.

The actresses who portrayed the female members of the Manson cult had to appear later in the film with bald heads. Of course, none of the actresses were willing to have their own lovely locks shaved, so Chase used plastic skullcaps. He found this a very difficult job to do but considers that it worked out very well.

Chase's first opportunity to make his own appliances came on the television movie *Brenda Starr*. Chase had to disguise actor Ted Allan. The before and after pictures of Allan show what a remarkable job Chase did. By using a false nose, false jowl pieces, stretch rubber around the lips, false dental caps (that Chase made himself), a wig, and a false beard and moustache, Chase definitely succeeded in creating an entirely new person out of Ted Allan.

For the television special "Eleanor and Franklin: The White House Years" Chase designed and made the foam-latex appliances to aid the actors in looking like the historical figures they portrayed, and he received an Emmy for his achievements.

Chase considers that, to date, this involved his longest preliminary work. He met with the director to decide about the concept. Chase felt it would be a mistake to try to make the actors look exactly like Franklin and Eleanor Roosevelt. It could be done, but the large amount of prosthetics necessary to create a real lookalike would be too restrictive for comfortable movement and artistic expression. They decided to settle for a similarity in appearance.

There are four major characters in the film where foam-latex appliances are used to effect the correct look. Jane Alexander as Eleanor and Edward Herrmann as Franklin are shown in the film at ages ranging from their early twenties to early sixties progressively. Rosemary Murphy is seen as Sara Roosevelt at the ages of forty-seven, seventy-eight, and eighty-seven. Actor Walter McGinn had to be aged to play sixty-two-year-old Louis Howe.

Chase took impressions of the actors, made up a positive model, and then sculpted the look that he wanted to achieve, complete, on both heads. Then he had the director come to his home and view what he had done. The director liked what he was doing,

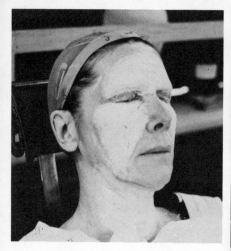

Actress Rosemary Murphy during a makeup application to portray the role of eighty-seven-year-old Sara Roosevelt. (*Ken Chase*)

Rosemary Murphy in makeup for her role as Sara Roosevelt. (*Ken Chase*)

Jane Alexander during makeup application. Here she wears eye bags, nasal labial folds, and jowls. False teeth were an important part of the makeup. (*Ken Chase*)

and from there it was a matter of making individual molds for each prosthetic device.

The procedure is to make a flexible mold of the original positive cast and, from that, duplicate section molds. For example, if Chase were to make an appliance that was just to fit under the actor's eye, he would make a separate mold of just that area and do a sculpting on that positive, then make a negative mold of that. Totally there were approximately forty molds just to do Eleanor and Franklin.

Chase researched books about Eleanor and Franklin and studied countless pictures of them both. It was time-consuming, taking several weeks, but Chase believed it was vital to obtain a feeling of what they really looked like. He believes that Ed Herrmann looked more like the real Franklin than Jane Alexander looked like the real Eleanor, but Jane Alexander has a very petite face, which is completely unlike that of Eleanor Roosevelt's.

It was necessary to create two different age categories—two different looks. They had to simulate the actors in their forties, fifties, and then, ultimately, Franklin at the age of sixty-three and Eleanor at the age of sixty-one. Thus, there were three complete sets of appliances.

In Franklin's oldest makeup he wore ten separate appliances. These consisted of a false forehead, pieces under the eyes, cheekbone pieces, labial full pieces, nostrils, a piece that fit above his upper lip, a piece that fit below his lower lip, and a neck.

Eleanor wore a little less than that. She had a forehead, the cheekbone pieces with puffs under the eyes, nasal labial full pieces, a neck, and false teeth. Chase made the dental caps to give her a protruding lip and also that bucktooth appearance that Eleanor Roosevelt had.

Chase states that his most favorite makeup to date was on "Eleanor and Franklin: The White House Years," on actress Rosemary Murphy, who portrayed Franklin's mother. In the last film she needed to be aged to ninety years of age, and it was a situation where there was not a lot of preparation time. Chase was very pleased with the results. He had only a weekend to design the makeup, make the molds, make the casts, and pour the foam rubber, yet Rosemary Murphy was able to perform that Monday.

Chase took a cast of her face and hands, then sculptured the look he wanted. He made his flexible mold, reproduced all his section molds, did the individual sculpting

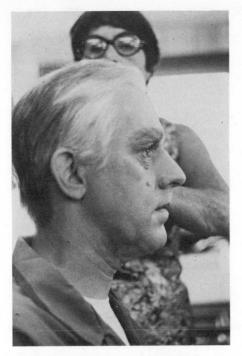

Profile of Ed Herrmann as Franklin D. Roosevelt at the age of sixty-one. The makeup included the following appliances: forehead, nostrils, upper lip, lower lip, labial folds, cheekbones, eye bags, neck, and a hairlace wig. His teeth were stained, and makeup was applied to his hands to create liver spots. (*Ken Chase*)

Chase won an Emmy for his successful achievements in makeup for the television series "Eleanor and Franklin: The White House Years." Here Chase poses with Jane Alexander in makeup and costume for her role as Eleanor Roosevelt. (*Ken Chase*)

on those molds, capped the molds, mixed the foam latex, put it in the oven, and baked it.

The makeup consisted of a very old forehead and pieces that fit over almost the full size of her face. An appliance was created to fit right on top of her own lower lip, making it look quite old and taking away the existing youthful shape of her mouth. Some prosthetics were needed for her hands, making them appear like the hands of an old lady.

Although Chase recognizes foam-latex appliances as the only way to make tremendous changes in the way someone looks, he still believes some of the old techniques still hold up and are very useful when there is not a great deal of preparation time.

Chase faced a very real challenge in his makeup expertise for the film *The Stunt Man* because director Richard Rush's style of directing employs the use of extreme close-ups. These conditions demand the utmost in makeup. For this film, Chase aged young Barbara Hershey to about seventy years of age. To accomplish this, he designed appliances which nearly covered Hershey's entire face. Dental caps were employed to slightly change the shape of her mouth and conceal her perfect teeth.

In addition to this major makeup, Chase also designed and employed many appliances when battle scenes in the film called for graphic wounds, such as severed limbs and missing eyes.

For public television's "Meeting of Minds" Chase designed a makeup for Jayne Meadows, who portrayed an aged Florence Nightingale. The appliances Chase employed were a nose and upper-lip appliance and pieces to add high cheekbones and bags under the eyes. In addition to the appliances, liquid latex was used on her eyelids, forehead, chin, and neck, which proved very effective. Makeup artist Larry Abbott applied the makeup.

In 1977 Chase opened the Ken Chase Studio, where he employs other craftsmen to assist him in his laboratory. His ambition when he started the studio was to work only on films that require special makeup designs.

Chase took on an extremely interesting and exciting project in 1978 when he became Makeup Designer and Supervisor for "Roots: The Next Generation," the sequel to

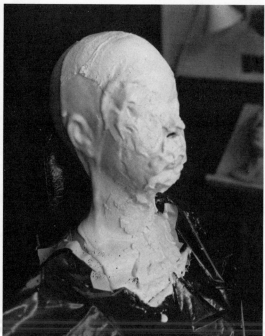

Lynne Moody patiently waits for her impression to set in the Ken Chase studio. (*Ken Chase*)

Old-age appliances for hands must not be overlooked, and Lynne Moody must suffer this procedure as well. (*Ken Chase*)

the Wolper television production of Alex Haley's best-selling novel *Roots*. Chase's staff was comprised of Joe DiBella, who also worked with Chase and who won an award for makeup on "Eleanor and Franklin: The White House Years"; Zoltan Elek, and Tom Miller, with David Dietmar in the lab. Chase considered this to be one of the biggest makeup films ever produced on television with one of the largest makeup budgets ever.

All the designs and molds were made at the Ken Chase Studio in Tarzana. Because of the outstanding success of the first series, the budget for the sequel had been treated with much respect. Chase also felt that he had enough prep time, including makeup tests for each character as their makeup was completed.

Avon Long portrayed the character Chicken George, which was played by Ben Vereen in the first *Roots*. Long did not require the aging that Vereen did because Long was the correct age for the character. There were approximately thirteen actors to age with prosthetics and many who aged

progressively through the series. Among those were Georg Stanford Brown, Lynne Moody, Richard Thomas, Marc Singer, Paul Koslo, and Debby Morgan.

Lynne Moody wore six appliances. Chase stained her teeth and added a wig supplied by Vivienne Walker. He used a rubber mask makeup, which is made from castor oil and color pigment. Chase used a prosthetic grade impression cream, which is the same alginate used by dentists, over Moody's hands and face. The material sets in approximately ten minutes, but the subject must remain in a fixed position for about twenty minutes for the entire process, which includes a plaster bandage too.

Chase did not use cosmetic contact lenses in his aging makeup because none of the characters were aged beyond seventy years, and he didn't feel they are necessary prior to that age.

We are convinced Ken Chase's future holds many promising and interesting makeup challenges. His realistic characterizations have an important role in the film industry.

Chapter 23

STAN WINSTON

Stan Winston, at the modest age of thirty, has already received two Emmys and three nominations for his makeup expertise.

While growing up, Winston shared the same enthusiasm and curiosity for filmdom's various creatures as did many makeup artists. When he attended the University of Virginia, he majored in Fine Arts, with a minor in Drama, and he became a member of the Virginia Players. As a Fine Arts major, Winston developed his painting and sculpting skills. There was no Makeup Department for the Virginia Players, so Winston created one.

When Winston went to the West Coast, it was to act, not to become a makeup artist. He went from agent to agent, showing them his portfolio and while he tried to find an agent, it was necessary to keep working. Instead of following the usual route and parking cars or shining shoes, he fell back on his love for makeup and applied to the makeup apprenticeship program.

Being a Fine Arts major, a painter, and a sculptor, Winston had all the proper qualifications and was extremely fortunate in being accepted into the apprenticeship program, and a year later he was placed under the skillful guidance of Robert Schiffer at the Disney Studios.

Winston credits much of his success to his three-year apprenticeship. During these years he was able to employ his skills of sketching, drawing, sculpting, while also learning the lab work. Winston became so involved in makeup that his career in acting began to recede into the background. He began to realize just how important and exciting makeup could become as he delved into the heavier character makeups.

It was after he had completed his apprenticeship and was a new journeyman makeup artist that Winston heard of Marlin Entertainments' production of *Gargoyles*. Winston went to Del Armstrong, head of their Makeup Department, and asked Armstrong to allow Winston to work on the background creatures because that was what he wanted to do more than anything else.

Ellis Burman designed the leader of the gargoyles, who was portrayed by actor Bernie Casey, and Winston designed the background gargoyles, of which there were approximately twenty. Although some sketches were done before Winston became involved, there were only two weeks of preproduction time allotted. The script called for creatures that were part man, part bird, part lizard, part animal.

"What it amounted to," Winston related, "is that when I got my hands into the clay, my mind 'went bananas,' so to speak. I had reptile books in front of me, bird books in front of me; and the gargoyle became more

Three background creatures Winston designed for Marlin Entertainment's television 1972 production of *Gargoyles. (Stan Winston)*

Ellis Burman's design of the lead gargoyle, played by actor Bernie Casey, in *Gargoyles. (Stan Winston)*

of a reptilian birdlike creature, rather than the gargoyle creatures of ancient times."

Bernie Casey, leader of the gargoyles, was designed to look more like a devil/demon creature. His skin was of a reptilian quality, yet his face was more manlike. He had enormous wings that actually beat. It was a heavy, cumbersome, trying makeup. Casey and Winston became close friends, and because of their camaraderie and the stress Casey was under in portraying this creature, Winston took on the job of applying Burman's creation. Winston did design the demon gargoyles' teeth.

The background gargoyles wore slip-rubber (over-the-head) masks. Because they had only two weeks in which to accomplish the entire job, the suits themselves were designed by special effects man Ross Wheat. The suits were basically wet suits, and everyone pitched in to apply the scales. The heads, face, and hands of the gargoyles were what was designed by the Makeup Department, that is, Burman and Winston.

One sequence at the end of the film called for two baby gargoyles to crack forth from their eggs. The design of these little creatures fell to Winston. To Winston's way of thinking, baby "anythings" are cute, and of anything he designed on the film, the most challenging for him was to design two "cute" baby gargoyles. One of the baby gargoyles was actually one of the producer's sons.

Winston believes that *The Autobiography of Miss Jane Pittman* was the best assignment he has ever had and, for television, probably the easiest. This is because they spent the time, and they spent the money for the manpower. Winston feels he had the time to do a proper old-age makeup, and he had a very talented man working with him. He and Rick Baker worked together on one face, and even though it was for television, where there is usually a constant rush and tight budget, this production gave ample preproduction time, and Winston feels this is one reason why the makeup looked as well as it did.

For the film *W. C. Fields and Me* (1977), Winston's intention was not to mask Rod Steiger but to keep him looking like himself and yet be the essence of W. C. Fields. Winston worked a month and a half developing his character, doing various sketches, and arriving, finally, at a perfect concept. Winston shaved and stripped Steiger's hair and used hairpieces. He shaved and redid his eyebrows and used an appliance nose.

In 1977 CBS presented the musical special *Pinocchio*, starring Sandy Duncan, Danny Kaye, Flip Wilson, and Liz Torres. Winston again found his time limited for preparation, but the characters were easy for him not only because they were what he likes to describe as "cartoon" but because of his background at Disney Studios and his work on the Pinocchio character for *Disney on Parade*.

Winston didn't attempt to present Sandy Duncan as a boy but to turn her into Pinocchio. The mechanics of the growing nose was designed for Winston by the Burmans, and it became Winston's job to figure out just how to fasten the nose on Duncan's face. As Pinocchio is madly telling lies and dancing, the final, huge nose appears. Winston's problem was to keep the nose from flopping around as Duncan danced.

The nose was made from foam rubber with a metal bar inside to keep it rigid. Without even time to test it, Winston had Duncan lie down, and he sewed monofilament through the tip of the nose and brought it around to the back of her head and tied it in different directions. It was like an antenna on one's roof with strands of wire leading down to each side to keep it erect and rigid. Duncan did her entire dance without the nose flopping at all, and so it was very effective.

There is always more than one person making decisions on films, and Winston feels the only thing anyone can do about it is to make your work as good as is possible. Winston has his makeup credits read "Makeup designed by Stan Winston" because, as he has so often told the producers, he considers himself as clever as a costume designer.

"Often makeup artists will have the costume designer design the entire character, and then their makeup must match that character; but I design my makeups, and I feel there is a big difference. This is why my credits read as they do, and not 'Makeup by Stan Winston.' "

Winston was associate producer and makeup artist for the film *Mansion of the Doomed* (1977), which starred Richard Basehart as Dr. Chaney. The film concerns an eye surgeon whose daughter loses her

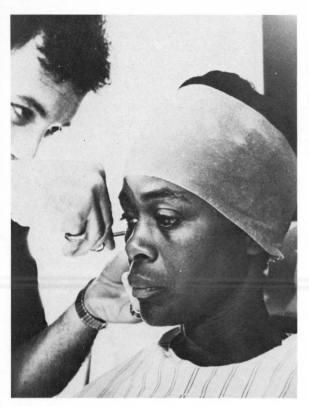

Cicely Tyson prepares for the makeup application which will take her to age one hundred and ten. (*Stan Winston*)

Cicely Tyson as the one-hundred-and-ten-year-old Miss Jane Pittman in the television film *The Autobiography of Miss Jane Pittman*. (*Stan Winston*)

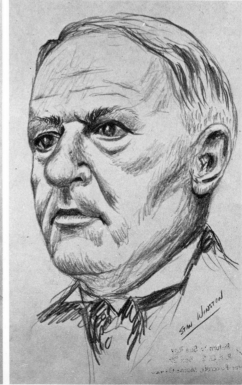

Winston's intention was not to mask Rod Steiger but to keep him looking like himself and yet be the essence of W. C. Fields. (*Stan Winston*)

Winston employed these sketches to aid him in the transformation of Rod Steiger to W. C. Fields for the film *W. C. Fields and Me*. (*Stan Winston*)

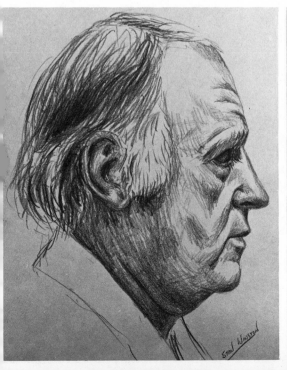 

The mechanics of Pinocchio's growing nose were designed for Winston by the Burmans, but it became Winston's job to figure out how to fasten the nose on Sandy Duncan's face. (*Stan Winston*)

Sandy Duncan and Danny Kaye in the CBS musical special *Pinocchio*. (*Stan Winson*)

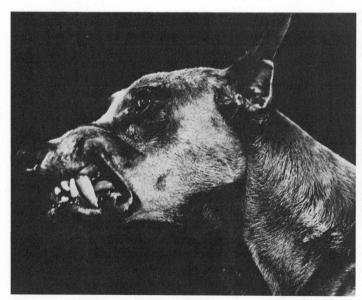

The mad Dr. Chaney screams in terror at his own gouged-out eyes; a victim of his own obsession in *Mansion of the Doomed*. (*Stan Winston*)

Dracula's Dogs presented Winston with many problems, one of which was to make these vicious canine teeth. (*Stan Winston*)

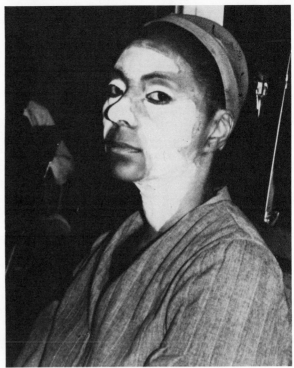

When the stars of *Roots* won rave reviews and the presentation broke all television records, Stan Winston had the distinct pleasure of knowing his makeup had been a part of it. Ben Vereen turned in a magnificent performance as Chicken George. (*Stan Winston*/ABC)

Leslie Uggams wears the appliances that will aid her in her role as Kizzy, child of Kunta Kinta in *Roots*. (*Stan Winston*/ABC)

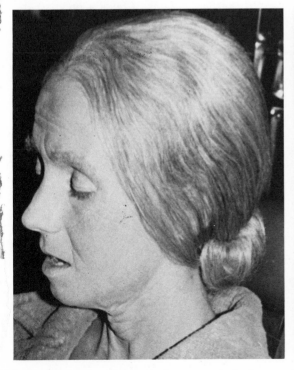

Sandy Duncan in old-age appliances and wig for her part as the elderly Missy Anne. (*Stan Winston*/ABC)

The kind features of Chuck Connors are gently molded into the cruel features of Massa Tom Lea. (*Stan Winston*/ABC)

sight in an auto accident that he is to blame for. He becomes obsessed with restoring her vision. A cornea transplant doesn't work, but there is a series of eye transplants that will.

Dr. Chaney begins to operate on and transplant the eyes of unwilling donors, and this works, but only for a short period of time. He does it again and again. The audience assumes the donors are being killed, but then it is learned that they are being held in a cell in the basement.

Even though these people are grotesque with their missing eyes, it is the normal-appearing Richard Basehart as Dr. Chaney who is in actuality the monster. Chaney does care about these people he has so deformed, and in the final sequence he is attacked in the cell by a huge man who has gone totally berserk. He tears Basehart's eyes out of his head, and the last shot is of the mutilated Basehart standing there screaming, and his eyes in the hands of the man who has ripped them out.

Winston had to reconstruct the entire upper half of Richard Basehart's face to give depth to the eyes. The face was built outward, and halfway up it had to closely match the actual bone structure beneath. It was an enormous challenge to not have the whole makeup resemble goggles. Because it was extended so far forward, there was a tendency for that to happen; however, Winston knew realism was essential here, and realism is what the audience saw.

The complete sets of vampire teeth used in the film *Blackula* (1975) were made by Winston. One of his more difficult teeth jobs was for the film *Dracula's Dogs* (1977). It presented many problems in itself because a dog's mouth is not shaped like a human's.

Special impression trays that would fit a dog's mouth had to be made. And quite understandably, taking impressions of a Doberman pinscher's mouth was not something Winston relished doing. Fortunately, they were extremely well-trained dogs and no problems at all to work with.

Winston had to work out a way to secure the dentures in the dogs' mouths without the dogs being able to pull them out. Because the teeth in a dog's mouth point out to the sides, a solid bridge could not be used. Winston made each tooth independent of the other and secured them with a series of hooks and straps.

Each tooth had a hook near the gumline and then elastic straps which went across the front of the gumline and the inside cavity of the mouth. In one set of teeth, Winston installed a bleeding device, so when the dog bit or tore into anything, it would allow blood to run from his mouth, giving a very effective makeup shot.

One of Winston's finest makeup jobs was the aging of the five major characters in the television production of Alex Haley's bestselling novel *Roots*.

It was an enormous job, with very little time allowed, but Winston's aging of Ben Vereen, Leslie Uggams, Chuck Connors, Sandy Duncan, and Olivia Cole will be long remembered along with the film and the novel. Unlike *The Autobiography of Miss Jane Pittman,* with which Winston had six weeks preproduction time and a talented assistant, for *Roots* he had two-and-a-half weeks to prepare and only himself to do the five characters. He feels it could have been better.

Winston, at this writing, is doing a three-day job for his friend Mary Tyler Moore, and a Diana Ross special in which she will portray three different women.

Chapter 24

RICK BAKER

Rick Baker may describe himself as being "ape-crazy," but ever since Dino De Laurentiis's *King Kong* (1976) hit the World Trade Center, Baker has certainly been tagged with the slogan "the man in the monkey suit."

Baker's life began in 1950 in Binghamton, New York. Son of artist Ralph Baker, it was quite natural that Baker should lean toward creative art. As most other nine- or ten-year-olds do, Baker discovered monsters and found them a curiosity, but his interest didn't stop there. He had to know how they were made, and he went to his father for the answers. His father explained that they were created by makeup artists.

An explanation that simple wouldn't satisfy the young Baker, so his father bought him a tube of greasepaint and showed him a few basics with highlights and shadows. It became a hobby with Baker, but a very meaningful one. The more he played, the more he learned.

He would smear on the greasepaint, add some heavy shadows here and there, and mess up his hair. Monsters that one can create with just paint such as vampires, ghouls, and zombies can usually be done quite effectively. These specters, Baker feels, are probably the easiest and best makeup oddities to start with. One can then get into buildups with mortician's wax and

nose putty, and then small appliances—cast rubber noses, eyepieces, and the like. One can progress to making rubber masks, then to working with foam.

Baker knows that it is more important how a makeup looks, not how it was done. He feels that all too often an apprentice makeup artist is shown a way to do makeup, and he believes that it is the only way, or the "right" way. Baker recognizes this as a drawback and feels that anything that works is right.

In the summer of 1968, before he was out of high school, Baker was hired by Art Cloakey Productions, which did stop-animation programs such as *Gumby* and *David and Goliath*. He became close friends with stop-motion animators Jim Danforth, Doug Beswick, and David Allen. It was with their help that Baker began to learn the professional way to create appliances and to do makeup.

Baker got his first real assignment for a creation while he was still an art major in college. He and Doug Beswick created the creature for *The Octoman,* a low-budget television production.

In 1971, at the age of twenty, Baker applied all his skills and experimental techniques to create the creature for *Schlock,* a feature film about a missing link, the Schlockthropus, an ape-man/monster. The monster-comedy flick was written and directed by the then-twenty-one-year-old John

Landis, who also played Schlock. Landis became winner of the 1973 Trieste Science Fiction Film Festival. Baker met John Chambers at this time when Chambers took a break from makeup and made his acting debut as the National Guard captain in *Schlock*.

Chambers, after viewing Baker's work in this film, was quoted as saying, "I can't recall any feature film requiring such detailed and inventive makeup being handled by such a young person. Rick should be one of the leading makeup artists of the future."

Baker created a four-piece face for *Schlock*, giving Landis the facial flexibility that was so necessary because the role called for a wide range of expressions.

In 1972 the film *The Thing with Two Heads* starred Ray Milland, Rosie Grier, and Baker as the Thing. Baker created a two-headed gorilla costume which he wore in this film about a doctor who experiments with grafting a head onto a body. Once the grafted head "takes," the doctor then amputates the original head.

Baker worked with Dick Smith on *The Exorcist* (1972), which entailed lab work on the demons that possessed Linda Blair, and necessitated travel to New York and Iraq.

"My most challenging job on a monster movie has to be making the baby monster for the film *It's Alive!* (1975). The producer, Larry Cohen, called me in New York while I was assisting Dick Smith on *The Exorcist*.

Baker got his first real assignment while he was still an art major in college. He and Doug Beswick created the creature for *The Octoman*, a low-budget television production. (*Photo courtesy of Rick Baker*)

At the age of twenty, Baker created the creature for *Schlock*, played by John Landis, who also wrote, directed, and won the 1973 Trieste Science Fiction Film Festival award for this film. Here Baker touches up Schlock's makeup. (*Photo courtesy of Rick Baker*)

Baker created and wore this unusual ape costume for his role in *The Thing with Two Heads*, which also starred Rosie Grier and Ray Milland. (*American-International/Rick Baker*)

Baker gained invaluable experience when he was involved in lab work with Dick Smith on *The Exorcist.* Here Baker effects a possessed Regan makeup on his wife, Elaine, for a Halloween show. (*Photo courtesy of Rick Baker)*

He told me the idea of the story. For some strange reason a monster baby is born from normal parents and kills everyone in the delivery room except the mother. It then escapes to terrorize the city.

"Cohen told me that he didn't want to show the baby monster for more than a split second and asked me what I suggested. I gave him several possible solutions to the problem; the easiest and cheapest one be-ing the construction of a foam-rubber baby-sized dummy with a wire armature, so it could be repositioned for different shots. Since he didn't want to show the baby for more than a split second, it didn't matter that it didn't move.

"When I returned to California from New York, the picture was already in production, so time was short. I quickly made up a foam-rubber baby-sized monster. Once the

One of Baker's most challenging assignments was a baby monster for *It's Alive!* (*Photo courtesy of Rick Baker*)

Producer Larry Cohen hadn't planned to shoot much of the monster baby, but he was so impressed with Baker's horrific creation that he wanted to show more of it, and he also wanted it to move. That sent Baker scurrying back to his lab for more ideas. (*Photo courtesy of Rick Baker*)

Baker completes modeling of the full-sized baby monster head. (*Photo courtesy of Rick Baker*)

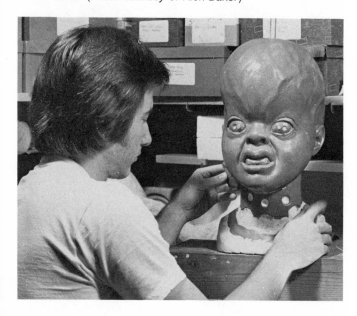

Clawed gloves, small monster baby, full-sized monster head appliance, and teeth appliances used in *It's Alive!* (*Photo courtesy of Rick Baker*)

producer saw it, it was so much better than he realized it could be that he wanted to show it more. He also wanted it to move.

"Because the baby I had created wasn't made to move, I had to do something more. I decided the fastest and most effective thing would be to make a foam-latex mask to fit a human actor, which, once glued to the actor's face, would be very flexible and could assume many expressions. I also had to make other parts of the baby—such as the hands and torso sections—for other insert shots.

"My wife Elaine volunteered to be my subject for this makeup. After I took a live cast of her head, I modeled the baby mon-ster face in oil-base clay. Some small changes had to be made, as the baby wasn't designed to fit an adult face. Once the sculpture was finished, a special plaster mold was made and the head was then cast in foam latex and applied. With clever photography and cutting, the baby seemed to be alive in the film."

Baker is now creating three mechanical monster babies for Cohen's sequel to *It's Alive!* entitled *It Lives Again!*

Dick Smith recommended Baker for the film *Live and Let Die* (1973) which starred Roger Moore as James Bond. Baker created a special effects head for actor Geoffrey Holder, who is shot in the head. The

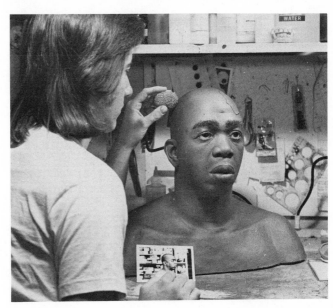

Baker created a special head of actor Geoffrey Holder for the film *Live and Let Die*. A shot blows part of the head away, and the eyes roll back up into the head. Baker also created the eye mechanism. (*Rick Baker*)

shot blows part of his skull away, and his eyes roll back up into his head. Baker created the head and the eye mechanism. He also created a special effects head for Yaphet Kotto who has a gas pellet forced down his throat in the film. His head inflates like a balloon, and it was Baker who created this strange head of Kotto.

In addition to creating special makeup effects for various commercials, Baker also created a special death mask for David Carradine in *Death Race 2000* (1975) and preproduction development of special makeup effects for *Squirm*.

Squirm is about bloodworms who become active after an unusual storm. Baker had to create the effect of a man's face being attacked by bloodworms that are boring through his skin. Baker became involved in a much larger project at this time and turned over the makeup application of *Squirm* to Norman Page.

Considering his interest in gorillas, Baker's involvement in *King Kong* seemed to come as a natural extension of the way he has directed his career. Good friends of Baker were interested in the possibility of stop-motion animation for the ape in *King Kong*, and they approached De Laurentiis's people concerning this. When they were informed that stop-motion would not be employed in the film and that a man in a suit would be used instead, Baker's friends recommended him as being the man who could build them a realistic suit.

Baker and friend Jon Berg combined their skills and approached the executive producer Federico De Laurentiis, director John Guillermin, and the Italian art director Mario Chiari, to discuss the possibility of creating the gorilla costume for *King Kong* (1976).

Berg, who has a great mechanical mind, was working on a gorilla suit for himself and had developed a pair of extended arms for it. The hands on the extended arms were so well made that each finger could be manipulated individually. They were capable of very intricate movements, and could grasp objects and hold them. The wrists not only moved but locked into place so that the actor in the suit could walk on his hands.

Baker had sculptured different gorilla heads and presented his portfolio. It was his impression that with the combined material he and Berg had to present, they would

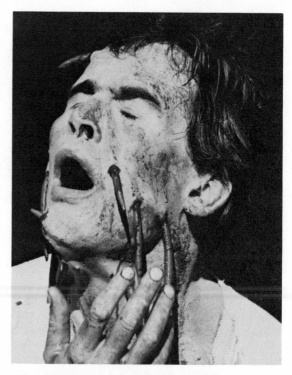

When bloodworms become activated after an unusual storm, you have *Squirm*. Baker designed and created this unusual effect but turned the application over to Norman Page. (*Photo courtesy of Rick Baker*)

make quite an impression.

"We went in there and they appeared to have a rather strange attitude. We showed them the arm extension, which we thought would surely convince them that we could do a great job. But they said, 'Well, that's very nice, but we don't want to use anything like this because our Kong isn't going to be a gorilla. Our Kong is going to be an ape-man, a kind of a primal man, the missing-link type.'

"Jon and I looked at each other and said, more or less to ourselves, 'Oh, oh!' We said, 'What do you plan to do about the Tyrannosaurus fight?' They told us, 'We haven't really decided about that. I don't think that we're going to put that in there.' 'Well,' we said, 'what about all the fantasy? Kong was such a fantasy picture, you know. Kind of a Beauty and the Beast type of thing.' They said, 'No, no, no. That's the old Kong; our new Kong is a disaster picture. Kong is just like any other modern-day disaster, and that's how we're going to treat it—no romance, no fantasy, whatever.' "

Baker and Berg received the script of *Kong* that day, but after reading it, Berg pulled out, feeling the quality of the film under its present direction was questionable. Baker still felt he had much to contribute to the film and wanted an opportunity to try.

De Laurentiis's people assured Baker they wanted to have him work for them, and they asked Baker if he would have any objections to a sculptor working with him.

"I questioned them as to why they'd want a sculptor working with me, and they said that someone had to do the sculpting. I explained that I had sculpted the articles I had brought in myself, and they had said, 'Oh, you sculpt, too. Well, how about if a makeup man works with you?'

" 'That's what I do!' I told them. 'I do makeup. See these. I did all these appliances and makeups myself.' They simply replied something to the effect of 'We see.'

In the beginning we all seemed to have a very strange perception of each other."

Baker's first objective was to convince the producers that King Kong had to be a gorilla. Only a gorilla, in Baker's opinion, could convey the feeling of strength and massiveness that was essential to King Kong. To achieve his goal, he invited Federico De Laurentiis, John Guillermin, and the production managers to his home. Most of these people had never seen a man in a gorilla suit. Baker had an old one which was not very good, but good enough, he felt, to aid him in relating his concept.

"They were all sitting quite comfortably in my living room while my wife assisted me with my suit in the bedroom. Suddenly, I came out on all fours. I charged right toward them, leaping over the love seat and, frankly, scaring the shit right out of them. You know, it left quite an impression in Guillermin's mind, which he never really forgot."

Baker wasn't just satisfied with designing and building the complex Kong costume, he wanted to *be* Kong. He knew that he alone had the intense desire and drive to portray Kong as he should be portrayed. (*Photo courtesy of Rick Baker*)

After impressing on John Guillermin and Federico De Laurentiis that King Kong simply had to be a gorilla and not the "missing-link" concept they were contemplating, Baker signed on with Dino De Laurentiis to present *King Kong* by Christmas of 1976. (*Paramount*)

Baker puts the finishing touches on an early Kong concept. (*Photo courtesy of Rick Baker*)

Baker sculpted the torso of Kong's body over a cast of Baker's own body. (*Photo courtesy of Rick Baker*)

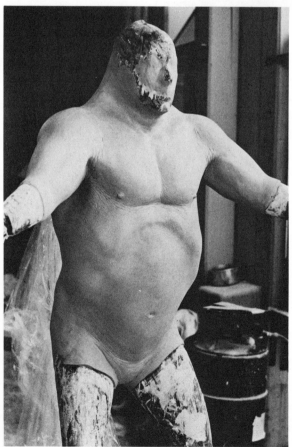

Baker was given some drawings of the missing-link conception, which he completely disregarded, and began creating a test suit. He and Carlo Rambaldi were to each have their test suits done in a month on the same day.

Working night and day, seven days a week with limited funds and in his own home, Baker completed his suit on the day expected. Rambaldi was building his suit at MGM. Although at first Guillermin didn't appear too pleased with Baker's suit, they did film it and study the tests. They never did ask Baker why he didn't follow the missing-link theory they had expected him to.

"Carlo did do his suit along the lines of the missing link, and when Guillermin saw it, he did not like the suit."

John Guillermin in an interview with Charles Chapman of the *Los Angeles Times* mentioned Baker's personally financed, single-handed feat and stated that Carlo Rambaldi didn't come up with the first version of his suit until March. Guillermin was then quoted as saying, "It was a two-hundred-dred-thousand-dollar disaster. I put Baker

The final King Kong concept by Baker, modeled in Plasticine. (*Photo courtesy of Rick Baker*)

and Rambaldi together, and two months later they came up with what became Kong. Rick played Kong for nine sweaty months, and he deserves a very large medal."

Baker found that he did make compromises on his test suit that he wishes he hadn't. He would have preferred a nice big chest and round face. However, he did create a very hefty gorilla, aging him by silvering his fur.

When the design of Rambaldi's suit came in, Guillermin began to believe that Baker's concept was right, noting the strength his suit conveyed. He felt this was a powerful animal.

Having worked with gorilla suits so much, Rick knew that one can get only a limited amount of expression from one mask, even with a very sophisticated mechanism. He suggested that he create some different faces with sculptured expressions which the mechanism would then accentuate.

They began with what they called the generic head, which was the normal Kong face with his mouth closed, looking very peaceful. Baker then created an angry head, which was similar to the generic head with the brows in an angry sort of frown. The mouth was open a bit. There was an "angry-roar" head with the mouth full-open. A "blowing head" was created with lips pursed in a blowing expression for the scene where Kong blows Jessica Lange dry.

Baker wanted to play Kong. At first the company toyed with the idea of having a muscle man play Kong. "I said to them," Baker relates, "If you get a muscle man, you may have somebody who's built more like a gorilla but who can't act, and he may not be able to convey what you want to convey. Even if he can do that, he may not want to wear the suit. For the amount of time the person is going to have to be in that suit he's going to really have to want to do it. In the first place, most actors don't like to be covered up. They want as much of themselves to show as possible; even in a character makeup they want it to be them. And add to that the fact that wearing that suit is going to be a tremendous strain." They eventually decided on Baker.

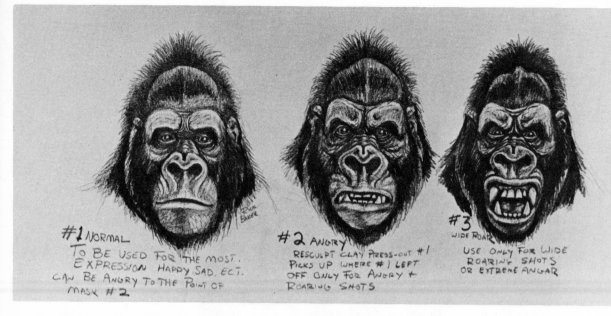

#1 NORMAL
TO BE USED FOR THE MOST.
EXPRESSION HAPPY SAD, ECT.
CAN BE ANGRY TO THE POINT OF
MASK #2

#2 ANGRY
RESCULPT CLAY PRESS-OUT #1
PICKS UP WHERE #1 LEFT
OFF ONLY FOR ANGRY +
ROARING SHOTS

#3 WIDE ROAR
USE ONLY FOR WIDE
ROARING SHOTS
OR EXTREME ANGER

Having worked with gorilla suits so much, Baker knew that one can only get a limited amount of expression from one mask, even one with a very sophisticated mechanism. He suggested that he create some different faces with sculptured expressions which the mechanism would then accentuate. (*Photo courtesy of Rick Baker*)

Baker did about ninety percent of the Kong scenes in the picture with a very small percentage done by the mechanical Kong: about six individual shots. Rick picked Bill Sheppard as his relief man but says Guillermin wouldn't hear of it. He thought Baker was the only person to play Kong properly.

Sheppard did the scene of Kong falling into the pit of chloroform, and the major portion of the snake fight, after Baker did the first couple of shots. Baker found the snake fight very difficult because of the combined weight of the suit—about forty pounds—and the snake, which weighed at least thirty pounds. When Sheppard took over, he did most of the snake fight lying on the ground making it much easier to handle the snake because he didn't have to contend with holding up the weight of it.

One thing that Baker has felt was truly a crime was the use of the black bearskins for the Kong suits. Anywhere from six to nine bearskins were used for each suit. Not only did Baker object to the obvious wasteful cruelty of killing so many bears for a Kong suit, but it wasn't even feasible. The suit was too hot, too heavy, and not very flexible. Ba-

ker felt there were other answers. The face, chest, and hands were foam latex. The padding was made out of urethane foam sheet rubber and built up with polyfoam.

It usually took Baker about thirty minutes to get into the Kong suit. Considering the hours it took to prepare for such classic makeups as *Frankenstein* (1931) and *The Mummy* (1932), it's amazing how the art of makeup has advanced.

To begin, Baker would strip to his underwear, then don the "panty," which was basically a one-piece item, zipped up the back. He would apply makeup around his eyes and insert the contact lenses. He then added the chest and rear-end padding, and finally the fur suit.

In the beginning, the contact lenses presented a problem for Baker.

"A gentleman by the name of Dr. Braff made the lenses. I'd wear them for about ten minutes, and the whites of my eyes would be solid red. Tears would be running down my face, and I'd be going insane from the pain. I kept going back to Dr. Braff and telling him the problems. He did some work on the lenses, but he didn't really know what the problem was. He thought I was just a chicken and didn't want to wear them. I explained to him the fact that I wanted to wear the lenses very much. It was my idea to use them, and I wasn't just being a baby about it. I felt he didn't really accept this, so I ended up going to Dr. Greenspoon who makes many lenses for people out here in Hollywood. It was Greenspoon's father who invented this type of lens in the first place. He knew the problem and explained that it was common.

"It seems that my eyes were very sensitive to the lack of oxygen. They drilled a little hole in the lens to get the oxygen in there, and then I could wear them for many hours. Eventually I could put them on first thing in the morning and wear them until lunchtime. I would take them off to eat my lunch, then put them back on and wear them until the end of the day. So there were days when I had them on almost ten hours. I didn't enjoy it, but most days it wasn't that painful. My vision was very limited, and I'd usually end up with a headache, but it wasn't as bad as it could have been."

Since gorilla arms are longer than man's, the Kong suit was equipped with arm and hand extensions. Baker says he couldn't do anything with the fingers other than bend them. They weren't made so that he could pick up anything with them. In scenes where Baker holds a doll-size model of Jessica Lange it was externally attached to the artificial hands. Any intricate movement was done with the huge mechanical hand. The extended hands made it impossible for Baker to use his own hands to put a breathing tube in his mouth, so he had to depend on someone else to do that.

With the exception of up-and-down movements of the head, Baker wasn't able to control the facial expressions of Kong. The faces were all maneuvered by external cables controlling mechanisms in the head. At times there were eleven cables coming from the back of the mask, running down the inside of Baker's suit and out his feet.

Each cable was controlled by a lever, and the levers were controlled by Italian-speaking technicians. When Guillermin wanted a

An angry Kong, sculpted in Plasticine. (*Photo courtesy of Rick Baker*)

certain facial expression, it was necessary to have a translator explain his wishes to the Italian technicians. At times Baker found it most frustrating to coordinate his body and eye movements with what the technicians were doing to the facial expressions.

Once the facial movements were coordinated with the body movements, they would do the shot—sometimes actually succeeding in getting it right quickly. Guillermin, however, always wanted to be sure they protected themselves, often saying, "That's perfect. That's a take. Let's do one more for safety." So they would end up doing several takes, even if they got a good one the first time.

The cables sometimes presented a very real hazard. Many times as Kong was crashing through the jungle or anywhere else at full speed with the cables dragging on the ground, they would become caught, which would yank Baker's head back, caus-

ing him to fall. Fortunately, he was never really hurt. Because of the extended arms, Baker didn't dare put his hands out to protect himself when he fell, because he was afraid the extended hands would bend his own hands too far back and break his wrists. Instinct seemed to tell him to fall on his side.

Getting into character to play a gorilla was no problem for Baker because he had played gorillas quite often. The problem was getting into the character of Kong as Guillermin wanted him portrayed. Baker had a different opinion of how Kong should be played but of course deferred to Guillermin.

Baker had studied the great apes and had read nearly every book about them he could get his hands on. He'd also put in a great deal of study time at zoos all around the States, spending hours watching the gorillas and their movements. All of this greatly helped him in his movements as Kong.

All of the things Baker did dressed as Kong were difficult because of the cumbersome, heavy, bearskin suit; but when he had to work with props, the difficulties were enormous. Here Kong's anger may just portray Baker's as well. When the elevator train sequence was filmed, the breakaway train top failed. It took a full day to get one good shot. (*Paramount*)

Although everything that Baker did was shot without sound, he found it helped him to create the Kong character by emitting gorilla noises as he played his scenes. All the Kong sounds were dubbed in later.

Because he didn't consider himself an actor, Rick was afraid that the scenes calling for him to show compassion with his eyes would be very difficult. However, compared to the enormous physical strain of wearing the heavy suit, Baker found it to be one of the easiest requirements of his role. He credits this to his ability to do makeups on himself and appliance makeups on others, so that he knew how much to exaggerate the movements of the eyes to make the point come across.

The weight of the suit was not the only drawback. It would become extremely hot, and Baker could easily lose five pounds in a day. His sweat would sometimes be so great that it would soak through to the fur. Breathing was difficult when he wore the mask, and he depended on the air tube inserted through the mouth for fresh air.

"On the average, I would wear the suit for four hours at a time. On good days I would have it on for much more time, and there were other days where we wouldn't have too much to do and I'd do a couple of takes and that would be it."

One of Baker's most physically demanding scenes was when Kong was required to come up out of the water. The foam latex of the suit soaked the water up and increased the weight of the suit to what seemed to Baker to be at least five hundred pounds. It was an enormous strain for him to climb out of the water and force himself to stand up, holding all that weight.

"I was in a water tank, which I think was about twenty feet deep. I had to walk on a little platform that had small guard rails on either side. I couldn't really see what I was doing or where I was in the water, and I was afraid that, with the suit absorbing the water like it was, I was going to step off the edge and go to the bottom. They had a man with a scuba tank there in case that happened, but I don't think it would have done much good because I don't think he could have gotten the air hose in my mouth through the gorilla suit.

"The closest I ever came to being hurt was the last few days of shooting. We'd already had a lot of trouble with the helicopters not working. When they finally got them all set up, something went wrong and one fell and smashed to pieces. They weighed about seventy pounds each.

"I was standing on top of a miniature World Trade Center, just the top few floors, and stood about thirty-five feet off the ground. Three miniature helicopters were suspended from wires seventy feet up in the air, flying around me. The action called for me to be getting shot at while I twirled around, watching the helicopters.

"Guillermin called 'action,' and I was very busy when I received a tremendous blow to my arm. I thought my arm was broken. I didn't know what happened, but I thought that one of the helicopters must be falling and was coming at me. Instinct told me to crouch, which I did, hoping that nothing else was going to hit me.

"Once I decided it was all clear, I learned that one of the wires that suspended a helicopter ran across a two-by-four that was up high on the stage, sheering off about four feet of it. By the time it hit me, it had built up quite a bit of speed, falling from the height that it did.

"It grazed my shoulder first, where I had a lot of padding, then hit me on the forearm. I think that if it wasn't for the fact that it hit the padding on my shoulder first, it probably would have broken my arm. Even more frightening was the fact that it hit only inches from my head—where there was no padding. If that had been the case, they would have had to find a new King Kong.

"The very final shot that we did was very late on a Monday night, and I was standing on the corner on the edge of the miniature World Trade Center. My toes were even hanging over the edge a little bit which made it pretty scary as I was up thirty-five feet. One of the miniature helicopters was on a wire, and I was supposed to look as though I was hitting the helicopter and it was to curve around and go into the building and explode. Well, it didn't work quite right, but once they blew up the helicopter, that was all we could do—that was it, the final shot. With careful editing, it looked fine in the film."

All of the things Baker did dressed as Kong were difficult because of the cumbersome suit, but when he had to work with props, it increased the difficulties enormously. For one thing, the more people involved in a shot, the greater the possibility of error.

When the helicopters weren't working, they filmed the elevated train scene. It took time to rig the set because it was necessary to prepare little powder charges, known as squibs, to go off, creating the effect of sparks as Kong tears off the top of the train.

When everything was finally set up, Kong charged to the train, lifted it up and attempted to rip off the top. The train was supposed to have a breakaway top and come apart easily, but it didn't. The film was stopped, the squibs set again, and Baker sat in the Kong suit, sweating. It eventually took five takes—a whole day—before they got a good take.

Baker summed up his feelings about the film: "There are a lot of people responsible for a picture like this, as in the case of any motion picture. But more so on a picture of this scale where so many things are happening at once.

"I think the Kong suit came off all right in most of the shots. It's definitely not the suit I wanted to build, and that upset me because I thought with all the money and time, I would be able to build the world's greatest gorilla suit. Everybody worked under a handicap on this picture because of the promise to have the picture out in a year's time."

Following his work on *King Kong*, but before it was released, Baker heard of a new film called *Star Wars*. A friend of Baker's advised him that George Lucas and producer Gary Kurtz were looking for a makeup artist to create additional aliens to be added to the cantina sequence, which had already been filmed. Baker gave them a bid but then became involved in *The Incredible Melting Man*.

It wasn't until Baker was well into his work for *The Incredible Melting Man* that he heard from the *Star Wars* accountant who informed Baker that they wanted him to make the aliens for the cantina sequence. Baker explained that he was now totally involved in *The Incredible Melting Man*, but they persisted in their desire for Baker's talent and asked if he couldn't work something out. Baker would assemble and set up a crew to do the work, with Baker supervising.

The team Baker formed consisted of Doug Beswick, Jon Berg, Laine Liska, Rob Bottim, and Phil Tippett, nearly all of whom are stop-motion animators. Because of a limited budget and only six weeks in which

Actor Alex Rebar, who plays the Incredible Melting Man, dons one of Baker's gruesome masks with Baker's help. (*Rick Baker*)

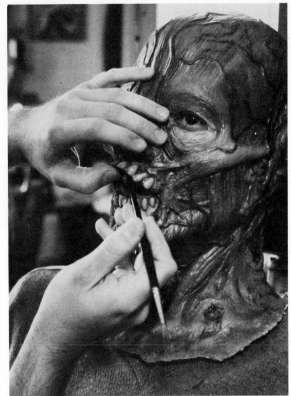

An eyeball is added to the grotesque creation. (*Rick Baker*)

Using spirit gum, Baker glues down the mouth area of the Melting Man's mask. (*Rick Baker*)

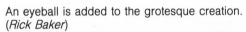

Although it looks as if Rick Baker is cleaning the teeth of the Incredible Melting Man, he is actually just adding a few finishing touches. (*Rick Baker*)

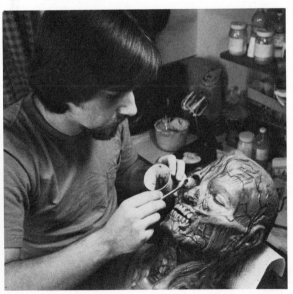

Opposite: Baker's work on *The Incredible Melting Man* consisted of four major latex full-head masks. Each one was altered slightly so that there were perhaps ten different versions of the makeup. (*Rick Baker*)

When makeup artist Stuart Freeborn became ill during the filming of *Star Wars*, George Lucas contacted Rick Baker to create some additional aliens for the cantina sequence. Baker was extremely busy on other projects at that time, but he gathered a crew under his supervision. These are two aliens created by Laine Liska and Doug Beswick. (*Rick Baker*)

to do the aliens, the crew basically prepared slit rubber masks which required a knowledge and ability to sculpt and make molds. Baker assisted them with anything unfamiliar.

Baker's work on *The Incredible Melting Man* consisted of four major latex full-head masks. Each one was altered slightly so that there were perhaps ten different versions of the makeup. The film concerns an astronaut who contracts a disease in outer space and begins to melt. The only way he can remain alive is by eating human flesh. The film called for some rather bizarre special makeup effects, including the head of a fisherman which is torn from his body by the

"Melting Man" and thrown into a stream. It tumbles over a waterfall and smashes on the rocks below, spewing forth blood and brain matter. Rob Bottim and Craig Reardon also assisted Baker. Although there was enough preproduction time, the film was shot in three weeks, and Baker feels there are areas of makeup in the film that are not the quality that he wishes they were.

It is certain that Baker's name will be well recognized in the makeup field. He never fails to accept a challenging assignment, and when he believes totally in a particular creation or concept, as he did with *King Kong*, he doesn't hesitate to "stick to his guns" and produce the best he has in him.

Under the supervision of Baker, Phil Tippett created these two cantina creatures. (*Rick Baker*)

Jon Berg adjusts the Hammerhead alien's mask that he created under Baker's supervision. Phil Tippett, in hood and sunglasses, sits to the alien's left. (*Rick Baker*)

Chapter 25

MORTON K. GREENSPOON

Dr. Morton K. Greenspoon is a third-generation optometrist. Greenspoon's grandfather was a watchmaker who came to America from Russia in the early 1900s and settled in New York State. In those years, most watchmakers and jewelers also handled spectacles. Itinerant peddlers traveled their area with a tray of spectacles, selling them to whomever needed them. When optometry laws were enacted in New York, they had a "grandfather clause," meaning that anyone already practicing optometry, including itinerant peddlers, automatically received a license to practice; so Greenspoon's grandfather became a licensed optometrist.

Greenspoon's father graduated from the University of Rochester School of Optometry in 1927. Optometry was a two-year course in 1927 and required two years of high school and two years of college. After graduation, the senior Greenspoon practiced briefly with William Feinbloom, who had a keen interest in contact lenses, which were made only in Germany by the Carl Zeiss Company at the time. Greenspoon also developed an interest in contact lenses. All contact lenses were constructed of glass. Negacol was used to take a mold of the eye, then plaster of Paris was poured into this to achieve the positive mold. A glass lens was blown over the positive mold, and then the prescription was ground in. This was the beginning of contact lenses in America.

Dr. Morton Greenspoon was born in New York City in 1929. In 1935 his father moved the family to California and opened a practice in downtown Los Angeles. He was the only optometrist in California at the time to understand how to fit the Zeiss lens. He spent many hours in his small workshop, grinding down and altering the glass lenses to make them fit. Because the lenses were made of glass, it was a long and tedious project.

After a number of years in the congestion of downtown Los Angeles, the senior Greenspoon decided to move to a rather quiet, secluded little community known as Beverly Hills. The California Bank Building at the corner of Wilshire Boulevard and Beverly Drive was the only high-rise building in Beverly Hills at the time, and since there was a vacant space, this is where Greenspoon moved his office. The California Bank Building also housed most of the theatrical agents in Beverly Hills, including the well-known William Morris Agency. Because of this, Greenspoon had a steady stream of actors and actresses going past his door, and when they needed the services of an optometrist, it was to his door that they turned. Greenspoon's patient roster began to read like a "Who's Who" in

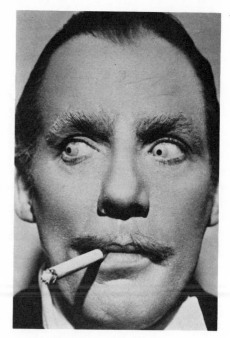

Miracles for Sale was a complicated mystery that required Henry Hull to have his own natural brown eyes, as well as light blue eyes. (*Morton Greenspoon*)

The senior Dr. Greenspoon fit Hull with the Zeiss lens, then fused a blue ceramic material to the outside of the corneal section. Greenspoon believes this was a first for Hollywood. (*Photo courtesy of Morton Greenspoon*)

Hollywood: Orson Welles, Rita Hayworth, Herbert Marshall, Ronald Colman, Eddie Cantor, and Esther Williams, but to name a few. Through his acquaintance with people in the film industry, he was eventually approached in 1939 to create a cosmetic effect.

The MGM film entitled *Miracles for Sale* (1939) was a complicated mystery that required Henry Hull to have his own natural brown eyes, as well as light blue eyes. The senior Dr. Greenspoon achieved this effect by first fitting Hull with the Zeiss lens. He then fused a blue ceramic material to the outside of the corneal section. The fusing was done in an oven in a bottle factory with everyone holding their breath. There was always the chance of the lens melting or changing due to the amount of heat necessary to fuse the color on. The procedure was successful and the results quite effective. Greenspoon believes this was the first time in motion picture history that a cosmetic contact lens was used to create a special effect in a film.

While his father was busy bringing a new

cosmetic medium to the ever-changing film industry, Morton Greenspoon was developing an interest in motion picture photography. After graduation from Beverly Hills High School, he spent six months in the Camera Department of Twentieth Century-Fox, where he decided the life of a motion picture cameraman was not for him. In 1947 Greenspoon entered the University of Southern California in a premed course to follow in the family footsteps of optometry. After graduation he spent the next year in practice with his father. He then set up his own practice in the San Fernando Valley in Sherman Oaks.

When Greenspoon's father retired and sold his practice to two other optometrists who had no knowledge or interest in cosmetic contact lenses, young Dr. Greenspoon inherited that portion of the practice. Located in Sherman Oaks, he was ideally situated in relation to Universal Studios, Warner Brothers, and quite near Twentieth Century-Fox, so it proved to be a very advantageous location for his cosmetic lens practice.

Orson Welles's left eye had to appear blind in Twentieth Century-Fox's production of *Jane Eyre*. (© *Twentieth Century-Fox Film Corporation*)

The first cosmetic creation Greenspoon recalls making was for blue-eyed Debra Paget for her role as a brown-eyed Indian in *Broken Arrow* (1950). Paget wanted the role very badly, and Darryl Zanuck jokingly told her if she could change her eyes from blue to brown she could have the role. The determined young actress approached Dr. Greenspoon with her problem, and they were able, with the use of cosmetic lenses, to send her back to Zanuck, brown eyes intact. Zanuck gave her the role, which she portrayed so successfully that it led to her often being cast in the role of dark-eyed Semitic characters in biblical roles. She used the brown contact lenses in many films.

That was the beginning for Dr. Greenspoon, and since then, he has managed to share the best of two worlds in his field, his "real" world of general practice and the exciting world of film "make-believe." He gave blue-eyed Alan Reed brown eyes for his role as the Mexican bandit Pancho Villa in *Viva Zapata!* (1952). Even though the film was black and white, blue eyes would have filmed too light to have passed for brown. He also helped wrestler Tor Johnson to appear blind and grotesque for his role in *The Monster* (1952). In 1957 he created the illusion of blindness for Van Johnson's role as a blind detective in *Twenty-three Paces to Baker Street.*

As a result of working on Audrey Hepburn in *Wait Until Dark* (1967), Dr. Greenspoon had to institute a new procedure for the studios using his services. After fitting Hepburn with the appropriate lenses to portray her blindness, Greenspoon felt that an optical technician should be on the set during shooting. The studio wouldn't hear of it. They saw it as an unnecessary expense. But when shooting began, Greenspoon received an urgent call demanding his presence that very moment, as no one on the set was able to insert Hepburn's lenses. Greenspoon visited the set and inserted the lenses. He was also able to find a contact lens technician who could remain on the set to attend strictly to Hepburn's needs during the filming. Now it is Greenspoon's policy that there always be a contact lens technician on the set to keep the lenses clean, to see that they are properly inserted, and that the individual does not wear the lenses beyond a safe length of time. Such a policy has undoubtedly prevented many serious injuries.

When working with the eyes of actors and actresses, Greenspoon is working with a priceless commodity. He is extremely proud that during his twenty-two years of cosmetic contact lens placements he has never caused a stoppage of production because of an eye injury or abrasion due to his

Laurence Naismith wore Greenspoon's silver-mirrored contact lenses as Merlin, the magician, in *Camelot*. (*Morton Greenspoon*)

lenses; nor has any actor or actress had discomfort caused by a contact lens he has fitted. He credits this to the role of the technician on the set and the fact that the technician is answerable only to him.

Curt Jurgens's eyes were changed from blue to brown for his role as the Eurasian general in *Inn of the Sixth Happiness* (1958), and Peggy Wood received brown eyes for her role as the biblical character in *Ruth* (1960). In 1963 José Ferrer's and Diane Baker's eyes were changed from blue to brown for their roles as Hindus in *Nine Hours to Rama* (1963). When producer George Stevens took on the life of Jesus Christ in *The Greatest Story Ever Told* (1965), Dr. Greenspoon had the pleasure of working on Ed Wynn, who played the part of Old Aram, the blind man whose sight was restored by Jesus. Contact lenses were employed to achieve the effect of blindness and removed after the miracle was performed.

In 1967 Dr. Greenspoon fitted Laurence

Naismith with silver-mirrored contact lenses to create an effect for his role as Merlin, the magician, in *Camelot*. This was the first time this effect was used, and it remains one of Greenspoon's favorites. The cameraman zoomed into the eye, and the audience could then see what Merlin saw in a wide-angle effect. He created this type of contact lens again for Yul Brynner's portrayal of a robot gunslinger gone mad in *Westworld* (1973). He credits the cameraman on *Westworld* with doing a superb job of lighting the mirrored lenses. At the end of the film Brynner walks down a long hall in an underground complex which is lighted by a series of overhead lights. As he passes each overhead light, it is caught in the convex mirrors in his eyes and his eyes flash eerily. Greenspoon feels much can be achieved with this effect.

In 1968 *Planet of the Apes* kept a multitude of people busy, including Dr. Greenspoon, who cooperated with makeup artist John Chambers to turn every blue-eyed feature actor into a brown-eyed one. Tony Curtis's eyes became brown for his role as *The Boston Strangler* (1968). Dr. Greenspoon also helped achieve the look of

blindness for Master Po in the highly successful television series "Kung Fu." Similar effects were used on several actors in the "Six Million Dollar Man" television series.

Joey Green, who portrayed a possessed African native in *Exorcist II: The Heretic*, was fitted by Greenspoon for yellowish-green contact lenses. Linda Blair who was so successful as the possessed Regan in *The Exorcist* did a repeat performance in this sequel wearing the same lenses Dr. Greenspoon had created for her first role. Her stand-in also wore similar lenses.

Dr. Greenspoon was requested to come up with a lens that would help create the effect of an eighty-year-old General MacArthur for Gregory Peck's portrayal of that role. It was felt that old-age makeup would not be fully effective unless the eyes looked old and senile. Greenspoon created the lenses with what is known as an *arcus senilis* around the edge of the iris, which dimmed the eye. Combined with the old-age makeup, the desired effect was quite successful.

Generally speaking, when a makeup artist approaches Dr. Greenspoon, he usually knows the type of lens that is needed to cre-

Yul Brynner wore Dr. Greenspoon's mirrored lenses for his portrayal of the robot gunslinger gone mad in *Westworld*. (*Morton Greenspoon*)

Dr. Greenspoon created these eyes for Lou Ferrigno and Bill Bixby in the television series "The Incredible Hulk." (*Morton Greenspoon*)

ate a convincing makeup design so that the eyes do not look out of place. Dick Smith, for example, knew exactly what he wanted for lenses in *The Exorcist*. On the other hand, the studio heads will seldom know precisely what they are looking for. In these instances Dr. Greenspoon will show them a photograph album of special cosmetic contact lenses he has created in his over two decades of special effects work. The producer and director can then usually find the lens that will do the trick.

Even Dr. Greenspoon has had a hand in the world of the vampire. He created scleral lenses for Barry Atwater's role as a vampire on the loose in Los Angeles for the ABC Movie of the Week *Nightstalker*. The role required bulging green eyes. Scleral lenses were painted with a special acrylic paint

which became part of the plastic and gave Atwater's eyes the appearance of being green and bloodshot. Usually Dr. Greenspoon creates a desired effect of this nature using large corneal lenses of his own design. They must be large to restrict their movement, and they must be designed so that there is sufficient interchange of tears and oxygen under the lens.

Despite all Dr. Greenspoon's precautions, it is sometimes the actor who creates problems. When Yul Brynner requested some medication to clear up his bloodshot eyes during the filming of *Westworld*, Greenspoon had no qualms in filling his request. Brynner apparently believed that if a little did that much good, twice as much would do that much more, so he made the same request of the set doctor.

Late that evening Greenspoon received a frantic call from the assistant director. Brynner's eyes were extremely dilated, he was having difficulty seeing, and everyone was quite concerned. After a chat with Brynner, Greenspoon discovered the problem, reassured Brynner that he would be fine once the medication wore off, and cautioned him against overmedicating himself in the future.

One of Dr. Greenspoon's more recent effects is used by Lou Ferrigno and Bill Bixby in the television series "The Incredible Hulk," Bill Bixby wears white contact lenses with green edges as he begins his transformation. Lou Ferrigno then picks up as the massive green "Hulk."

On occasion, Dr. Greenspoon is called upon to expand upon his cosmetic eye effects. In the case of the film *The Fury* (1978), Greenspoon was asked if he could create a stage blood that would be safe for the eyes. The film concerns two teen-agers with incredible psychic powers. During the course of the film, they use their powers to cause wounds to bleed excessively. John Cassavetes became the unhappy object of one of the teen-ager's wrath, and his eyes turn to a bloody pulp. He wore a pair of red scleral contact lenses created especially for his role by Dr. Greenspoon. For the blood which flowed from Cassavetes's eyes, Greenspoon employed a chemical, used many times in routine practice, called gonioscopy fluid. It is a rather thick fluid used mainly for putting special lenses on the eye when optometrists wish to view the anterior angle of the eye using a slit lamp. Greenspoon then located a red dye which could be safely used in the eye and dyed the fluid red.

Dr. Greenspoon also created scleral lenses for use by Joe Gibb who portrayed the part of a four-hundred-year-old Indian medicine man, Misquamacus, in William Girdler's *The Manitou* (1978).

Although Greenspoon's usual cosmetic eye lenses are very often created to distort or drastically change the eyes, one of his recent efforts was to change an unusual natural eye color to a more average-appearing eye color. Meg Foster, who stars in *A Different Story* (1978), has very light blue eyes. They are so light that when photographed in Technicolor, they appear to be albino or blind. Unless that type of effect is specifically required, it is very distracting. Dr. Greenspoon fitted her with blue contact lenses to make her eyes a more normal blue.

Dr. Greenspoon is an integral part of the makeup artists' world. He has contributed to many brilliant screen characterizations. He recognizes the vulnerability and the pricelessness of one's eyes and has strived throughout his career to combine his medical expertise with the needs of the motion picture industry. Hollywood owes a real debt of gratitude to three generations of Greenspoons.

Blazing contact lenses add a horrific effect to this creature from the "Bionic Woman" series. (*Morton Greenspoon*)

Index